THE RICH CHRISTIAN
in the CHURCH
of the EARLY EMPIRE:
CONTRADICTIONS
and
ACCOMMODATIONS

THE RICH CHRISTIAN
in the CHURCH
of the EARLY EMPIRE:
CONTRADICTIONS
and
ACCOMMODATIONS

BY

L. Wm. COUNTRYMAN

THE EDWIN MELLEN PRESS
NEW YORK AND TORONTO

FOR

SARAH HOLMES

I, II, AND III

ACKNOWLEDGMENTS

This work began as my dissertation for the degree of Doctor of Philosophy at the University of Chicago. The present publication has given me the opportunity to revise it by expanding certain sections and by taking account of some important works to appear in the last few years. I have not, however, altered any of my major conclusions. My thanks to Herbert Richardson, editor of this series, for the opportunity to do this revision and for some valuable criticisms.

It is a pleasure to acknowledge the many personal debts incurred as I wrote. The work owes its origin to the stimulation of course work under Robert M. Grant, who also supervised the dissertation and helped give it its present shape with his judicious criticism. My other readers, Bernard McGinn and Jonathan Z. Smith, were also most helpful; and Constantine Trypanis and Peter Brown both provided me with helpful suggestions.

I completed writing the dissertation in Springfield, Missouri, where I must thank Gerrit ten Zythoff and my other colleagues at Southwest Missouri State University and at the Southwest Missouri Ecumenical Center who fostered and encouraged this project.

For financial support in my graduate education, I am indebted to the University of Chicago, to my father-in-law, Earl Elberfeld, to the Continuing Education Fund of the Diocese of Southern Ohio, and above all to the Episcopal Church Foundation, whose generosity was extraordinary. For a subsequent opportunity of research and learning, I should like to thank the National Endowment for the Humanities for the invaluable experience of a Summer Seminar in the Social World of Early Christianity under Wayne A. Meeks.

My thanks to Helen K. Bailey and to Una Crist who typed this work with such care in both its incarnations.

Finally, my wife Sally deserves thanks under all the headings above—as critic, protector of working time, principal bread-winner of the family during my years of course-work—also, for help with typing and, most especially, for creating a home for us.

L. Wm. Countryman
Brite Divinity School
Texas Christian University

March 1980

CONTENTS

INTRODUCTION... 1

    History of the Modern Discussion................. 1
    The Method and Scope of the Present Work......... 18
    Rich and Poor in the Greco-Roman City........... 22
    Wealth and Poverty in Palestinian Judaism....... 26
    Limits of This Study............................ 33
    Footnotes....................................... 35

CHAPTER ONE.   WEALTH AND ALMSGIVING: THE
THOUGHT OF CLEMENT OF ALEXANDRIA................. 47

    Is Christian Wealth Legitimate?................. 47
    Detachment and Simplicity....................... 52
    Almsgiving or Communism?........................ 54
    Conclusions..................................... 60
    Footnotes....................................... 64

CHAPTER TWO.   EARLY CHRISTIAN ATTITUDES
TOWARD WEALTH................................... 69

    Detachment...................................... 69
    Simplicity...................................... 73
    Communism....................................... 76
    Righteous Poor and Wicked Rich.................. 81
    Conclusions..................................... 89
    Footnotes....................................... 92

CHAPTER THREE.   ALMSGIVING: THE RELIGIOUS
VALUE OF WEALTH................................. 103

    Almsgiving in Judaism and the Greco-
      Roman World................................. 103
    Alms for the Poor.............................. 107
    The Redemptive Power of Almsgiving............. 108
    Alms from the Rich: Abandonment................ 114
    Alms as the Cement of the Churches............. 118
    Conclusions.................................... 120
    Footnotes...................................... 122

CHAPTER FOUR. THE DANGER OF RICHES TO
    THEIR POSSESSOR................................. 131

    The Weakness of the Rich....................... 131
    The Rich as Potential Apostates................ 135
    Implications of Apostasy....................... 142
    Footnotes...................................... 145

CHAPTER FIVE. THE DANGER OF THE RICH TO
    THE CHURCH..................................... 149

    Tension Between Rich and Poor.................. 149
    Insubordination of the Rich.................... 151
    Roles of the Rich Layman and the Minister...... 157
    Church and Club................................ 162
    Occasions of Conflict.......................... 166
    Conclusions.................................... 171
    Footnotes...................................... 174

CHAPTER SIX. CYPRIAN OF CARTHAGE: A CASE STUDY IN
    THE THEORY AND PRACTICE OF CHRISTIAN RICHES..... 183

    Cyprian of Carthage and His Abandonment
        of Wealth.................................. 183
    The Decian Crisis: Before and After............ 188
    Almsgiving: The Only Solution.................. 195
    Conclusions.................................... 199
    Footnotes...................................... 201

CONCLUSION... 209

    Summary.. 209
    Implications for Further Work.................. 210
    Footnotes...................................... 215

LIST OF ABBREVIATIONS.............................. 216

BIBLIOGRAPHY....................................... 217

    Texts and Translations of Ancient Jewish
        and Christian Works........................ 217
    Background and General Works................... 219
    Early Christianity and its Society............. 223
    Works on the New Testament..................... 230
    Works on Later Christian Authors............... 236

THE RICH CHRISTIAN
in the CHURCH
of the EARLY EMPIRE:
CONTRADICTIONS
and
ACCOMMODATIONS

INTRODUCTION

HISTORY OF THE MODERN DISCUSSION

The topic to which the present work is devoted has called forth a great deal of literature over the last century and a quarter, largely because it has been caught up in the modern collision between capitalism and communism. Apologists for a variety of political tendencies have sought to use the early Christians as champions of their own or as whipping boys for the opponents' point of view. Many of these works tell us less about the early days of Christianity than they do about the political struggles of the nineteenth and twentieth centuries. Nonetheless, it is worthwhile to narrate the history of the discussion as it is reflected in the major works, if only to point out what way I hope to set the enquiry on a different track.

As early as 1733, a German church historian felt obliged to counter the "common opinion" that understood the primitive church at Jerusalem to have practiced compulsory communism. In his "De vera natura communionis bonorum in ecclesia Hierosolymitana commentatio," Johann Lorenz Mosheim insisted on the voluntary nature of the practice and called attention to Luke's use of Greek philosophical parallels in describing the primitive Christian community. Thus he recognized the apologetic character of "communist" language in early Christian writings.[1]

The true beginning of the modern discussion, however, must be dated to the middle of the nineteenth century when, as a contemporary author ambivalently asserted, "the heroes of 1848...perfidiously perplexed and envenomed the issue."[2] Even before 1848, there had been, at least

1

in France, an effort tò link Christianity with the plight
of the industrial working classes.[3] Yet, whatever claims
the socialist leaders of the Revolution made on early
Christian precedent belong to the history of politics
rather than that of scholarship. It is a different matter
when we examine the response to their claims. In the conservative aftermath of 1848, the French Academy offered a
prize for the best essay on the subject of early Christian
charity; their hope was to find a scholarly author who
would refute all claims that the primitive church had recommended or practised communism and show that the true Christian social principle was charity, not economic equality.
The successful claimant was a Swiss Protestant, Étienne
Chastel, whose work was published in 1853. That the study
was concerned with the present as well as the past is evident from its title: *Études historiques sur l'influence de
la charité durant les premiers siècles chrétiennes, et
considerations sur son rôle dans les sociétés modernes.*[4]

Chastel distinguished sharply between the political
motives of the revolutionaries and the purely spiritual
purpose of the Gospel; of charity, he said:

> It is not a political virtue that [Jesus]
> comes to establish among men; it is a reli-
> gious sentiment that he desires to teach
> them, and this much less for the present
> happiness of those who will be the objects
> of it, than for the eternal felicity of
> those who are called upon to exercise it.

Chastel was aware of the revolutionary possibilities in a
new religion, particularly one which "seems favorable to
the ill favored classes"; and he evoked the specters of the
Peasants' Revolt and the militant Anabaptists of the Reformation Era. The apostles, he argued, had been quick to
suppress all such tendencies. Thus, Paul had not only emphasized the duties of work and obedience (II Thess. 3:6,
14), but had actually threatened excommunication, which

must have involved loss of charitable support, for the un-
ruly.[5]

Chastel's work soon appeared in an English translation made by a fellow Swiss, resident in the United
States.[6] G. A. Matile's introduction to his translation
makes it plain that he shared Chastel's political concerns.
Although it is not clear what Matile saw in the American
situation to alarm him (indeed, he was not altogether opposed to the revolutions of 1848), it may be important
that the Perfectionist followers of Robert Humphrey Noyes,
as well as other, more secular groups, had already begun
experiments with communism in this country.[7]

The debate, however, about early Christianity and
wealth has historically been rooted in Europe rather than
America, and Matile's effort to transplant it remained
isolated on the western shore of the Atlantic for some
time to come. In France, Charles Périn reinforced the
conservative outlook in his *De la richesse dans les
sociétés chrétiennes*.[8] This is an effort at "Christian
economics," however, rather than history; and it is of
little use for our purposes. In a more historical vein,
Edmond Le Blant attempted to vindicate the importance of
the rich in early Christianity by calling attention to the
large number of rich martyrs; but he was uncritical in his
use of martyr acts.[9]

Beginning in the 1880s, German scholars took the
lead in the study of the historical questions. G. Uhlhorn
wrote a monumental treatise on early Christian charity,
which was soon translated into English. His political
stance seems similar to that of Chastel, though he is much
less obvious about it. The work is written in a pietistic
vein, as a panegyric on the unspotted love of the earliest
Christians, which expressed itself as a purely voluntary
but fully adequate concern for the poor.[10]

About the same time, H. Holtzmann dealt with the
problem of communism in Acts by denying the historicity of
the whole account. He dated Acts to c. 125 and proclaimed
that the whole motif of communism was *heidenchristlich*.[11]
W. Haller, on the other hand, analyzed attitudes of second-
century Christians toward wealth and concluded that the believers were indeed poor——and were kept that way by church
restrictions on their occupations and by the constant demands of charity.[12] In neither Holtzmann nor Haller is
there any apparent concern for contemporary political questions. Yet, there were others to deal with such issues,
if scholars did not. It was at this time that Frederick
Engels published an article claiming early Christian communism as a remote precedent for the modern workers' movement: "...'socialism' did in fact, as far as it was possible at the time, exist and even become dominant——in Christianity."[13]

German-speaking scholars in the first decades of
this century produced useful works on several aspects of
our topic. R. Knopf and Andreas Bigelmaier explored the
social composition of the early Christian communities and
showed that they were composed of a mix of people drawn
from various social strata.[14] Unfortunately, their work
was overshadowed by the more popular and romantic conclusions of Adolf Deissmann. Deissmann asserted that Christianity was always *volkstumlich,* basing his argument on
such data as language and occupation. One post-War writer,
Rudolf Schumacher, returned to the line of enquiry set by
Knopf and Bigelmaier, but it is only in the decade of the
70s that Deissmann's image of the early Christians as uniformly poor has been effectively broken. Scholarship was
no longer insulated at this time from political developments, for both Deissmann and Schumacher respond sharply
to writers of the political Left.[15]

The period also saw the production of a number of
works dealing with Clement of Alexandria, whose importance
for our subject was thus already recognized. While some
of these are concerned primarily with Clement's relationship to Stoicism and to the issue of asceticism,[16] others
confront the issue of wealth directly, concluding that
Clement qualified the Christian's freedom in regard to
riches without actually banning them.[17] Here, too, there
are signs that at least one scholar wrote in full aware-
ness of the political implications of his work.[18]

The real political battle, however, was fought more
openly. The opening salvo was fired not by a Leftist, but
by an ardent free-trade economist, Lujo Brentano. As Rec-
tor of the University of Munich, he delivered a lecture in
1901 in which he claimed that the early Christians had exhibited an unnatural antagonism toward the acquisition of
property. He defended his position the next year in the
Sitzungsberichte of the Munich Academy.[19] This attack from
an unexpected quarter called forth replies from Roman
Catholic moderates. F. X. Funk answered Brentano at once
with an essay "Über Reichtum und Handel im christlichen
Altertum," which Funk still thought worthy of inclusion in
his collected essays five years later. Even after the
World War, Odulphus van der Hagen took pains to refute
Brentano in his Utrecht dissertation on Clement of Alex-
andria.[20]

The more serious challenge, however, came from the
political Left. In *Die Entstehung des Christentums,* Albert
Kalthoff portrayed the early church as seeking to live out
a messianic communism under the forms of the Greek club. A
few years after Kalthoff's work, there appeared Karl
Kautsky's *Der Ursprung des Christentums,* which proved a
nightmare for theologians who were trying to maintain a politically moderate position. Kautsky was a major figure in

German Marxism; his popular book caught the public imagination and was in its ninth edition within eleven years; moreover, it seems to have had great appeal for young Roman Catholics, to judge by the energy with which that church's theologians set out to refute it. Like Kalthoff, Kautsky portrayed the early Christians as the spiritual ancestors of modern Marxism, although he also criticized the inadequacy, as he saw it, of all ancient notions of communism.[21]

From the Roman Catholic side, Ignaz Seipel had taken up the Leftist gauntlet even before Kautsky's book appeared; but his *Die wirtschaftsethischen Lehren der Kirchenväter* was not an adequate response. It is a highly synthetic work, frequently glossing over real differences among the Fathers; and its author is often guilty of taking one or two proof-texts as grounds for saying, "The Fathers teach...." A more adequate treatment appeared the next year, Otto Schilling's *Reichtum und Eigentum in der altkirchlichen Literatur*. This remains to this day a thorough and balanced presentation of the basic sources for the early Christian theory of wealth, though it ignores actual practice. Both Schilling's and Seipel's works are open to the objection that they treat the subject in an apologetic way, for partisan purposes. In 1891, Leo XIII had issued an encyclical, *Rerum novarum,* in which he laid down an official line on the question of private property: that it is a legitimate, but by no means an unqualified right. Schilling and Seipel expected to find the Fathers saying exactly this, and they were not disappointed.[22]

The lines had now been drawn for the struggle. Socialist authors, some of them Christian, others not, insisted that early Christianity was essentially akin to the socialist stance; but they failed to bring to their work any serious historical scholarship. The theologians and

academicians who responded to them maintained that the
early Christians had not been unfriendly to the principle
of private property; and they tended to minimize even the
episode of apparent communism in the primitive church in
Jerusalem. The only author who resists easy classification in this way seems to be the Capuchin, Ephrem Baumgartner, who argued that communism had indeed been an important
element in early Christianity, though only on a voluntary
basis and in accordance with the doctrine later to be defined in *Rerum novarum*.[23]

The one other major work produced before World War
I was Ernst Troeltsch's study of Christian social teaching.
Troeltsch argued that the communism of the early church was
a purely voluntary "love-communism," which did not compromise the principle of private property. This harks back to
the nineteenth-century works on charity by Chastel and,
more especially, Uhlhorn, although Troeltsch works the
whole conception out in a far more unified and theological
way than his predecessors. According to Troeltsch, early
Christianity did not make the healing of social wrongs the
goal of its charity, but rather the actualization of brotherly love. (The early church is treated only as an element
in a sweeping survey of all church history.)[24]

Most of the works which I have found from the period between the wars did little more than echo what had already
been said. Johannes Behm and Paul Fiebig wrote attacks on
Kautsky and on those who had repeated his arguments. Andreas Bigelmaier produced a fairly conventional essay which
does have the value, however, of presenting a survey of the
debate to the year 1921, including some works I have not
been able to consult. Franz Meffert summed up the polemical
situation as a two-fold attack on the church (particularly
the Roman Catholic Church): on one side stood the nineteenth-century liberals, such as Brentano, who attacked all

Christianity as socialistic, while on the other the socialists attacked the modern church as the ally of the capitalists, while claiming Jesus and his immediate followers for
themselves.[25]

   After the early twenties, the controversy seems to
have collapsed of exhaustion caused by the endless repeti-
tion of the same arguments. Despite its near disappearance from the learned journals, however, the question remained in the air. As late as 1933, Otto Schilling felt
obliged to publish an angry article in defense of the
earlier Roman Catholic works on the subject of property
(e.g., his own and Seipel's). Against charges that the
theologians had deliberately neglected the more collecti-
vist passages from the Fathers, Schilling affirmed that
his earlier work had attempted to set forth their social
ethic *ohne jegliche Tendenz.*[26] In this way, the German
politico-historical controversy had at length bogged down
in a morass of claims and counter-claims.

   As a sign of hope for the future, there were, however, a couple of exploratory works which at least laid a
foundation for future discussion. Friedrich Hauck published a detailed study of the position of early Christianity on labor and money, in which he argued that Jesus had
simply reversed the Old Testament's favorable view of
wealth. The successors of Jesus, according to Hauck, faith-
fully preserved his general attitude, though their teaching
gradually assimilated to the philosophical critique of
wealth current in the Greco-Roman world. Hauck's work, however, is marred by the conventional German tendency to create an excessively sharp contrast between Christianity and
Judaism—so much so that Hauck was driven to deny that the
Rabbis had ever countenanced any doctrine of poverty as
piety. In the same year that Hauck's work was published,
Ernst Lohmeyer brought forth a discussion of social atti-

tudes in the church of the New Testament. He concluded
that, even though Christianity was a child of its times
and of certain urban tendencies, which made it attractive
to artisans, the early Christians were actually quite indifferent to contemporary social questions, since they saw
them only in the light of eternity.[27]

During the first quarter of the present century,
the subject of early Christian attitudes toward wealth was
also being canvassed in English-speaking countries, but in
almost total isolation from the German discussion. Only
one American author took public account of Kautsky's work—
Patrick J. Healy, who published a long series of articles
in the *Catholic University Bulletin* for 1911. The first
and last of these ("Historic Christianity and the Social
Question" and "The Materialistic Interpretation of Early
Christian History") contain specific attacks on Kautsky.
In the second ("Social and Economic Questions in the Early
Church"), Healy admitted that the early Christians were
inclined to denounce wealth and power, but insisted that
they had not meant this in any revolutionary sense. The
American scholarly community, however, took little notice
of Healy's work; nor did it affect the discussion in Ger-
many on which it was based.[28]

The Americans, instead, were under the influence of
the Social Gospel, which sought justice and compassion for
the lower classes within the existing framework of society
or, at least, without violent revolution. On the whole,
the American scholars were friendly toward the philanthrop-
ic rich. Shailer Mathews, writing in 1897, could explain
Jesus' recommendation that one should be "faithful in un-
righteous mammon" (Lk. 16:11) with the words "Wealth is a
public trust."[29] About the same time, F. G. Peabody, Profes-
sor of Christian Morals at Harvard, argued that the Christian rich are trustees, responsible for their own moral

use of wealth.[30]

Few of the works in English contribute much to our
understanding of the historical questions. Orello Cone's
Rich and Poor in the New Testament was a serious work of
scholarship; but the revolutions in New Testament studies
since Cone wrote have rendered much of what he had to say
out-of-date. Gerald D. Heuver, *The Teachings of Jesus Concerning Wealth,* gives evidence of wide reading in the contemporary discussion of wealth—but little evidence of com-
prehension. W. E. Chadwick, in *The Social Teaching of St.
Paul,* sought to show that the teachings of Jesus and Paul
agreed with "modern sociology"; he rejected "'compulsory'
socialism."[31]

Other contemporary works in English inclined to
the homiletical—a tone which distinguished these writers
from the more polemical Germans, but which did not encourage solid attention to historical detail. Such are the
works of Louis Wallis and Charles Foster Kent. C. W. Votaw
claimed the Christians as an idealistic ethical movement,
and he then went on to explain away their apparent devotion
to apocalyptic and their notable lack of reforming zeal.
Thus, the homiletical needs of the present were allowed to
reshape history in the most radical way.[32] Similar studies
by Mathews, Walter Rauschenbausch, Charles Ryder Smith, and
Chester Charlton McCown continued to appear on through the
1920s.[33]

It was also in the 1920s, however, that American
and British scholarship on this subject began to reach a
degree of maturity. In Britain, C. J. Cadoux published a
monumental collection of material on a great variety of social issues in early Christianity. It remains in print
even now and has become the standard English-language volume on wealth in early Christianity. Cadoux made no secret
of his stance as a Christian Socialist; yet, he presented

the material fairly, if not always in a well-digested way.
His work makes little effort to interpret the early Christian writers in terms of their own social and cultural
context, for Cadoux was primarily interested in establish-
ing precedents for the handling of ethical questions in
the modern church.[34]

Less thorough, but more promising, were the works
of Shirley Jackson Case, a leader of "The Chicago School."
Scholars associated with the Divinity School of the University of Chicago had shown an interest in our topic for
some time: Mathews, Heuver, Wallis, and Votaw were all associated with the School in one way or another. It is in
Case, however, that their concerns reached the level of
genuine and imaginative historical scholarship. In his
two works on the social world of early Christianity, he
described the church as one of the few institutions of antiquity to take a specific and sweeping interest in the
poor as such, and he argued that Christian social concern
had been a major element in the expansion of the church.
Although Case's political presuppositions do not seem to
have been socialist, they are not avowedly capitalist,
either; indeed, it is one of the triumphs of his work that
he focused on antiquity for its own sake, without keeping
one eye cocked on the current political scene. Case's
work also represented an advance on the best European
scholarship, such as that of Schilling, in that he was
concerned about what early Christians did as well as what
they thought and said.[35]

Case had few immediate followers in the task,
although Donald Wayne Riddle's interesting and scepti-
cal study of *The Martyrs* acknowledges his lead. Other
English and American scholars, however, were beginning to
pursue similar lines of inquiry. Of importance are F. C.
Grant's work *The Social Background of the Gospels* (openly

anti-socialist but a careful piece of scholarship), Charles
Stanley Phillips' *The New Commandment,* and Amos Niven
Wilder's *Eschatology and Ethics in the Teaching of Jesus.*
In all these, current politics take second place to a
real interest in history. The early Christians are seen
as antagonistic toward wealth, but not as "socialists" in
the modern sense. By the late 1920s, the subject had at-
tracted enough attention in the English-speaking world to
justify the production of a bibliography on it by Norman
H. Baynes.[36]

     The general tendencies of American and English re-
search during this period became available to the general
public in an interesting and neglected work of 1942: Holmes
Rolston's *The Social Message of the Apostle Paul.* This is
a popular work, but the author, in his careful treatment
of the Pauline materials, shows that he was aware of the
difficulties involved in social analysis of early Christianity. He argued that Paul was conservative as regards
the existing economic order, but sought to ameliorate it
through a voluntary sharing of wealth within the church.
Rolston thus detached Christianity from the defense of
capitalism, but without suggesting any specific alternative. The standard Roman Catholic approach to our subject
also became available to English-speaking audiences in a
popular form during the war years, with the publication of
two works by Igino Giordani: *The Social Message of Jesus*
and *The Social Message of the Early Church Fathers.* Neither work is original or particularly interesting in its
own right.[37]

     Since the Second World War, there has been no lack
of popular or pious works on the question of early Christian attitudes toward wealth. I mention a few of the English and American works here only to show what kind of
needs and interests inspired writers on the subject.

Popular works on New Testament ethics, such as those by L.
H. Marshall and William Lillie, tended to include a chapter on wealth. If one digs through the inspirational language, one finds such authors saying that wealth is an individual problem for Christians and that Jesus and his
early followers were neutral toward the social order. There
is no great effort to explore the early Christians' own
social situation. Such works, of course, came largely
from "establishment" writers. From the other side of the
fence came Howard Thurman's *Jesus and the Disinherited*
(1949), which discusses what Jesus means for "those with
their backs against the wall." The difference in view-
point is instructive; but, again, the work is not historical. However useful these books may have been to church
people of the time, they do not further our study, since
they ignore the historical particularity of the documents.
Indeed, this approach was so broadly accepted that Hendrik
Kraemer, in a little tract called *The Bible and Social
Ethics*, almost managed to discuss his topic without reference to the Bible itself.[38]
      On the scholarly level, English-language studies
of our subject continued at first in the pre-war vein. In
1956, Amos Wilder and F. C. Grant contributed articles to
a major collection on New Testament background and eschatology; but these do not represent a great advance on
their earlier works. Ray Petry's work on eschatology and
social thought only skirted the areas of primary concern
to us here. Perhaps the most interesting treatment of attitudes toward wealth in early Christianity was an essay
by G. E. M. de St. Croix, who maintained that, with the exception of Jesus himself and a few heretics, the early
Christians had never seriously questioned the institutions
of slavery and private property. These conclusions, to be
sure, would not have been remarkable were their author not

a Marxist, who thus broke with tradition of Engels and
Kautsky.[39]

   The important developments of this period came not
from a reappraisal of the familiar evidence about Early
Christian attitudes toward riches, but rather from a revival of interest in the general social life of early
Christianity, beginning with the pioneering efforts of an
Australian scholar, E. A. Judge. In a short work, published in 1960, Judge called attention to the supreme importance of the social milieu for understanding early
Christianity. This first effort was insufficiently docu-
mented and showed an inadequate acquaintance with New Testament scholarship; but it served to launch an investigation which has been pursued more extensively by Judge himself, in subsequent articles, and by other scholars. It is
this interest which has inspired two important recent
studies. One is Robert M. Grant's *Early Christianity and
Society,* which includes several chapters pertinent to our
subject (note especially the chapters on property and almsgiving) and which looks at early Christian attitudes toward wealth and alms in the context of ecclesiastical practice. Abraham J. Malherbe's *Social Aspects of Early Christianity* is not concerned primarily with questions of
wealth, but it adds depth to our conception of two subjects
closely linked to the study of the rich within the church—
the level of education and the institution of the house
church.[40] In addition to these longer works, a number of
articles have appeared recently, which deal with specific
aspects of our topic with careful attention to the actual
practice of the early Christians and to their social
milieu. Other studies of early Christianity from a sociological or social-anthropological standpoint, such as John
Gager's *Kingdom and Community,* may contribute to our study
of wealth indirectly, but do not make that a primary

concern.[41]

A similar development of sociological interest took place in Germany in the late 1960s. Before this, most writers in German who dealt with our subject had done so without any serious effort to place the early Christians in the social framework of their own age and culture. A partial exception was the work of Rudolf Schumacher, who argued that the Christians of the apostolic age were not all poor; Schumacher's argument, however, was entangled with an anti-Communist polemic, which lessened its value.[42] The 1967 articles of Heinz Kreissig on social organization of Early Christian communities and of Henneke Gülzow on the Roman church under Callistus thus broke new ground, subsequently worked also by Werner Eck, in an article on Christians in the senatorial *ordo,* and by Gerd Theissen in a series of articles pointing the way to a new understanding of the social order in both Palestinian Christianity and the church at Corinth. In these works, wealth is not the central issue, but their authors set a new standard for the discussion—one which takes the historical, cultural, and social milieu as seriously as the ideas expressed in our surviving documents. It is necessary now for the scholar to work conscious of practice as well as theory in the early churches.[43]

This does not mean that the discussion of theory has lapsed. The aftermath of World War II and the partitioning of Europe into two political camps encouraged continental theologians to revive the old Marxist-conservative contest of the 20s and 30s. In France, for example, Stanislas Giet published research which he had originally undertaken to refute a Marxist writer of 1931, Gérard Walter.[44] Giet's conclusions are similar to those of the earlier Roman Catholic writers we have noted. Other French writers have been inspired by related purposes. Paul

Christophe was moved by the needs of the "social teaching
of the church" in writing his discussion of property
rights; he concentrates mainly on the patristic teachings
and concludes that Christianity always recognized the
right of private property, but under the obligation of
charity. The rich are *intendants* of wealth. A little
later, S. Légasse undertook a form-critical study of Jesus'
summons to the rich man (Mk. 10:17-31) at least partly because of concern about the rationale for the Religious
Life. He concluded that the passage as we have it is a
creation of Mark and that the hard words there addressed
to the rich were originally intended for all people alike.[45]

      Among writers of German, there was an early effort
by Konrad Farner, a Swiss writer, to distance himself from
both Marxist and Christian theoreticians and to present an
original and independent approach to the subject. He accused the former of suppressing individual freedoms, the latter of emphasizing only one side of the evidence. His
work, however, is not sufficiently historical for our purposes, since it depends almost entirely on secondary writings. Other authors adhered to more traditional lines.
Johannes Leipoldt published a moderately conservative interpretation of social thought in early Christianity.[46]
Martin Dibelius argued that Jesus was only indirectly concerned with social ethics——through the primary Christian
concern for brotherly love. A comparable conclusion issues
from Werner Georg Kümmel's article on private property in
the New Testament, where the author declares that private
property like everything of this world is radically subor-
dinated to the Kingdom, but not, for that reason, absolute-
ly rejected. Hans-Joachim Degenhardt wrote an interesting
study of riches and poverty in the Gospel of Luke, concluding that Luke aimed at imposing an ideal of voluntary
renunciation of possessions on all the Christian ministers

of his day. This work is vitiated, however, by Degenhardt's insistence that the disciples in the Gospel are
nothing more than surrogates for the clergy of Luke's own
day. An article by Wolf-Dieter Hauschild in 1972 suggests
that the early Christian suspicion of the rich might rea-
sonably have led to some sort of socialism and ponders why
it did not—without reference to the cultural and social
circumstances of the ancient church.[47]

The best recent book from the continent of Europe
to deal specifically with the question of wealth in early
Christianity is that of Martin Hengel, though it began
life not as a work of scholarship, but as a lecture given
"to an audience of Bavarian lawyers on the theme of 'Property in the New Testament.'"[48] In detachment and historical sophistication, Hengel's book is much superior to
those of Seipel or Kautsky. Yet, the same basic problem
remains. The modern author is interested in showing the
relevance of ancient ideas to modern circumstances, with
the result that he is always tempted to view his material
in an anachronistic light or, at best, to treat the social
doctrine of the ancients as an abstraction. In fact, we
cannot hope to detach the social teachings of early Christian writers from their original social setting and still
find them fully intelligible eighteen centuries later in a
very different social milieu.

It is impossible, of course, for any modern student of this subject to be completely indifferent to the
outcome of his research. He almost certainly has some
feeling about the economic system under which he lives, and
he may well wish to implicate the ancient Christians either
in his own ideas or in those of his opponents. The inves-
tigator who wishes to understand the ancient church in its
own terms, however, must first set his modern concerns at
a distance for the moment and let the early Christians be

themselves, indifferent to the moral questions of the
twentieth century.

If we attempt to see the words and theories of
early Christian writers first as reflecting concerns of
their own specific age and culture rather than as univer-
sals of human experience, we may hope to arrive at a concrete notion of what these authors were saying to the
people they themselves knew—as opposed to some hypothetical message they may have sent to a twentieth century of
which they could scarcely have conceived. This is the approach which Shirley Jackson Case christened "social emphasis," admonishing scholars that

> Whether the interests of the present are in
> strict agreement with those of the past may
> often be open to question. But the function
> of interpretation is, at all costs to modern
> wishes, to allow the life of the ancients to
> throb afresh through the veins of the his-
> torical documents.

It may well be that the social experience of the Early
Christians will still, for many, have relevance to the
economic controversies of our time. But it seems that,
for the present, the first step toward discovering that
relevance would be to turn one's back on the modern issues
and concentrate on the life of the ancient world. That is
the extent of my purpose here.[49]

THE METHOD AND SCOPE OF THE PRESENT WORK

In pursuing this objective, we have two principal
problems to overcome. The first of these concerns the nature of our data, the second, the scope of the enquiry.
Something must be said of each of these problems and the
way in which I hope to overcome them.

First, the data we have to work with are almost exclusively literary in character and general in expression.

There is little in the way of material remains from the
Christianity of the first two and one-half centuries A.D.;
and the literary remains are seldom specific about wealth.
Thus, when we find references to the rich, we shall not be
able to specify *how* rich they were or to what order of society they belonged. We can only be sure that the early
church included both richer and poorer members and that
these were readily enough identified at the time. Unfortunately, we cannot hope to locate our subjects precisely
on the map of Roman society.

In addition, our materials are fragmentary in nature. Some of them are literal fragments—picked from the
sands of Egypt or quoted in later authors. (Fragments are
of no use for the present study when it is impossible to
replace them in their original social context.) Even
where we possess a complete work or a corpus of works by
one author, any reference to rich Christians in it is usually incidental—fragmentary in a metaphorical sense. Consequently, much of the potential material for a study such
as this consists of isolated statements which we can place
with assurance neither in the context of their author's
overall thinking nor in that of his practical experience.
The problem, then, is to find some way of organizing and
understanding this material without importing twentieth-
century preconceptions into the very foundations of our
study.

There is a partial remedy for this problem in that
one Early Christian author did leave us a sustained discussion of the rich and their wealth: Clement of Alexandria. Only in his works do we have a large enough and
coherent enough treatment of the topic that we can be relatively confident of representing his thought correctly;
with the other authors, we are forced to assume too much at
every step. I should not wish to suggest that Clement can

be taken as typical of Early Christian thought about the
rich, or even to assume that the early church had any typical approach. But we can make use of Clement to provide
the basic outlines of our discussion, so that the assumptions of our argument (even if they should prove unrepresentative of the Early Christian writers as a whole) are
at least drawn from known second-century concerns, not
twentieth-century ones.

        The first chapter, then, of the present work is
devoted to a study of the thought of Clement of Alexandria,
to be used as a basis of comparison in ascertaining the
overall tendencies of Early Christian thinking on the subject of wealth. But it must be supplemented and corrected
by a detailed comparison with the other ancient authors.
This endeavor occupies the two succeeding chapters, one of
which is devoted to attitudes toward wealth as such, the
other to the related topic of almsgiving, its purpose and
rationale.

        At this point, we meet the second basic problem of
our study—that of scope. In the first three chapters,
the present study has the same scope as earlier treatments
of the topic, though it proceeds according to the different method outlined above. Thus far, it is a study of
Early Christian *ideas*. Here, however, the resemblance
ends. Social doctrine is intelligible only in terms of
social experience, and therefore the doctrinal material
studied in the first three chapters must be set against
its social context. We begin to ask, "What was the *role*
of the rich in the early church?" It is a question that
has seldom been asked and never answered in any comprehensive way.

        Accordingly, Chapters Four and Five draw together
available information about the behavior of the Early

Christian rich and the way in which contemporary writers regarded them. I have interpreted this material in the light of ancient social parallels in an effort to define the normal role of the rich layman in any ancient congregation. If the premises of this work are correct, this effort should go far to demonstrate why Early Christian authors expressed themselves in just the way that they did on the topic of wealth, when other attitudes, whether more negative or more positive, were familiar to them from the resources of Greek philosophy and Hebrew scripture.

Finally, to test the results of the whole study, I have reserved the works of one author, Cyprian of Carthage, to a separate chapter. His discussion of wealth does not challenge that of Clement of Alexandria for coherence, but he provides much the broadest picture we possess of the interaction of ideas and social realities in the ancient church. If the results of our investigation furnish a valid description of the ancient church's social situation, they will show it by throwing light on Cyprian's experience and doctrine, where these have hitherto been obscure.

It is appropriate to say something, too, at this point about the *temporal* limits of this work. Historians of the early church are used to dealing with the whole pre-Constantinian era as a unity. From the doctrinal point of view or even the aspect of church organization, this approach makes a certain sense, for the conditions of development after the conversion of Constantine were radically different from those before. The topic here, however, is an aspect of *social* history; and it is a truism of ancient social history that the great divide between early and late Roman empire, between principate and dominate, lay somewhere in the time of troubles that overwhelmed the latter part of the third century. By the time of Constantine, Roman society was radically different from what it had been

even in the reign of Septimius Severus. Indeed, the society of Constantine was closer, in some ways, to that of
Justinian than to that of Augustus.

        Our study of Christian social history must adhere
to the same limits as those of secular social history.
Cyprian is, therefore, the latest author included in the
present work. In his time, we do not yet see the enormous
development of imperial bureaucracy or the extraordinary
wealth of a limited number of senatorial families that
would come to dominate the Empire of the fourth century.
He still reacted in terms of an older social structure
that focused on the individual city as its unit.

RICH AND POOR IN THE GRECO-ROMAN CITY

        A brief sketch of the social structure of the
Early Roman Empire is in order here, to provide the back-
drop for what we shall have to say in the coming chapters.
We shall introduce a more detailed discussion of relevant
aspects of ancient society as these become useful; but
there are certain key elements that call for attention at
once.

        The early Christians formed a segment of that an-
cient urban culture which we call for convenience Greco-
Roman, although it included other peoples as well, notably
the Jews. Christianity first arose in the province of
Palestine, with roots in the rural district of Galilee as
well as in the city of Jerusalem; but it quickly spread to
other Hellenistic cities around the eastern part of the
Mediterranean. In the West, too, it was at first limited
to the cities, or, more precisely, to Greek-speaking en-
claves within them.[50] The differences between Palestine
and the rest of the Roman Empire should not be exaggerated,
for in many respects society had the same type or organization in both milieus. Nonetheless, there were differences,

especially in the symbolic values of wealth and poverty.
We must therefore consider two distinct backgrounds for
early Christianity.

The population of the ancient Greek city was
stratified into a social hierarchy, and wealth was but one
of several criteria which determined a person's rank within this system. We are apt to speak, casually, of "upper,"
"middle," or "lower classes" in the ancient world; but
this terminology, borrowed from modern social arrangements,
is misleading. Among us, a "class" is a social group informally determined by wealth and by relationship to the
means of production. Birth is irrelevant except insofar
as it determines inheritance of wealth; and members of all
classes usually enjoy the same rights of citizenship in
the modern state. But among the Greeks and the Romans of
antiquity, one's position in society depended on birth and
legal classification as well as on wealth.[51]

Since the ancient social order rested on basically
different presuppositions from ours, we can best understand it by abandoning the term "class" altogether and
substituting the more appropriate concepts of "order" and
"status." Unlike the informally constituted class, an
order is a legally defined social group for which a certain degree of wealth may be a necessary, but not a sufficient, qualification and which has a special relationship
to the state, with attendant civic rights and obligations.
A modern American may move from the lower to the middle
class by shifting from a badly-paid job as a menial laborer to a well-paying job as office manager; but the ancient
Roman could move upward from order to order only by being
formally translated by the appropriate authority, no matter
how his income might increase.[52]

This is not to say that wealth was insignificant
in the constitution of orders. Members of the upper orders

in Rome itself—senators and equestrians—were required to
possess a certain minimum wealth (called *census*).[53]   But
wealth alone did not determine social prestige; and one
might find rich men scattered throughout the Roman hierarchy, from the senatorial order at the top to the order of
freedmen at the bottom. Wealth often functioned socially
by conferring on its possessor a certain prestige (which
we shall call "status" here) that modified his place in
the hierarchy of orders without actually affecting his membership in a certain order. Thus a rich freedman might
wield more influence than a (relatively) poor senator, despite being far below him in terms of order.[54]   It will
thus be apparent that wealth and social distinction were
not identical in Greco-Roman society, even though riches
were one source of social power and prestige. We must not
make the common mistake of identifying the rich with the
members of one or a few orders.

To be rich, in terms of classical society, meant
to live on one's investments and by the labor of others.
The rich man *par excellence* was the gentleman farmer; for
agriculture on the grand scale, with slave bailiffs over-
seeing tenants and other slaves, was the most eminently respectable of investments. The man who engaged *actively* in
trade or industry, in his own person, was the opposite of
rich, no matter how large his capital.[55]   There was a tendency for the rich to become members of the highest orders
of society; and the governing class of each city was made
up of rich citizens. (Some of the rich were excluded from
citizenship because of their low or foreign birth.) The
larger and richer the city, however, the more likely that
there would be too many rich citizens for all to enter the
charmed circle of decurions (councilmen), so that it was
not unusual for commoners to be rich, too.[56]

The poor, by contrast, were those who lived by

their own labor.   Here we must distinguish between two
groups of people for whom the Greeks and Romans had distinct terms, but whom we commonly lump together in English
as "the poor." At the bottom of the economic scale stood
those whom the ancients called *ptōchoi* or *indigentes*; we
shall refer to them here as "the indigent," that is, people
utterly without resources. They owned nothing by way of
property or tools of trade, and they lived a hand-to-mouth
existence, dependent on day-labor or begging. At a higher
level stood the *penētai* or *pauperes*. Unfortunately, we
have no distinct word for them in English—only the catch-
all term "poor." They were small shopkeepers, artisans and
farmers, people who owned property and the tools of their
trade and could expect a reliable income from their own
labor. Even if a man owned a considerable staff of slaves
and a prosperous shop, he was "poor" as long as he engaged
actively and directly in the business.[57]

The distinction between rich and poor was only
partly economic in nature. Wealth, being associated with
the upper orders, implied certain social rights and obligations. The rich citizens of the ancient Greek city almost
always enjoyed special distinctions: their property qualified them for a special grade of citizenship and opened to
them offices to which the many could not aspire. In return,
the city reserved the right to call upon the funds of the
rich in emergencies—for example, to build warships or to
buy grain in a famine. In Roman times, no one could hold
major public office without being rich, since officials
were expected to provide games, feasts, and other public
benefits at their own expense. (Indeed, in some cities,
they were expected to pay *summae honorariae* for the privilege of holding office at all.)[58]

To a great extent, the rich performed their obligation through the medium of the state. But we have already

observed that not all the rich belonged to the class of
decurions—much less to the imperial elite of equestrians
and senators. Insofar as these "outsiders" wished to as-
similate themselves to the highest orders of society, they
necessarily had to imitate the benefactions of their su-
periors and show that they, too, were public spirited.
Those who were not eligible for public office could still
benefit smaller groups of their fellow-citizens by becoming
patrons of clubs—a topic we shall discuss at greater
length in Chapter Five. The objective of the rich, then, at
every level of society was to behave *as* rich toward people
poorer than they, while looking, often as not, for similar
benefits for themselves from those richer than they.[59]

WEALTH AND POVERTY IN PALESTINIAN JUDAISM

        The role of wealth in Palestinian society was simi-
lar in many ways to that in Greco-Roman society, particularly in the city of Jerusalem itself, which was dominated
by a group of rich, priestly families. These families
were large landowners and also politically powerful, since
they had the right to have the high priest chosen from
among them. There were also wealthy laymen. But the vast
mass of people were "poor" in the sense that they worked
for a living. At the bottom of the scale, here as in the
Greek world, lay the destitute—beggars and day-laborers.
        Religious considerations, however, played a role
in Jewish society unknown among Greeks. The political parties of Palestine were also religious sects, for whom social and theological issues tended to merge. Since the
primitive church at Jerusalem arose in this sectarian cli-
mate, the social composition and the social attitudes of
the Palestinan Jewish sects are of interest to us here, although they present a number of difficulties.
        The simplest sect to characterize socially is that

of the Sadducees, which was centered around the great high-
priestly families already mentioned, no doubt including
their dependents. It was not, in the first century A.D.,
a party of broad, popular appeal; but its very cohesiveness
combined with its powerful political and economic base to
give it great authority.[60]

The principal sect in opposition to the Sadducees
was, of course, that of the Pharisees; and it has often
been assumed by modern writers that they therefore represented the "people" as opposed to the aristocracy. They
have even been characterized more precisely as "middle
class." But this is to oversimplify the matter and, indeed, to reinterpret in terms alien to the age. The heart
of the Pharisaic movement lay not in an economic class, but
in an authoritative religious order—the scribes, who
served as interpreters of Jewish Law and therefore as
judges in all matters touching on it. The scribes were
overwhelmingly lay in origin, as opposed to the priestly
Sadducees. They were, as Finkelstein characterized them,
"urban plebeians," for the most part, which did not exclude
them from being rich, as the constituency of the important
school of Shammai undoubtedly was.[61]

Josephus and other ancient writers also mentioned
the Essene sect, which Josephus described as practicing a
kind of philosophical communism. The fact that they practiced community of goods tells us nothing in itself about
the social origin of the sect's members, but Josephus suggests that they were recruited from among both rich and
poor, who then shared equally from the common chest.[62] The
Dead Sea Scrolls and other remains found at Qumran in this
century are probably those of an Essene community. Among
the Scrolls, there are two rule books, one of which, the
Community Rule, does indeed call for a kind of communism,
while the other, usually called the *Damascus Rule,* presup-

poses a community of prosperous, independent farmers.
Since both rules make careful provision for disposition of
the members' property, the membership can scarcely have
been recruited from among the indigent.[63]

There was also a series of revolutionary groups in
first century Palestine, which Josephus grouped together
as a "fourth philosophy" of Judaism. There may have been
an economic basis for this variety of Jewish sectarian
life, for one of the first acts of revolution in A.D. 66
was the burning of the Records Office in Jerusalem, to procure abolition of debts. The revolutionaries did not, however, bring about a thorough-going social reversal, for the
leadership of the Revolt itself remained in the hands of
men of education and even social standing, such as Josephus
himself.[64]

As for the great majority of Jews, the *amme-ha-*
arets, they belonged to none of these sects. While the
Pharisees scorned them for their lack of education in Torah, they were not identified with any single social or
economic group. Thus, the party structure of Jewish society was clearly related to economic strata only at the
top—a result of the historical development in Jewish society.[65]

Under the Hasmonean monarchy, Sadducees and Pharisees alike first rose to prominence as court parties, vy-
ing for influence with the Jewish priest-king. Of the two,
the Sadducees were much more successful and held power almost uninterruptedly from the time of John Hyrcanus (135-
105 B.C.) onward. Even after Pompey incorporated Palestine into the Roman Empire, neither the family of Herod
nor the successive Roman governors tried to rule the country without the cooperation of its most prominent families.
The Pharisees thus found themselves in the unhappy position
of an opposition party permanently deprived of public in-

fluence, except for one brief moment of glory under Alexandra Salome (78-69 B.C.).[66]

As for the other Jewish sects, the Essenes were in a permanent opposition to the Sadducees, whose priestly predecessors had had some part in an early suppression of the Essenes. The Fourth Philosophy saw the rich priests as collaborators with the Romans and, at the very beginning of the Revolt of A.D. 66, attacked both their economic dominance and their priestly prerogatives.[67] The opposition of all these groups to the Sadducees was not only political but religious as well. After all, the Sadducees were in control of the paramount symbol and center of ancient Judaism, the Temple of Jerusalem. The High Priest was both the head of the Jewish nation and its most sacred personage. Since every Jewish sect, relying on the confidence that it alone taught a religion truly pleasing to God, believed firmly in its right and obligation to lead the Jewish people, the religious and political success of the Sadducees was a stumbling-block to Pharisees, Essenes, and the Fourth Philosophy, all alike.

This situation, however, changed radically after the Revolt of 66-70. With the burning of the Temple, the diversion of the former Temple tax to the treasury of Jupiter Capitolinus, and the general destruction wrought by the war in Palestine, the Sadducees lost their base of power. The Essene community is no longer heard from after the War and was probably destroyed. The Fourth Philosophy, though it certainly lingered as a revolutionary temper which would again burst forth at a later date, was discredited for the time being. The only sect which survived the debacle in sufficient strength to assume the leadership of the nation was that wing of the Pharisaic party led by Johanan ben-Zakkai. Even if all rivals did not disappear at once, the whole complexion of Jewish politics was now

changed, for the leadership belonged no longer to wealthy
and aristocratic priests, but to scribes whose qualifications were educational rather than economic or hereditary.
The only organized opposition to this state of affairs was
that of the Ebionites, or Jewish Christians, whom the
Pharisees eventually succeeded in reading out of the Jewish nation.[68]

The social and economic relationships of the Jewish sects were thus complex. The literature of the age,
however, makes them seem even more complex than they were
in fact. We have already seen that, except for the Sadducees themselves and perhaps the Fourth Philosophy, the
sectarian divisions were not economic in character. It is
the more remarkable, then, to find that members of the pre-
66 opposition consistently characterized themselves as the
pious *poor*. At Qumran, indeed, the term *'ebyonim* ("poor,"
adopted also by the Jewish-Christians) became virtually
the community's own title for itself. The same motif appears, more sparingly, in the *Psalms of Solomon,* often at-
tributed to the Pharisees, and in a variety of apocalyptic
writings which we cannot attribute to any one sect.[69] How
could Pharisee or Essene characterize himself as poor,
when these sects actually recruited from more than one
stratum of society?

The solution lies not in the Pharisees or Essenes
themselves, but in their opponents. The Sadducean leaders
were unquestionably rich, and it is no surprise that the
sectarians described these "wicked" men as such. As a
class, Pharisees and Essenes were no doubt poorer than the
establishment in the Temple, even if they were not "the
poor" in terms of society at large. To some degree, then,
they were merely speaking in terms of a dramatic, rhetorical antithesis, which conveniently ignored technical realities. The Essenes, in addition, may have applied the

motif to themselves in the sense of "voluntarily poor," that is, as practitioners of communism, though there is nothing to suggest that they were conscious of such a connection. Neither of these explanations, however, is sufficient by itself to explain the widespread popularity of the motif of the pious poor.

The principal reason for the use of this motif was that it brought with it a sense of scriptural authentication for those who used it. The sacred language of the Psalms had already bestowed on poverty a connotation of piety and devotion amid difficult circumstances.[70] In its national laments, Israel represented itself to God as oppressed and needy and therefore deserving of his help, as contrasted with the wicked who trust in their power and wealth. This language must have owed much to the ancient Israelite conviction that God exercises a special protection over beggars and other helpless people. The Pharisee or Essene who availed himself of this motif of poverty was characterizing himself as Israel, deprived of its right and deserving of vindication.[71]

The sectarian rhetoric of poverty, then, was a religious protest against rich and successful Sadducees rather than a literal description of the poverty of those who made use of it. This is confirmed by the virtual disappearance of the motif of the pious poor after A.D. 70 (apart from one major exception, discussed below). This motif, which was a common feature of apocalyptic works written before the Jewish Revolt, becomes rare under the new conditions which followed it. One work of the latter period even reversed the old rhetoric, numbering it among the evils of the Last Days that "the poor shall have abundance beyond the rich"; for the author of *II Baruch,* this was simply a violation of good order.[72] Once the Sadducees had disappeared as the dominant religious force within

Judaism, the motif of the pious poor lost its point.

The one exception to this development is found
among the Jewish-Christians, who went by the name "Ebionites" (*'ebyonim*, "the poor"), just as the Essenes had at
an earlier date. Why did they preserve the motif of the
pious poor at a time when it was disappearing elsewhere in
Judaism? It is possible that it had become for them,
after a period of persecution during the Jewish Revolt and
continuing antagonism on the part of the Pharisees, simply
a literal description of their economic status. But we
do not know anything certain about their social condition.[7]

What we do know is that the motif of the pious
poor had become a fixed part of their tradition (and of
all Christian tradition) well before A.D. 66. Among Hellenistic Christians, it quickly lost its sectarian significance and, as we shall see, became fossilized. But Ebionites passed from an era of oppression by Sadducees to one
of oppression by Pharisees. If the rhetoric of poverty
was no longer so apposite as it had once been, it still
served the purpose of defining "us" against "them," the
oppressed against the oppressor, the pure against the
wicked.

The evaluation of wealth in Jewish-sectarian
thought was important for Christianity at its time and
place of origin. For this reason, we have been compelled
to devote some attention to it at this point, to show that
the rhetoric of the day was not, as is sometimes supposed,
a simple reflection of social or economic realities. It
is these realities, particularly in the Hellenistic world
to which Christianity quickly moved, that will most interest us, for it was the role of the rich in Greco-Roman society which provided the principal context for developing
Christian thought on the subject.

LIMITS OF THIS STUDY

Finally, before we enter upon the main body of our
study, it is appropriate to mention two topics that the
reader will *not* find treated here, even though they may appear at first glance to be integral parts of our subject.
First, I have excluded all references to wealth and poverty that are explicitly metaphorical. If Clement of Alexandria speaks of people who are poor in vices and rich in
virtues, it is clear that he is not making economic distinctions as such. The metaphorical values of wealth and
poverty were already largely determined for the Greek language before the advent of Christianity; and passages which
merely reflect that established usage contribute nothing to
the present study.

Second, this work includes no analysis of the class
membership or social rank of the early Christians. This is
an important and interesting topic; but it contributes little to our understanding of the role of the rich, for, as
we have seen, wealth and social rank were by no means the
same thing in antiquity. Our writers, however, did not
distinguish between rich people of different ranks: they
lumped them together according to their economic status.

The one important thing to recognize about the social structure of the early church is that its membership
was not drawn from a *single* order or economic status.
There is no need to prove the point here, since the following pages will, I think, put it beyond doubt. The early
church included rich and poor, privileged and non-privi-
leged. It is important to state this truth here in the
Introduction because many readers will still assume that
the early Christians were all impoverished or even destitute.[74] But no one can long retain that impression when
faced with the large quantity of Early Christian writing
which dealt directly with the question of the rich Chris-

tian in the church. It is to that material that we now
turn.

   The thesis of our study will be this: Early Christian attitudes toward wealth were composed of curiously
incompatible elements, some negative, some positive. This
configuration was determined neither by tradition nor by
the demands of logical coherence, but by the requirements
of the early church's social life, in which rich laymen
played an essential role but also gave rise to a variety
of problems. Thus, Early Christian attitudes toward the
rich can be understood only in terms of the roles which
the rich actually played in the community.

FOOTNOTES

[1]The treatise is found in Mosheim's *Dissertationum ad historiam ecclesiasticam pertinentium,* 2 vols. (Altona and Flensburg: Fratres Korte, 1733-43), 1:1-53.

[2]The quotation comes from the translator's introduction to Étienne Chastel, *The Charity of the Primitive Churches: Historical Studies upon the Influence of Christian Charity During the First Centuries of Our Era, with Some Considerations Touching its Bearing upon Modern Society,* trans. G. A. Matile (Philadelphia: J. B. Lippincott & Co., 1857), p. iii.

[3]Alec R. Vidler, *A Century of Social Catholicism, 1820-1920* (London: S. P. C. K., paperback edition, 1969), pp. 45-49. See also pp. 83-88 on developments in Belgium.

[4]Paris: Capelle, 1853. Similarly, the bishops of France urged a "revival of catholic teaching and piety and private charity"; Vidler, p. 45.

[5]Chastel, (Eng.), pp. 38, 64-69.

[6]See above, n. 2.

[7]Richard DeMaria, *Communal Love at Oneida: A Perfectionist Vision of Authority, Property, and Sexual Order,* Texts and Studies in Religion, vol. 2 (New York: The Edwin Mellen Press, 1978), pp. 1-37.

[8]2d ed., rev. (Paris: V. Lecoffre, 1868). On the purpose of such works under the Second Empire, see Vidler, pp. 75-76.

[9]"La richesse et la christianisme à l'âge des persécutions," *Revue archéologique,* Ser. 2, vol. 39 (1880):220-30.

[10]*Die christliche Liebestätigkeit in der alten Kirche* (Stuttgart: D. Gundert, 1882). Eng., *Christian Charity in the Ancient Church,* trans. Sophia Taylor (Edinburgh: T. & T. Clark, 1883).

[11]"Die Gütergemeinschaft der Apostelgeschichte," in *Strassburger Abhandlungen zur Philosophie* (Freiburg in Breisgau: J. C. B. Mohr [Paul Siebeck], 1884), pp. 25-60.

[12]"Das Eigentum im Glauben und Leben der nachapostolischen Kirche," *Theologische Studien und Kritiken* 64(1891):478-563.

[13]Eng., "On the History of Early Christianity," in Karl Marx and Frederick Engels, *On Religion* (Moscow: Progress Publishers, 1975), pp. 275-300. The article appeared originally in *Die neue Zeit* 1(1894-95), pp. 4-13, 36-43. Another, antithetical work of the period, which I

have not been able to consult, is H. Köhler, *Sozialistische Irrlehren von der Entstehung des Christentums und ihre Widerlegung* (Leipzig, 1899).

[14] R. Knopf, "Ueber die soziale Zusammensetzung der ältesten Heidenchristlichen Gemeinden," *ZTK* 10(1900):325-47. Andreas Bigelmaier, *Die Beteiligung der Christen am öffentlichen Leben in vorconstantinischer Zeit, Ein Beitrag zur ältesten Kirchengeschichte* (Munich: J. J. Lentner, 1902). Bigelmaier's work remains the best survey of the subject as a whole, embracing virtually all the pre-Constantinian material.

[15] [Gustav] Adolf Deissmann, *Das Urchristentum und die unteren Schichten,* 2d ed. (Göttingen: Vandenhoeck & Ruprecht, 1908); this is a brief, popular work, written for the *Evangelisch-sozialen Kongress* in Dessau in 1908. Deissmann regarded the early Christians as uniformly poor; yet, he attacked both Kalthoff and Kautsky as inaccurate, since he insisted that the church was always a movement of individuals, never a mass movement.
Rudolf Schumacher, *Die soziale Lage der Christen im apostolischen Zeitalter* (Paderborn: Ferdinand Schöningh, 1924), is more accurate; but Schumacher's shrill, polemical tone no doubt lost him credibility.

[16] Markgraf (no first name preserved), "Klemens von Alexandrien als asketischer Schriftsteller in seiner Stellung zu den natürlichen Lebensgütern," *Zeitschrift für Kirchengeschichte* 22(1901):487-515. Wilhelm Wagner, *Der Christ und die Welt nach Clemens von Alexandrien: Ein noch unveraltetes Problem in altchristlicher Beleuchtung* (Göttingen Vandenhoeck & Ruprecht, 1903).

[17] Ludwig Paul, "Welche Reiche wird selig werden?" *ZWT* 44(1901): 504-44. See also the Dutch scholar, Odulphus Josephus van der Hagen, *De Clementis Alexandrini sententiis oeconomicis, socialibus, politicis* (Utrecht: Dekker & V. D. Vegt, 1920).

[18] See below, note 20.

[19] Lujo Brentano, "Die wirtschaftlichen Lehren des christlichen Altertums," *Sitzungsberichte der philosophisch-philologischen und der historischen Klasse der kgl. Akademie der Wissenschaften* (Munich, 1902) pp. 141-93.

[20] Van der Hagen (see above, n. 17). Funk's essay appeared first in *Historisch-politische Blätter* 130(1902):888-99; it was reprinted in F. X. Funk, *Kirchengeschichtlichen Abhandlungen und Untersuchungen,* 3 vols. (Paderborn: Ferdinand Schöningh, 1897-1907), 3:150-59.

[21] Albert Kalthoff, *Die Entstehung des Christentums* (Leipzig: E. Diederichs, 1904). See also Kalthoff's earlier work, *Das Christus-Problem: Grundlinien zu einer Sozialtheologie,* 2d ed. (Leipzig: E.

Diederichs, 1903), and the prompt response by Julius Thikötter, *Dr.
Kalthoff's Schrift "Das Christusproblem" beleuchtet* (Bremen: J. Morgenbesser, 1903).

Karl Kautsky, *Der Ursprung des Christentums, Eine historische
Untersuchung,* was first published in 1908. I have seen only the 9th
edition (Stuttgart: J. H. W. Dietz Nachf., 1919). Kautsky suggested
that an inadequate understanding of economics and unusual pressure of
circumstances combined to cause early Christian communism to degenerate
into a kind of mutual-aid system; this in turn created a constant need
for funds, which made the rich ever more important to the church. See
the English translation of his work: *Foundations of Christianity,*
trans. Henry F. Mins (New York: Russell & Russell, [1953]), pp. 357-59.

[22]Seipel's work was published as number 18 of the Theologische
Studien der Leo-Gesellschaft (Vienna: Von Mayer & Co., 1907). Seipel
wrote partly in response to a Leftist work outside the limits of our
subject, Theo Sommerlad's *Das Wirtschaftsprogramm der Kirche des
Mittelalters* (1903).

Otto Schilling, *Reichtum und Eigentum in der altkirchlichen
Literatur: Ein Beitrag zur sozialen Frage* (Freiburg in Breisgau:
Herdersche Verlagshandlung, 1908).

[23]Ephrem Baumgartner, "Der Kommunismus im Urchristentum,"
Zeitschrift für katholische Theologie 33(1909):625-45.

[24]Ernst Troeltsch, *Die Soziallehren der christlichen Kirchen und
Gruppen, Gesammelte Schriften,* Bd. 1 (Tübingen: J. C. B. Mohr [Paul
Siebeck], 1912). Eng., *The Social Teaching of the Christian Churches,*
trans. Olive Wyon, introduction by Charles Gore (London: George Allen
& Unwin, 1931); see especially pp. 133-36.

[25]Johannes Behm, "Kommunismus und Urchristentum," *Neue kirchliche
Zeitschrift* 21(1920):275-97. Paul Wilhelm Julius Fiebig, *War Jesus
rebell? Eine historische Untersuchung zu Karl Kautsky, Der Ursprung des
Christentums, mit einem Anhang: Jesus und die Arbeit* (Gotha: F. A.
Perthes, 1920). Andreas Bigelmaier, "Zur Frage des Sozialismus und
Kommunismus der ersten drei Jahrhunderte," in *Beiträge zur Geschichte
des christlichen Altertums und der Byzantinischen Literatur: Festgabe
Albert Ehrhard,* ed. Albert Michael Königer (Bonn: Kurt Schroeder, 1922);
see pp. 73-76 for the survey. Franz Meffert, *Der "Kommunismus" Jesu
und der Kirchenväter* (M[ünchen]-Gladbach: Volksvereinverlag, 1922).

[26]Otto Schilling, "Der Kollektivismus der Kirchenväter,"
Theologische Quartalschrift 114(1933):481-92.

[27]Friedrich Hauck, *Die Stellung des Urchristentum zu Arbeit und
Geld* (Gütersloh: C. Bertelsmann, 1921). Ernst Lohmeyer, *Soziale Fragen
im Urchristentum* (Leipzig: Quelle & Meyer, 1921).

[28]Patrick J. Healy, "Historic Christianity and the Social Question," *Catholic University Bulletin* 17(1911):3-19; "Social and Economic

Questions in the Early Church," ibid., pp. 138-53; "The Social Value
of Asceticism," ibid., pp. 233-56; "The Economic Aspects of Monasticism," ibid., pp. 318-36; "The Fathers on Wealth and Property," ibid.,
pp. 434-58; "The Materialistic Interpretation of Early Christian History," ibid., pp. 656-77.

[29]Shailer Mathews, *The Social Teachings of Jesus: An Essay in
Christian Sociology* (New York: Macmillan Co., 1897), p. 155.

[30]Francis Greenwood Peabody, *Jesus Christ and the Social Question:
An Examination of the Teaching of Jesus in its Relation to Some of the
Problems of Modern Social Life* (New York: Grosset & Dunlap, 1900), pp.
223-25.

[31]Orello Cone, *Rich and Poor in the New Testament: A Study of the
Primitive-Christian Doctrine of Earthly Possessions* (New York: Mac-
millan Co., 1902). Gerald D. Heuver, *The Teachings of Jesus Concern-
ing Wealth,* Introduction by Herrick Johnson (Chicago: Fleming H.
Revell, 1903); this work was a thesis at the University of Chicago
Divinity School. William Edward Chadwick, *The Social Teaching of St.
Paul* (Cambridge, England: University Press, 1906).

[32]Louis Wallis, *Sociological Study of the Bible* (Chicago: University of Chicago Press, 1912). Charles Foster Kent, *The Social
Teachings of the Prophets and Jesus* (New York: Charles Scribner's Sons,
1917), speaks of his subjects as "above all else social teachers and
reformers" (p. v). Clyde Weber Votaw, "Primitive Christianity an
Idealistic Social Movement," *American Journal of Theology* 22(1918):54-
71.

[33]Shailer Mathews, *Jesus on Social Institutions* (New York: Macmillan Co., 1928); this work is based largely on Mathews' earlier
book (see above, n. 29).   Walter Rauschenbusch, *The Social Principles of Jesus* (New York: Association Press, 1925). Charles Ryder
Smith, *The Bible Doctrine of Wealth and Work in Its Historical Evolution* (London: Epworth Press, 1924). Chester Charlton McCown, *The
Genesis of the Social Gospel: The Meaning of the Ideals of Jesus in
the Light of Their Antecedents* (New York: Alfred A. Knopf, 1929).
McCown is an interesting study in contradictions who maintains that
Jesus was fundamentally opposed to riches as such and yet denies that
abandonment of wealth is the proper response to Jesus' teachings (pp.
3-6); he also maintains that Jesus *cannot* have meant to commend poverty, since poverty in itself is purely evil—and what Jesus cannot have
meant, he did not mean (pp. 350-53).

[34]Cecil John Cadoux, *The Early Church and the World: A History of
the Christian Attitude to Pagan Society and the State Down to the Time
of Constantinus* (Edinburgh: T. & T. Clark, 1925).

[35]Shirley Jackson Case, *The Social Origins of Christianity* (Chicago: University of Chicago Press, 1923), and *The Social Triumph of*

the *Ancient Church* (New York: Harper & Bros., 1933). Case's work is
still stimulating, but the great changes in the understanding of the
social and economic life of the Roman world since the 1930s have made
it partly obsolete.

[36]Donald Wayne Riddle, *The Martyrs: A Study in Social Control*
(Chicago: University of Chicago Press, 1931). Frederick C. Grant, *The
Economic Background of the Gospels* (London: Oxford University Press,
H. Milford, 1926). Charles Stanley Phillips, *The New Commandment: An
Inquiry into the Social Precept and Practice of the Ancient Church*
(London: Society for Promoting Christian Knowledge, 1930). Amos Niven
Wilder, *Eschatology and Ethics in the Teaching of Jesus* (New York:
Harper & Bros., 1939). Norman H. Baynes, *The Early Church and Social
Life (The First Three Centuries), A Selected Bibliography,* Historical
Association Leaflet No. 71 (London: G. Bell & Sons, 1927).

[37]Holmes Rolston, *The Social Message of the Apostle Paul* (Richmond, Va.: John Knox Press, 1942). Igino Giordani, *The Social Message
of Jesus* (Paterson, N. J.: St. Anthony Guild Press, 1943) and *The
Social Message of the Early Church Fathers* (Paterson, N. J.: St.
Anthony Guild Press, 1944).

[38]L. H. Marshall, *The Challenge of New Testament Ethics* (New York:
Macmillan Co., 1947). William Lillie, *Studies in New Testament Ethics*
(Edinburgh: Oliver & Boyd, 1961). Howard Thurman, *Jesus and the Disinherited* (New York: Abingdon-Cokesbury, 1949). Hendrik Kraemer, *The
Bible and Social Ethics* (Philadelphia: Fortress Press, Facet Books,
1965). A more historical treatment is found in Richard Batey, *Jesus
and the Poor* (New York: Harper & Row, 1972).

[39]Amos Niven Wilder, "Kerygma, Eschatology and Social Ethics,"
and Frederick C. Grant, "The Economic Background of the New Testament,"
both in *The Background of the New Testament and Its Eschatology,* ed.
W. D. Davies and David Daube (Cambridge: Cambridge University Press,
1956). Ray C. Petry, *Christian Eschatology and Social Thought: A
Historical Essay on the Social Implications of Some Selected Aspects
in Christian Eschatology to A.D. 1500* (New York: Abingdon, 1956). G. E.
M. de Ste. Croix, "Early Christian Attitudes to Property and Slavery,"
in *Church, Society and Politics,* Studies in Church History, vol. 12,
ed. Derek Baker (Oxford: Basil Blackwell, 1975). I cannot say what
course recent Soviet scholarship may have taken, but up until 1960 it
was still following the lead of Engels, according to Bernhard
Stasiewski, "Ursprung und Entfaltung des Christentums in sowjetischer
Sicht," *Saeculum* 11(1960):157-79.

[40]E. A. Judge, *The Social Pattern of the Christian Groups in the
First Century: Some Prolegomena to the Study of New Testament Ideas of
Social Obligation* (London: Tyndale Press, 1960). Compare his later
articles on Paul: "Paul's Boasting in Relation to Contemporary Profes-
sional Practice," *Australian Biblical Review* 16(1968):37-50, and "St.
Paul and Classical Society," *Jahrbuch für Antike und Christentum*

15(1972):19-36. Robert M. Grant, *Early Christianity and Society:
Seven Studies* (San Francisco: Harper & Row, 1977). Abraham J. Malherbe, *Social Aspects of Early Christianity* (Baton Rouge, La.: Louisiana State University Press, 1977).

[41]It would serve no purpose to present a long list of articles
here, all of which will reappear later in this work. The book by Gager
is *Kingdom and Community: The Social World of Early Christianity*
(Englewood Cliffs, N.J.: Prentice-Hall, 1975).

[42]See above, p. 36, n. 15. As part of the Roman Catholic apologetic effort, the work is shrill, but apparently accurate.

[43]Heinz Kreissig, "Zur sozialen Zusammensetzung der frühchristlichen Gemeinden im ersten Jahrhundert u.Z.," *Eirene* 6(1967):91-100.
Henneke Gülzow, "Kallist von Rom: Ein Beitrag zur Soziologie der
römischen Gemeinde," *ZNW* 58(1967):102-21. Werner Eck, "Das Eindringen
des Christentums in den Senatorenstand bis zu Konstantin d. Gr.,"
Chiron 1(1970):381-406. Gerd Theissen, "Wanderradikalismus: Literatursoziologische Aspekte der Überlieferung von Worten Jesu im Urchristentum," *Zeitschrift für Theologie und Kirche* 70(1973):245-71; "Soziale
Schichtung in der korinthischen Gemeinde: Ein Beitrag zur Soziologie
des hellenistischen Urchristentums," *ZNW* 65(1974):232-72; "Die Starken
und Schwachen in Korinth: Soziologische Analyse eines theologischen
Streites," *Evangelische Theologie* 35(1975):155-72. The Palestinian
church is presented at a more popular level in Theissen's *Sociology of
Early Palestinian Christianity,* trans. John Bowden (Philadelphia:
Fortress Press, 1978); the original German edition was published in
1977.

[44]Gérard Walter, *Les origines du Communisme, judaiques,
chrétiennes, grecques, latines* (Paris: Bibliothéque historique, 1931);
I have not seen this work. Stanislas Giet, "La doctrine de l'appropriation des biens chez quelques-uns des Pères," *Recherches de science
religieuse* 35(1948):55-91.

[45]Paul Christophe, *L'usage chrétien du droit de propriété dans
l'Ecriture et la tradition patristique* (Paris: P. Lethielleux [1964]);
the quotation comes from p. 9. S. Légasse, *L'appel du riche (Marc 10,
17-31 et parallèles): Contribution à l'étude des fondements scripturaires de l'état religieux* (Paris: Beauchesne, 1966).

[46]Konrad Farner, *Christentum und Eigentum* (Berlin: A. Francke,
1947); this was Farner's dissertation, later revised and reprinted as
the first part (pp. 9-90) of his *Theologie des Kommunismus?* (Frank-
furt/M.: Stimme-Verlag, 1969). Johannes Leipoldt, *Der soziale Gedanke
in der altchristlichen Kirche* (Leipzig: Koehler & Amelang, 1952); this
was later reprinted by the Zentralantiquariat der Deutschen Demokratischen Republik (Leipzig, 1970), though I cannot see that it favors a
Marxist position.

[47]Martin Dibelius, "Das soziale Motiv im N.T.," in *Botschaft und Geschichte: Gesammelte Aufsätze*, 2 vols. (Tübingen: J. C. B. Mohr [Paul Siebeck], 1953-56)1:178-203. Werner Georg Kümmel, "Der Begriff des Eigentums im Neuen Testament," in *Heilsgeschehen und Geschichte*, Marburger theologische Studien, 3 (Marburg: N. G. Elwart Verlag, 1965), pp. 271-77. Hans-Joachim Degenhardt, *Lukas, Evangelist der Armen: Besitz und Besitzverzicht in den Lukanischen Schriften: Eine traditions- und redaktionsgeschichtliche Untersuchung* (Stuttgart: Verlag kath. Bibelwerk, 1965). Wolf-Dieter Hauschild, "Christentum und Eigentum: Zum Problem eines altkirchlichen 'Sozialismus,'" *Zeitschrift für Evangelische Ethik* 16(1972):34-49. Another recent German work is Karlmann Beyschlag, "Christentum und Veränderung in der alten Kirche," *Kerygma und Dogma* 18(1972):26-55; it is so very abstract and oriented toward modern questions that I did not find it useful for the purposes of this work.

[48]Martin Hengel, *Property and Riches in the Early Church: Aspects of a Social History of Early Christianity*, trans. John Bowden (Philadelphia: Fortress Press, 1974); the German original was published a year earlier.

[49]Case, *Social Origins*, p. 31.

[50]The first Roman Christian to write in Latin seems to have been Novatian, in the middle of the third century; Johannes Quasten, *Patrology*, 3 vols. (Utrecht: Spectrum Publishers, 1962-63), 2:212-16. At Lyons, the official account of the martyrdoms of c. 177 was written in Greek; and one of the martyrs was an immigrant from the East. At Carthage, Greek was still in common use among Christians at the beginning of the third century; Timothy David Barnes, *Tertullian: A Historical and Literary Study* (Oxford: Clarendon Press, 1971), pp. 68-69.

[51]For a fuller discussion of "class" and related terms, see T. B. Bottomore, *Classes in Modern Society* (New York: Vintage Books, 1966), pp. 12-28.

[52]My use of the terms "order" and "status" follows that of M. I. Finley, *The Ancient Economy* (Berkeley: University of California Press, 1973); see especially pp. 45-51. The Latin *ordo* was applied only to the upper orders of society and, occasionally, to freedmen; but Finley extends the meaning of the term "order" to include every group that meets the definition given here.

[53]Equestrians were required to possess property worth 400,000 sesterces; senators 1,200,000 (sometimes the figure is given as 1,000,000). But for practical purposes, a senator could not manage on less than HS8,000,000. Richard Duncan-Jones, *The Economy of the Roman Empire: Quantitative Studies* (New York: Cambridge University Press, 1974), p. 4, n. 2; p. 18. Epictetus mentions a man at Rome who thought himself ruined when he was left with only HS1,500,000 (*Diss.* 1.26.11-12).

"The pittance allowed to impoverished noblemen to enable them to keep
up their station was half a million [sesterces] a year"; A. H. M.
Jones, *The Roman Economy: Studies in Ancient Economic and Administra-
tive History,* ed. P. A. Brunt (Totowa, N.J.: Rowman & Littlefield,
1974), p. 126.

[54]The element of social incongruity made the rich freedman a fa-
vorite object of attack in Roman satire, e.g., by Petronius in his
Satyricon or by Juvenal, *Sat.* 1.102-16. Ironically, the ancient *Vita*
(whose reliability, however, is in doubt) tells us that Juvenal was
the son or foster-son of a rich freedman.

[55]Finley, pp. 40-42 (citing Cicero, *Off.* 1.150-51), 58, 75-76,
116-17, 120-22.

[56]In small cities as many as one-tenth of the free adult males
might be members of the council; but since councils tended to include
no more than one hundred men, larger cities could set higher conditions on the honor. Duncan-Jones, pp. 283-87. There are indications
that not all local wealth was included in the decurionate, especially
in the East; Peter Garnsey, *Social Status and Legal Privilege in the
Roman Empire* (Oxford: Clarendon Press, 1970), p. 256.

[57]*TDNT, s. vv.* πένης, πενιχρός, by Friedrich Hauck, and πτωχός,
πτωχεία, πτωχεύω by Friedrich Hauck and Ernst Bammel. On slave-hold-
ing, see Finley, pp. 79-80.

[58]Finley, pp. 150-54; Duncan-Jones, pp. 63-65, 80-88. From the
time of Hadrian on, the Empire bestowed more and more legal privileges
on the upper orders; see Garnsey, pp. 107, 126, 169-70, 221, 270, and
John Crook, *Law and Life of Rome* (Ithaca, N.Y.: Cornell University
Press, 1967), pp. 97, 273-75.

[59]For a general survey of club life, see Samuel Dill, *Roman Society from Nero to Marcus Aurelius,* 2d ed. (London: Macmillan & Co.,
1925), pp. 268-82. On philanthropy for the rich, see below, p. 106.
There was a strong resistance to admitting the "poor," e.g., persons
engaged in trade, to city councils; this was still true even in the
third century, when it was "becoming difficult to fill the council";
A. H. M. Jones, *Roman Economy,* pp. 40-41.

[60]Victor Tcherikover, *Hellenistic Civilization and the Jews,*
trans. S. Applebaum (New York: Atheneum, Temple Book, 1970), p. 261.
Joachim Jeremias, *Jerusalem in the Time of Jesus: An Investigation into Economic and Social Conditions during the New Testament Period,*
trans. F. H. and C. H. Cave (London: SCM Press, 1969), pp. 27-28, 96-
99.

[61]For the Pharisees as "middle class," see Prosper Alfaric,
Origines sociales du Christianisme, ed. Jacqueline Marchand, pref. Jean
Sarrailh (Paris: Union Rationaliste [1959], pp. 54-55. The most

comprehensive treatment is that by Louis Finkelstein, *The Pharisees: The Sociological Background of Their Faith,* 2 vols. (Philadelphia: Jewish Publication Society of America, 1938); see 1:1-6, 11-20, 82-91 *et passim.* For the role of the scribes and their lay emphasis, see Leo Baeck, *The Pharisees and Other Essays,* English translation with intro. by Krister Stendahl (New York: Schocken Books, paperback edition, 1966), pp. 20-22, 40-44.

⁶²Josephus, *Bell.* 2.8.3; *Ant.* 18.1.5. In the latter passage, Josephus specifies τὰ χρήματά τε κοινά ἐστιν αὐτοῖς, ἀπολαύει δὲ οὐδὲν ὁ πλούσιος τῶν οἰκείων ἢ ὁ μηδ' ὁτιοῦν κεκτήμενος . If this language has any concrete meaning, it is that some Essenes were rich to begin with, others poor.

⁶³*Community Rule,* col. VI; *Damascus Rule,* col. XII. Chaim Rabin, *Qumran Studies* (New York: Schocken Books, paperback edition, 1975), pp. 22-27, has questioned whether the *Community Rule* really prescribes full-fledged communism, since the normal method of punishment was through the levying of fines. Rabin concludes from this that the Qumran community was not Essene; but we might equally well conclude that Josephus "oversold" the Essenes to his Greek audience by assimilating them more closely to the Pythagoreans than the facts warranted. Efforts to reconstruct the economy of the Qumran community tend to be very hypothetical; e.g., W. R. Farmer, "The Economic Basis of the Qumran Community," *TZ* 11 (1955):295-308.

⁶⁴Josephus, *Bell.* 18.1.6; *Ant.* 2.8.1, 17.6. One of the leaders of the Revolt was Eleazar, son of the high priest; *Bell.* 2.17.2. See also S. G. F. Brandon, *Jesus and the Zealots: A Study of the Political Factor in Primitive Christianity* (Manchester: Manchester University Press, 1967), pp. 53-56. Some of the earlier revolutionaries (before the Revolt of A.D. 66) were probably little more than bandits; Morton Smith, "Zealots and Sicarii," *HTR* 64 (1971):1-19, especially pp. 18-19.

⁶⁵See Aharon Oppenheimer, *The 'am ha-aretz: A Study in the Social History of the Jewish People in the Hellenistic-Roman Period,* trans. I. H. Levine (Leiden: E. J. Brill, 1977), pp. 18-22.

⁶⁶Josephus, *Ant.* 13.10.5-6; 13.5; 16. Tcherikover, pp. 253-55, 261-64.

⁶⁷The "Wicked Priest" had attacked the Essenes' own "Teacher of Righteousness" and driven him and his followers into exile. See the collection of data and interpretation by Geza Vermes, *The Dead Sea Scrolls in English* (Harmondsworth: Penguin Books, revised reprint, 1968), pp. 58-68. Even later, the Essenes refused to have anything to do with the Temple service; Josephus, *Ant.* 18.1.5. Cf., however, B. E. Thiering, "Once More the Wicked Priest," *JBL* 97(1978):191-205.

The Zealots not only burned the Records Office in Jerusalem, thus abolishing debts, but also replaced the Sadducee high priest with a non-entity of "purer" descent; Jeremias, *Jerusalem,* pp. 192-93.

[68]Baeck, pp. 21-22; Jacob Neusner, *First Century Judaism in Crisis: Yoḥanan ben Zakkai and the Renaissance of Torah* (Nashville: Abingdon Press, 1975), pp. 176-92.

[69]For Qumran, see the *Thanksgiving Hymns* (1QH), cols. II and V, and discussion in TDNT, *s.v.* πτωχός, πτωχεία, πτωχεύω, by Friedrich Hauck and Ernst Bammel.
    Psalms of Solomon 10:7 sets "the pious" and "the poor" in parallel. For attribution of this work to Pharisees, see R. H. Charles, ed., *The Apocrypha and Pseudepigrapha of the Old Testament,* 2 vols. (Oxford: Clarendon Press, 1913), 2:viii. For a more recent interpretation of the complexities of this problem, see D. S. Russell, *The Method and Message of Jewish Apocalyptic, 200 B.C.-A.D. 100* (Philadelphia: Westminster Press, 1964), pp. 25-28.
    The identification of wealth with wickedness is common in apocalyptic writings; e.g., I Enoch 46:7-8, 96:4.

[70]This is not to say that the Hebrew word ᶜ*ani* ever denoted "righteous" or "pious"—a position disproved by Ernst Percy, *Die Botschaft Jesu. Eine traditions-kritische und exegetische Untersuchung,* Lunds Universitets Årsskrift, N.F. Avd. 1, Band 49, Nr 5 (Lund: C. W. K. Gleerup, 1953), pp. 45-81. But Percy has ignored the importance of connotation in rhetoric and the possibility of figurative use of language.

[71]E.g., Ps. 86:1-2:
        "Incline thy ear, O Lord, and answer me,
            for I am poor and needy.
        Preserve my life, for I am godly;
            save thy servant who trusts in thee."
The true origins and significance of this rhetoric emerged only a few decades ago. See Harris Birkeland, *The Evildoers in the Book of Psalms,* Avhandlinger, Det Norske Videnskaps-Akademi i Oslo II, Historisk-Filosofisk Klasse, 1955, no. 2 (Oslo: Jacob Dybwad, 1955), pp. 57-69, 71-75; Sigmund Mowinckel, *The Psalms in Israel's Worship,* trans. D. R. Ap-Thomas, 2 vols. (Oxford: Basil Blackwell, 1962), 2:251; H. H. Rowley, ed., *The Old Testament and Modern Study: A Generation of Discovery and Research* (London: Oxford University Press, Oxford Paperbacks, 1961), pp. 170-72, 197-203.
    The special relationship of Yahweh to the poor is manifest both in the relief legislation of the Torah and in such warnings as Proverbs 22:22-23:
        "Do not rob the poor, because he is poor,
            or crush the afflicted at the gate;
        for the Lord will plead their cause
            and despoil of life those who despoil them."

[72]*II Baruch* 70:3b-5a. For the dating of *II Baruch,* see Russell,

pp. 64-65. The motif of the pious poor did not disappear completely
from rabbinic Judaism, but it lost the pre-eminence that it had among
the sects before A.D. 66. Cf. the references in *Encyclopaedia Judaica*,
s.v. "Armut im Talmud," by A. Marmorstein.

[73]H. J. Schoeps, *Jewish Christianity: Factional Disputes in the
Early Church*, trans. Douglas R. A. Hare (Philadelphia: Fortress Press,
1969), argues at one point that poverty was a fact of life for later
Ebionites (p. 107); but he also interprets their thinking on the subject as representing a "tendency toward abstinence" rather than a rejection of possessions as such (pp. 101-3).

[74]The notion that the early Christians were all poor goes back to
pagan detractors of the second century. Christian apologists admitted,
in reply, that the majority of the faithful were indeed poor (so, for
example, Minucius Felix, *Oct.* 36). It became a kind of modern orthodoxy, however, to identify the early Christians as almost invariably
poor: Marx and Engels, pp. 171, 177, 289-90; Kautsky (Eng.), pp. 272-74;
Louis Wallis, pp. 241-42. If this assertion "is meant to imply that
they did not draw upon the upper orders of the Roman ranking system [at
first], the observation is correct, and pointless"; E. A. Judge, *Social
Pattern*, p. 52. Adolf Harnack finally concluded that the Christians
belonged to the petit bourgeoisie; *The Constitution and Law of the
Church in the First Two Centuries*, trans. F. L. Pogson and H. D. A.
Major (New York: G. P. Putnam's Sons, 1910),pp. 139-40.
    A small, but capable series of modern treatments of the subject
has culminated in the description of the early Christians as "ein fast
getreues Spiegelbild der allgemeinen sozialer Schichtung im römischen
Reich"; Werner Eck, p. 382. Among the better treatments of the subject,
cited above, are Andreas Bigelmair, *Die Beteiligung*, R. Knopf, Troeltsch
(Eng., pp. 39-49), and Kreissig. See also Dennis Groh, "Upper-Class
Christians in Tertullian's Africa: Some Observations," *Studia
patristica* 14, pt. 3 (*TU*, 117, 1975):40-46.

CHAPTER ONE

WEALTH AND ALMSGIVING: THE THOUGHT
OF CLEMENT OF ALEXANDRIA

IS CHRISTIAN WEALTH LEGITIMATE?

Early Christian authors did not tell us much about the social role of wealth in the church of their day. The questions which twentieth-century students ask, they were not eager to answer. When they came to speak of wealth, they adopted not a sociological perspective, but an ethical one. They wished to define the moral dimensions of wealth and they expressed a certain attitude towards riches and their possessors. Any modern attempt to explore the social role of the rich must therefore begin at one remove; we must first define the ethical attitudes of Early Christian writers and only then move toward the concrete social realities which lay behind them and gave them content.

Unfortunately, the effort to define the Early Christian attitude toward wealth is itself beset with difficulties. Most important of these is the fact that most of our authors express their thoughts on the matter only incidentally and in passing—usually as an element in the discussion of some quite different topic. It is not easy to be sure, under such circumstances, what represents an author's own opinion and what represents mere rhetorical opportunism. And it is hardly ever possible to piece isolated fragments together convincingly to express one man's coherent doctrine of wealth.

There is only one author who gives us a clear and connected account of his ideas on wealth, and that is Clement of Alexandria—in a homily entitled *Who is the Rich*

Man that is Saved.[1] With this work and two others that
supplement and expand our knowledge of his thinking, we
can say with some assurance that we know what he believed.
We must perforce, then, begin here in our study, since it
is here alone that we have adequate evidence.

At the same time, there are dangers in this pro-
cedure of which we must remain conscious. Clement was
certainly not the first Christian to write about wealth,
nor was he ever a standard authority on the topic. Moreover, he differed from other Early Christian authors (except Origen) in the breadth and depth of his knowledge of
Greek philosophy and in his friendly attitude toward it.
There is always the possibility that in studying Clement
we shall be devoting our time to a maverick of Early Christian literature rather than a typical thinker; and we must
therefore test the results gained from him by careful comparison with the more fragmentary statements of other
writers. Still, he offers us our best hope of gaining a
coherent conception of the matter in hand.[2]

Clement was clearly at home with the subject of
wealth. He himself had enjoyed the benefits of a fine
education and of world travel in his search for teachers.
It is unlikely, therefore, that he was of the lowest
strata of ancient society. What is more, his audience in
the catechetical school of Alexandria was made up of rich
people. The moral instruction he gave there, exemplified
in his *Paedagogus,* was directed to people who had table
service of gold or silver and gold ornaments on their
clothes; the women wore jewels and slaves waited on them.
Clement's description of their wealth was, to be sure,
partly literary stereotype, but it was not for that reason
pure invention on his part. Much of the *Paedagogus* would
be completely irrelevant if addressed to any audience *but*
that of the rich. And Clement's hearers, if not neces-

sarily the cream of Alexandrian society, were at least
recognizable, by anyone's standard, as rich.[3]
  Some of these rich Christians had begun to fear
that it was impossible for them to be saved without
surrendering their wealth entirely. They had read in the
gospels the story of the rich man who came to Jesus and
enquired what he must do to be saved. Jesus answered that
he must obey the commandments; he replied that he was already doing so. "And Jesus looking upon him loved him,
and said to him, 'You lack one thing; go, sell what you
have, and give to the poor, and you will have treasure in
heaven; and come, follow me.'"[4] Does this saying not command all future Christians of wealth to follow the same
path of abandonment? The whole of the treatise *Who is the*
Rich Man that is Saved? is devoted to refuting that propo-
sition, to vindicating the possibility that the rich can
be saved even *as* rich.
  In the first part of the work (Chaps. 4-27), Clement shows Jesus did not exclude the rich from the Kingdom.
In the second part (27-41), he prescribes how the rich
must act to further their salvation. (The work also includes a short introduction [1-3]; the conclusion is now
partly lost.) The whole treatise is pertinent to our topic,
but we shall begin by examining Clement's reasons for thinking that the rich can be saved, despite what the gospels
seem to teach.
  Clement lays it down on principle that the passage
from Mark is not to be understood literally as saying that
the rich man was to abandon all his possessions: "...the
Saviour teaches His people nothing in a merely human way,
but everything by a divine and mystical wisdom" (5). This
must particularly be true in this case, Clement observes,
for the rich enquirer had already fulfilled the Law (im-
plicitly identified with the literal sense of Scripture)

and he was now coming to Christ as to the true source of
immortality. In other words, he was turning from a religion of eternal works to one of inward contemplation (6-
10). Once this point is established, how can anyone think
that what Jesus demanded was simply one more external work
of righteousness?[5]

The rich man is not "to fling away the substance
that belongs to him," but "to banish from the soul its
opinions about riches, its attachment to them." Poverty
is no virtue in itself, if it is not associated with knowledge of God (11). Even Greek philosophers sometimes cast
away their possessions in this way, and it is unthinkable
that mere pagans could have fulfilled the high and spiritual demands of Christ. At worst, such external abandonment
of wealth can even lead to evil. It may induce men to become "supercilious, boastful, conceited and disdainful of
the rest of mankind"; and the resulting poverty may distract a man from the pursuit of higher things (12).[6]

Money, on the other hand, may even subserve good
ends. The gospel contains commands that cannot be fulfilled without it: such commands as "make to yourselves
friends from the mammon of unrighteousness" (Lk. 16:9), or
"Lay up treasures in heaven" (Mt. 6:20). For almsgiving
and sharing are impossible without wealth (13). "We must
not then fling away the riches that are of benefit to our
neighbors as well as ourselves" (14). In any case, there
is no harm in wealth, so long as its possessor did not accumulate it after becoming a Christian. "For what wrong
does a man do, if by careful thought and frugality he has
before his conversion gathered enough to live on; or, what
is still less open to censure, if from the very first he
was placed by God, the distributor of fortune, in a family
abounding in riches and powerful in wealth?" (26). Clearly
such wealth violates no *Christian* principles for it was not

a Christian who desired or accumulated it.[7]

What, then, does Jesus demand of the rich enquirer?
Clement finds the key to the matter in the Stoic doctrine
that all material things are *adiaphora*—morally indifferent.[8] Virtue and vice reside in the soul alone and in the
way it *uses* wealth. Thus a soul that is poor in passions
and rich in virtues can be trusted to handle material
riches wisely and well (14-19). The important thing is
that nothing earthly should have a stronger grip on our
affections than God does (22-23).

> Can you...rise superior to your riches? Say
> so, and Christ does not draw you away from
> the possession of them; the Lord does not
> grudge. But do you see yourself being
> worsted and overthrown by them? Leave them,
> and cast them off, hate them, say good-bye
> to them, flee from them (24).

The harsh medicine of complete abandonment is thus called
for only in extreme cases. And the rich man of the Gospel
was mistaken when he took Jesus' words literally: "what
was hard he himself had made impossible" (20).[9]

Clement thus devoted much time and energy to
proving that "the Saviour has by no means shut out the
rich" (26). Clearly, the topic was an important one.
There may have been Christian teachers who were actively
discouraging the rich, for Clement refers once to people
who "behave with insolent rudeness towards the rich members of the church" (3). We cannot say just who these
were nor why they attacked the rich, but Clement, too, expressed the belief that wealth constituted a real danger
to the Christian, so that even he could not take it for
granted that the rich would be saved.[10] In the *Paedagogus,*
he compared riches to a snake, "which will twist round the
hand and bite, unless one knows how to lay hold of it without danger by the point of the tail."[11] In *The Rich Man,*
too, he often implies that the rich were particularly in

danger of sinning.

DETACHMENT AND SIMPLICITY

The rich Christian was thus in a position of some
difficulty, which required that he find and practice remedies for his weakness. Above all, he must constantly
practice detachment from wealth and simplicity of life.
These themes Clement treated at some length in the
Paedagogus and *Stromata*. (The second part of *The Rich Man*
concentrates on another remedy, almsgiving.) In the *Stromata,* particularly, Clement referred riches to the category of *adiaphora,* which become good or evil only as they
are used well or ill by a human agent. To use these things
well, however, requires effort and education, for we must
all overcome the effects of human weakness and bad nur-
ture.[12]

Riches, like other aspects of human life, give
rise to passions. The same is true of honors, marriage,
or poverty. But it is the passions that are evil, not the
things themselves. Just so, in the parable of the Great
Supper, the covetous men who rejected the summons did so
"not because of their possessing property, but because of
their inordinate affection to what they possessed."[13] The
remedy for this is clear—inner detachment from all the
pains and pleasures of the external world in which we must
necessarily live.[14]

This inner detachment has its counterpart in an
outer simplicity of life. In the *Paedagogus,* Clement recommended simple foods (those that do not have to be cooked
at all are best) and water as the normal beverage (Bk. 2,
Chaps. 1-2). He opposed the use of gold and silver ves-
sels (Chap. 3); he urged that clothes and shoes be func-
tional and not ornate (Chaps. 10-11); and he vehemently attacked any kind of personal adornment, especially cosmetics

and other means of beautification (Bk. 2, Chap. 13; Bk. 3,
Chaps. 2-3). He was not, to be sure, perfectly consistent,
and he even conceded that "the wearing of gold and the use
of softer clothing is not to be entirely prohibited"; but
he was determined that the rich Christian should not be a
voluptuary.[15]

Clement suggested several reasons why such simplicity must be the standard of Christian life. For one, it is
an imitation of God, who is completely self-sufficient in
his spiritual essence. While complete self-sufficiency is
impossible for a human being, one can at least approach it
"by requiring as few things as possible."[16] Again, simplicity is the natural mode of life for creatures, freely
supplied to them in the ordinary course of the universe:

> No one is poor as regards necessaries, and
> a man is never overlooked. For there is one
> God who feeds the fowls and the fishes and,
> in a word, the irrational creatures; and not
> one thing is wanting to them, though "they
> take no thought for their food." And we are
> better than they....

So confident of this principle is the gnostic (Clement's
"advanced" Christian) that he never prays for necessities,
"being persuaded that God, who knows all things, supplies
the good with whatever is for their benefit, even though
they do not ask."[17]

The Christian, therefore, can escape the temptations of wealth without literally abandoning it, if he
cultivates an inner detachment from it and an outer simplicity in his manner of life. Such a person will not, of
course, desire to *increase* his fortune; (this explains
Clement's implicit criticism of wealth gained after conversion to Christianity). But there can be no harm in keeping
a fortune that one did not gather as a Christian, so long
as one prevents it, through detachment, from becoming a

hindrance to salvation.[18]

ALMSGIVING OR COMMUNISM?

         There is also a more positive remedy that the rich
Christian can apply to his situation—that of almsgiving.
Ths is the principal topic of the second part of *The Rich*
Man, in which Clement attempts to explain how it is that
almsgiving can lead to salvation. The doctrine that alms
can save was itself no stranger to Clement or his audience.
Indeed, many of his hearers embraced it with a calculating
enthusiasm that disturbed Clement; and he attacked their
attitude in the *Stromata:*

                    We must...have recourse to the word of
                    salvation neither from fear of punishment
                    nor promise of a gift, but on account of
                    the good itself. Such as do so, stand on
                    the right hand of the sanctuary; but those
                    who think that by the gift of what is per-
                    ishable they shall receive in exchange what
                    belongs to immortality are in the parable
                    of the two brothers called "hirelings."

Yet, the doctrine had so far penetrated his own thought
that he dropped back into it a few chapters further on in
the same work, by promising different rewards for good
works done according to fear and those done according to
love.[19]

         In *The Rich Man,* Clement became an open advocate
of the doctrine of redemptive almsgiving: "What splendid
trading! What divine business! You buy incorruption with
money. You give the perishing things of the world and receive in exchange for them an eternal abode in heaven"
(32).[20] And he attempted to make this doctrine rationally
intelligible through a complex interpretation of relevant
Scriptural passages. The train of reasoning which Clement
followed in this process was involved and, in some respects
fundamentally alien to modern notions of Biblical exegesis.

In order to make it clear, we must lay the argument out
here step by step.

First, Clement appealed to the Summary of the Law
with its twin commandments—to love God with all one's
might and to love one's neighbor as oneself. The second
of these commandments could be taken as implying almsgiving, and Clement could have argued for alms as an expression of love, as some New Testament authors did. But
this was not, apparently, satisfactory to him. He therefore carried the subject a step further, observing that
Jesus had defined the term "neighbor" by telling the parable of the Good Samaritan. Who is the "neighbor" in this
parable? It is not, if one reads the story with strict
attention to grammar, the man who *received* the benefaction
(the traveler who fell among thieves), but rather the man
who *gave* it (the Samaritan). Our "neighbor" is our *benefactor*. And who fits this description better than Jesus?[21]
The neighbor, therefore, to whom I must direct my
love is none other than Christ, the supreme benefactor of
humanity; it is as much a duty to love him as to love God.
How does one do this? By loving Christ's friends. "For
whatever service a man does for a disciple the Lord ac-
cepts for Himself, and reckons it all His own.... 'He that
hath given a cup of cold water to a disciple in the name
of a disciple shall not lose his reward'" (30). By this
chain of reasoning, Clement brings us to the verse of
Scripture which is really, for him, the clearest rationale
for almsgiving: "Make to yourselves friends from the mammon of unrighteousness, that when it shall fail, they may
receive you into the eternal habitations."[22] One must
give alms precisely to those who have the power, by their
relationship with Christ, to give eternal life: "you should
personally seek out men whom you may benefit, men who are
worthy disciples of the Saviour" (31). The Lord will then

give the benefits of incorruption to you "because of your
esteem and favour and relationship with such men" (33).

By this involved argument, Clement explained that
almsgiving earns a reward because it is done, through the
Christian poor, to Jesus himself. The corollary of this
argument is that the sanctity of the recipient, which
makes him Christ's friend, is as important as his poverty.[2]
The object of the rich almsgiver is to recruit "an army of
God-fearing old men, of God-beloved orphans, of widows
armed with gentleness, of men adorned with love," by whose
prayers the attacks of this world will be thwarted (34).
These dependents will pray for their benefactor, admonish
him "with frankness" (and also treat him with the utmost
love and esteem in this world) (35). In this way, Clement
presents a rational scheme to explain the redemptive powers
generally ascribed to almsgiving: alms make spiritual
friends who have influence with Christ; therefore their
prayers and advice serve to protect the rich man from temptation in this world and to ensure his reception "into the
eternal habitation."

Some particularly holy man may even serve as the
rich Christian's spiritual director. His prayers will
support and enhance the rich man's own repentance for his
sins and will serve to guarantee God's favorable acceptance
of the penitent:

> Let [this man] spend many wakeful nights on
> your behalf, acting as your ambassador with
> God and moving the Father by the spell of
> constant supplications; for He does not
> withstand His children when they beg His
> mercies. And this man will beg them, if he
> is sincerely honoured by you as an angel of
> God and is in nothing grieved by you, but
> only for you. This is unfeigned repent-
> ance (41).

To prove that holy intercessors do indeed have such powers
Clement cites the story of St. John and the Robber. There

was a young man for whom the Apostle John had high hopes
when he first baptized him. Later, the man fell away from
the church and became a brigand, and his congregation gave
him up as lost. But John sought him out, brought him home
to the church, and there "interceded for him with abundant
prayers, helped his struggle by continual fasting, and by
manifold siren-like words laid a soothing spell upon his
mind" (42). John even consecrated him bishop; and this
sudden transition from robber to bishop should certainly
have convinced Clement's wealthy audience that they were
not beyond hope.[24]

Clement was unwilling, however, that the rich
should limit their benefactions to the holiest—those who
could actually serve in the capacity of spiritual advis-
ors.[25] He insisted that the rich must not try to distinguish the worthy poor from the unworthy, but must give indiscriminately lest they overlook "some who are beloved by
God, the penalty for which is eternal punishment by fire"
(33). Anyone "enrolled as a disciple" is worthy of assistance (33); and this assistance is not to be terminated
with one gift, but should extend to "complete relief and
long companionship" (32). Clement thus demanded a high
standard of almsgiving in order that the prayers of the
poor might win eternal rewards for the giver.[26]

Clement could also rationalize the doctrine of redemptive alms in another way. He wrote movingly in *The
Rich Man* of the love of God as motive for alms: "On behalf
of each of us He laid down the life that is equal in value
to the whole world. In return He demands this...from us
on behalf of one another" (37). The love that is expressed
here and now in generosity toward the brethren will go beyond this world of perishing things into the perfect con-
summation, when faith and hope have ceased to be of value
(38). This, then provides an alternate explanation of how

almsgiving in this life affects the life of the world to
come. But in the case of each explanation——that based on
the friendship and prayers of holy men or that based on
the power of love——the emphasis falls on the anticipated
reward.

        Even so, not all the rich heeded Clement's argu-
ments. There were rich women who preferred to spend their
money on lap dogs, birds and "monsters" and looked askance
at the Christian poor. They knew a special type of "poverty"——stinginess, "by which the rich are poor, having nothing to give away." They asserted that they had every
right to use the bounty that God had bestowed on them.[27]
In response to this intransigence, Clement occasionally had
recourse to a yet stronger argument in favor of almsgiving:
the argument that private property is essentially opposed
to God's purpose and that almsgiving is therefore nothing
more than an amelioration of sin.

        This topic requires our particular attention, since
it lies at the heart of the whole modern controversy over
Early Christian attitudes toward wealth. What did Clement
mean by resorting to this argument? Do we have here the
keystone of his thinking? Or are we dealing rather with a
rhetorical flourish, an extreme statement introduced purely
to form the basis for an *a fortiori* argument? The fact that
Clement introduces this teaching against private property
at only two places in his voluminous writings suggests that
it is hardly one of his leading intellectual motifs. But
we must examine these two occurrences carefully to see how
the argument runs in each case.

        One of the passages in question is in the *Paedagogu*
Clement is rebuking the female fondness for jewels and gold
ornaments. In the style of diatribe, Clement allows his
auditors to speak in their own defense; and they draw attention to the frequent mention of jewels in Scripture and

to the fact that God himself created them. After correct-
ing them on the meaning of these points, Clement continues:

> God brought our race into communion by
> first imparting what was His own, when He
> gave his own Logos, common to all, and
> made all things for all. All things
> therefore are common, and not for the
> rich to appropriate an undue share. That
> expression, therefore, "I possess and pos-
> sess in abundance: why then should I not
> enjoy?" is suitable neither to man nor to
> society. But more worthy of love is that:
> "I have: why should I not give to those
> who need?"... For God has given to us, I
> know well, the liberty of use, but only so
> far as necessary; and He has determined
> that the use should be common. And it is
> monstrous for one to live in luxury, while
> many are in want.

What is the point of this passage in context? That the
rich should surrender their property, or that Christians
ought to practice some kind of community of property? No.
The point is simply that the rich ought to use their wealth
to give alms rather than to adorn themselves. The wealth
remains at their disposal, but they have a duty to dispose
of it in accordance with the example set by God himself.
"How much more useful to acquire decorous friends than
lifeless ornaments!"[28]

The other pertinent passage is found in *The Rich
Man*. Clement has just cited Luke 16:9, with its reference
to "the mammon of unrighteousness," and he continues:

> Thus He declares that all possessions are
> by nature unrighteous, when a man possesses
> them for personal advantage as being entire-
> ly his own, and does not bring them into the
> common stock for those in need... (31).

Here, too, Clement appears to be condemning private property entirely; but he fails to draw the obvious conclusion.
Once again, he advocates not communism, but almsgiving.
Indeed, he treats the private fortune as a God-given bounty
for just this purpose:

> ...from this unrighteousness it is pos-
> sible to perform a deed that is righteous
> and saving, namely, to give relief to one
> of those who have an eternal habitation
> with the Father (31).

Even if wealth is, in some sense, intrinsically wrong, it
now acts as an opportunity for and the means to salvation
for those who possess it.[29]

Clement did advocate a voluntary equality of life
among Christians, "for it becomes those that are servants
of one God, that their possessions and furniture should ex-
hibit the tokens of one beautiful life."[30]   But he never
advocated communism of property; indeed, he actually rejected it (along with communism of wives) in his discussion of the views of the Carpocratians.[31]   He treated
wealth not as evil in itself, but rather as a danger or
temptation which the rich Christian might overcome by inner detachment, simplicity of life, and generous almsgiving.

> If...a man chooses to remain in his
> pleasures, sinning time after time, and
> values earthly luxury above eternal life,
> and turns away from the Saviour when He
> offers forgiveness, let him no longer
> blame either God or wealth or his previ-
> ous fall, but his own soul that will
> perish voluntarily.

On those rare occasions when Clement goes beyond this position to term wealth evil in itself, it is purely for the
sake of constructing an *a fortiori* argument: Since there
is no basis for private property in God's will anyway, you
must, all the more, give alms generously as long as you
retain your riches.[32]

CONCLUSIONS

Two different tendencies emerge from our survey of
Clement's thinking on wealth. On the one hand, Clement wa

qualifiedly negative about riches. Even though he did not,
as a rule, suggest that riches were an evil in themselves,
he did hold that they were an occasion of serious temptation to the Christian who possessed them. (Exceptionally,
he would declare all personal property evil as the first
step in an *a fortiori* argument.) As remedies against the
danger of riches, Clement advocated spiritual separation
from them—inner detachment and outer simplicity of life.
Thus far, his position was negative, but not radically so:
wealth is something to disentangle oneself from spiritually, but one may continue to possess it in material terms.

The other side of Clement's attitude was a high
theology of almsgiving, which granted to wealth a positive
role in the salvation of its possessor. He was reluctant
to endorse the doctrine of redemptive alms in the more
gnostic *Stromata.* Yet, he did so with energy in *The Rich
Man,* a work from which one might logically draw the conclusion that the potential benefit of riches more or less
counterbalanced their danger. The two sides of Clement's
thinking are not entirely at odds, for generous almsgiving
could imply a certain detachment from wealth on the part
of the giver. Nonetheless, there is an incongruity here,
the source of which lay in Clement's determination to com-
bine themes drawn from two distinct traditions—Hellenistic
philosophy and Jewish Wisdom.[33]

In the first aspect of his thought, Clement was the
child of his Greek philosophical education. We have already observed that he adopted the Stoic category of
adiaphora, "things morally indifferent," to explain the
ethical significance of wealth. There are other evidences
as well of his dependence on Stoic ethical thought. He
taught that God was *apathēs* (above passion) and that this
was an ideal for man as well. He insisted on simplicity
of life, following a long Stoic tradition of practical

guidance for daily life; indeed, many passages in Book II
of the *Paedagogus* are taken directly and without acknowledgement from the discourses of the first-century Roman
Stoic Musonius Rufus. (On this last topic, Clement had no
difficulty reconciling his philosophical background with
Scripture, for he was able to adduce quotations from the
Prophets and Wisdom writers, too, in support of simplicity
and against luxury.)[34]

This is not to say that Clement simply adopted
philosophical doctrine whole. That would scarcely have
been possible, for there was a variety of attitudes toward
wealth in the philosophical schools. To choose only the
two extremes, by way of illustration, philosophers might
teach anything from the Aristotelian acknowledgement of
wealth as a good and an appropriate attribute of the good
man to the Cynic abandonment of wealth as an impediment to
the philosophical life. Clement knew of these alternatives
and the gospels themselves appeared to support a more negative assessment of wealth: why then did he adhere so firmly
to basic Stoicism? How did Clement make this choice?[35]

Clement relied on the "school" philosophy of his
day—a Middle Platonism which had incorporated many Stoic
ethical doctrines, including those that Clement himself
accepted. The Middle Platonists rejected Aristotle's doctrine, which made human fulfillment at least partially dependent on external circumstances, and embraced the Stoic
ideal of *apatheia,* by which the virtuous man was to rise
above all fear and love of material goods.[36] The Cynic
doctrine of complete abandonment of possessions received
some lip service, but was little practiced by respectable
philosophers of Clement's time.[37] Thus, Clement's ethical
principles were those that were at home in the context in
which he himself was educated; they were essentially identical with those of the *prevailing* philosophy of his day.

Clement was not, however, simply the child of his philosophical education. He combined with it a doctrine of redemptive almsgiving derived from the Hebrew Scriptures. This teaching had a long history in Jewish religious thought before Clement's time (see the discussion in Chapter Three below) and was already popular with the lay members of the church, as we have seen from Clement's own writings. Clement's insistence on combining two disparate traditions shows that he had some end in view beyond simple faithfulness to one or the other. His aim was to say something relevant to the actual situation of the Christian rich.

Why this particular combination of doctrines? The answer to this question lies in the social structure of the early church. Before turning to that subject, however, we must consider whether Clement's attitude toward the rich is truly representative of the early church by comparing his thought with other, less systematic discussions of wealth and almsgiving in Early Christian literature. We shall first examine attitudes toward wealth to see how other authors handle the themes that we have isolated from Clement's work. We shall ask whether there are yet other themes represented in their works which are not found in Clement. Then, in a separate chapter, we shall consider the Early Christian teaching on almsgiving, with special reference to the doctrine of redemptive alms.

FOOTNOTES

[1]Τίς ὁ σῳζόμενος πλούσιος is generally referred to by its Latin
Quis dives salvetur? The point of the title is to distinguish the
rich man who is saved from the one who is damned. Since the title is
cumbersome in English, I shall use a shortened form, *The Rich Man.*
Despite its length, the work was originally an oral address; see Ludwig Paul, pp. 518-19.

[2]Clement was first to write on the subject "in ausführlicher,
zusammenhängende Weise" (Schilling, p. 41). Careful scholars have always recognized that the Early Christian authors on this matter differ
from each other at least in tone (idem, pp. 78-79). Only Seipel, p.
294, was unable to see any real differences among them. In a later
age, Basil the Great probably knew and used Clement's *Quis div.;*
Stanislas Giet, pp. 55-91.

[3]It has long been clear that Clement's portrayal of Alexandrian
luxury is partly literary stereotype; but this does not prove it
false, since an unrecognizable picture of his audience would have defeated his purpose. See Richard Bartram Tollinton, *Clement of Alexandria, A Study in Christian Liberalism,* 2 vols. (London: Williams &
Norgate, 1914), 1:245. Gustave Bardy collects the evidence for the
character of Clement's audience in *Clément d'Alexandrie* (Paris: J.
Gabalda, 1926), pp. 15-16. Clement himself must be thought of as cosmopolitan, but not "as a comfortable and worldly figure"; Henry Chadwick, *Early Christian Thought and the Classical Tradition* (New York:
Oxford University Press, 1966), p. 63.

[4]Mark 10:17-22. In *Quis div.* 4, Clement cites a text that has
been assimilated to Mt. 19:21, though he specifies that he is using
Mark.

[5]Quotations from *Quis div.* are given in the English translation
of G. W. Butterworth in Loeb Classical Library (London: William
Heinemann, 1919).

[6]It is sometimes suggested that Clement became more negative toward poverty over the years and more lenient toward wealth; so, for
example, Markgraf, pp. 511-12, and Tollinton, pp. 321-24. Hagen, p.
47, attempted to refute this claim by showing the basic consistency of
Quis div. with *Stromata* and *Paedagogus.* In any case, the chronological relation of these works is uncertain.
    It appears that Philo, whose lead Clement often followed, also
rejected the Cynic ideal of abandonment; F. Geiger, *Philon von Alexandreia als sozialer Denker,* Tübinger Beiträge zur Altertumswissenschaft, no. 14 (Stuttgart: W. Kohlhammer, 1932), p. 28. For a discussion of the Cynic-Stoic teaching, see Rainer Nickel, "Das Verhältnis
von Bedürfnis und Brauchbarkeit in seiner Bedeutung für das
kynostoische Ideal der Bedürfnislosigkeit," *Hermes* 100 (1972):42-47

[7]In his preference for inherited wealth, Clement resembles Seneca
(*Ep.* 20.10), who thought inherited wealth best because it is least distracting spiritually. See also *De brevitate vitae* 23.2. Despite his
rejection of acquisition, Clement does not seem to have condemned
trade; Hagen, pp. 19-20, 23.

[8]Wilhelm Capitaine, *Die Moral des Clemens von Alexandrien,* Jahrbuch für Philosophie und spekulative Theologie, Erganzungsheft 7
(Paderborn, 1902), pp. 191-94; Olivier Prunet, *La morale de Clément
d'Alexandrie et le Nouveau Testament* (Paris: Presses Universitaires
de France, 1966), p. 145.

[9]*Quis div.* 24: Δύνασαι καὶ τῶν χρημάτων ἐπίπροσθεν εἶναι; φράσον
καὶ οὐκ ἀπάγει σε χριστὸς τῆς κτήσεως, ὁ κύριος οὐ φθονεῖ, ἀλλ' ὁρᾷς
σεαυτὸν ἡττώμενον ὑπ' αὐτῶν καὶ ἀνατρεπόμενον; ἄφες, ῥῖψον, μίσησον,
ἀπόταξαι, φύγε.
It is hard to say what Clement meant by saying that the rich man
had interpreted Jesus' command in such a way as to make it impossible.
He had already noted the fact that some of the Greeks had abandoned
their wealth; it was not therefore impossible in the abstract. Some
of Clement's rich auditors, however, no doubt considered it impossible;
perhaps he is identifying himself rhetorically with their point of
view.

[10]The identity of these opponents of the rich is obscure. Hagen,
pp. 29-30, suggested that they were Gnostics, some of whom did advocate communism. Others have suggested that it was Clement's own
rigorous position in *Paed.* that had alarmed his hearers (Markgraf, p.
511; Tollinton, 1:304-5); but Clement would scarcely have referred to
himself in this derogatory manner. With these opponents who "behave
with insolent rudeness" (καταθρασυνομένους αὐθάδως), contrast the behavior Clement expected of the Christian poor, who will address their
patrons with frankness (μετὰ παρρησίας), but with such respect that
"they seem to touch not your flesh but each his own soul" (35).

[11]*Paed.* 3.35.1 (Chapt. 6). Translations from *Paed.* and *Strom.*
are based on those of W. Wilson (*The Ante-Nicene Fathers,* ed. Alexander Roberts and James Donaldson. American edition ed. A. Cleveland
Coxe, 8 vols. [Buffalo: Christian Literature Publishing Co., 1885-86]),
revised to make them more intelligible and to bring them into conform-
ity with the Greek text of Stählin (*GCS*). Chapter numbers, from *ANF*,
are added to the references for the convenience of readers who do not
have access to the Greek edition.

[12]*Strom.* 2.109.3-4 (Chap. 20).

[13]*Strom.* 4.31.1-5 (Chap. 6); cf. 3.4.1-2 (Chap. 1). The true
gnostic is ἀπάθης; see Walter Völker, *Der wahre Gnostiker nach Clemens
Alexandrinus, TU* 57 (1952):524-40, and Salvatore R. C. Lilla, *Clement
of Alexandria: A Study in Christian Platonism and Gnosticism* (London:

Oxford University Press, 1971), p. 217.

[14] See Lilla, pp. 109, 182.

[15] *Paed.* 3.53.1 (Chap. 11). Markgraf, pp. 487, 509-10, 513, called attention to the difference between Clement's rejection of luxury and Origen's more ascetic attitude.

[16] *Paed.* 3.1.1 (Chap. 1). This was an old philosophical theme; see *RAC,* s.v. "Autarkie," by P. Wilpert.

[17] *Paed.* 2.14.5 (Chap. 1); *Strom.* 7.46.1 (Chap. 7). Clement was too practical to press this argument to an extreme; elsewhere, he spiritualizes it, saying not that physical necessities are guaranteed, but that the one real necessity for the Christian is the Logos of God (*Paed.* 3.39.4-40.2 [Chap. 7]). On the importance of moderation and the ideal of nature in Clement's moral thought, see Eric Osborn, *Ethical Patterns in Early Christian Thought* (Cambridge: Cambridge University Press, 1976), pp. 53-56.

[18] Acquisition implied, for Clement, an unhealthy attachment to wealth. Cf. *Quis div.* 17: ὁ δὲ ἐν τῇ ψυχῇ τὸν πλοῦτον φέρων, καὶ ἀντὶ θεοῦ πνεύματος ἐν τῇ καρδίᾳ χρυσὸν φέρων ἢ ἀγρόν, καὶ τὴν κτῆσιν ἄμετρον ἀεὶ ποιῶν, καὶ ἑκάστοτε τὸ πλεῖον βλέπων, κάτω νενευκὼς καὶ τοῖς τοῦ κόσμου θηράτροις πεπεδημένος, γῆ ὢν καὶ εἰς γῆν ἀπελευσόμενος πόθεν δύναται βασιλείας οὐρανῶν ἐπιθυμῆσαι καὶ φροντίσαι;

[19] *Strom.* 4.29.4-30.1 (Chap. 6); cf. 4.113.6-114.1 (Chap. 18).

[20] The difference between *Strom.* and *Quis div.* is less one of theory than of audience. The reader of *Strom.* is assumed to be on his way to higher, gnostic spiritual attainments; the reader of *Quis div.* is but one of the faithful—and perpetually in danger of falling short of that. Clement recognized different ethical motives as appropriate to different spiritual levels; Capitaine, pp. 259-66.

[21] At first (*Quis div.* 28), Clement hints that Jesus told the parable of the Good Samaritan in order to expand the sense of the term "neighbor," which Jewish usage tended to limit to the meaning "fellow-Jew." But he does not develop this line of thought at all. Instead, in section 29, he defines "neighbor" with the words, "And who else can this be but the Saviour himself?" (τίς δ' ἂν ἄλλος οὗτος εἴη πλὴν αὐτὸς ὁ σωτήρ;). There follows a description of Jesus' work in terms of binding up wounds, on analogy with the parable. Schilling's treatment (p. 43) of *Quis div.* 28 as a call to universal almsgiving is therefore incomplete and misleading.

[22] Lk. 16:9.

[23] Clement does acknowledge elsewhere (*Strom.* 7, Chap. 12) that

alms should be given even to enemies, but here he thinks only of almsgiving to other Christians. The same point is made in Frag.
53 (GCS):
Ἐλεημοσύνας δεῖ ποιεῖν, ὁ λόγος φησίν, ἀλλὰ μετὰ κρίσεως καὶ τοῖς ἀξίοις·
ὥσπερ γὰρ ὁ γεωργὸς σπείρει οὐκ εἰς ἅπασαν γῆν, ἀλλ᾽ εἰς τὴν ἀγαθήν, ἵνα
αὐτῷ καρποφορήσῃ, οὕτω δεῖ σπείρειν τὴν εὐποιΐαν εἰς εὐλαβεῖς καὶ
πνευματικούς, ἵνα τῆς ἀπ᾽ αὐτῶν εὐκαρπίας διὰ τῶν εὐχῶν ἐπιτύχῃς. In
support of this position, Clement cites Sir. 12.2.

[24]The chaplain's power to procure forgiveness is doubly surprising in light of Clement's restrictions on the power of the penitential
discipline; A. Méhat, "Penitence seconde et péché volontaire chez
Clément d'Alexandrie," VC 8 (1954):225-33. Clement's concept of a
chaplaincy to the rich has never been properly explored, though it has
been noted: John Patrick, Clement of Alexandria (Edinburgh: William
Blackwood & Sons, 1914), p. 182; Henry Chadwick, Early Christian
Thought, pp. 63-64; and Osborn, pp. 64-65.

[25]There is some confusion between the role of the chaplain (who
must be of advanced spirituality, according to Quis div. 36) and the
role of ordinary poor Christians, to whom Clement gives responsibilities for spiritual direction in Quis div. 35.

[26]The gnostic knows how to distinguish the worthy from the unworthy; Strom. 7.69.2-3 (Chap. 12). But the audience of Quis div. is
composed of the "faithful." There is a distinction, then (contrary to
Seipel, p. 213) between worthy and unworthy recipients; Clement simply
refuses the faithful the right or the understanding to act on it.

[27]Paed. 3.30.2-4 (Chap. 4); 2.119.2 (Chap. 13). The first passage is exaggerated, even including the claim that these women expose
unwanted children. I know of no other suggestion that the early
Christians ever tolerated this practice; Athenagoras specifically denied it, Pres. 35.

[28]Paed. 2.120.3-6 (Chap. 12); the whole passage 2.119.1-121.1 is
relevant.

[29]Quis div. 31: φύσει μὲν ἅπασαν κτῆσιν, ἣν αὐτός τις ἐφ᾽ ἑαυτοῦ
κέκτηται ὡς ἰδίαν οὖσαν καὶ οὐκ εἰς κοινὸν τοῖς δεομένοις κατατίθησιν,
ἄδικον οὖσαν ἀποφαίνων, ἐκ δὲ ταύτης τῆς ἀδικίας ἐνὸν καὶ πρᾶγμα δίκαιον
ἐργάσασθαι καὶ σωτήριον, ἀναπαῦσαί τινα τῶν ἐχόντων αἰώνιον σκηνὴν παρὰ
τῷ πατρί.
Brentano, pp. 150-51, cited the passages from Paed. and Quis div.
as proof that Clement fostered communism; Hagen, pp. 27-28, demonstrated the inadequacy of this interpretation. This exchange did not,
however, bring the controversy to an end, despite the conclusiveness
of Hagen's argument—or of the texts themselves.

[30]Paed. 2, Chap. 3.

[31]Strom. 3, Chap. 2.

[32]*Quis div.* 42 end. Philo exhibits a similar lack of apparent
clarity in his discussion of private property; Geiger, pp. 30-31.

[33]The incomplete nature of Clement's synthesis has given rise to
widely varying estimates of the character and sources of his message.
He has been interpreted as an ascetic on the Cynic-Stoic model (so
Markgraf, p. 510, and Wilhelm Wagner, p. 78). Hagen (pp. 37-43), on
the other hand, insisted that Clement borrowed nothing from the Stoics
but language, which he completely transformed to the service of uniquely Christian doctrine. For more recent views, see Prunet, pp. 145-47,
and H. I. Marrou, "Morale et spiritualité chretiennes dans le Pédagogue de Clément d'Alexandrie," *Studia Patristica* 2, 2 pts. (*TU*, 63-
64), 2:541-44. Osborn, pp. 50-59, is not completely clear about
Clement's debt to philosophy.

[34]Henry Chadwick (*Early Christian Thought,* pp. 61, 147, n. 152)
has pointed out that the treatment of wealth in *Quis div.* is "closely
analogous to that of Seneca," *De beata vita* 20-22. On *apatheia,* see
Capitaine, pp. 287-88, and Lilla, p. 105. On *adiaphora,* see above,
p. 65, n. 8.

[35]At the extreme, Aristotle could claim that wealth was appropriate and good for the gentleman, but not for the many (*Eth. Eud.*
8.1249a6-15). The Cynics and Stoics, on the other hand, regarded too
much property as a distraction from the truly important—virtue and
understanding; Nickel, pp. 46-47. Real poverty, however, might be no
less distracting than wealth; Seneca, *Tranq.* 8.8, 9.1. Seneca encouraged Lucilius to devote himself to philosophy without waiting to
accumulate more wealth; but he based his argument on the fact that
Lucilius was already rich enough (*Ep.* 17.10). Clement did make use of
Aristotle's analytic method in dealing with ethical issues; so Elizabeth A. Clark, *Clement's Use of Arstotle: The Aristotelian Contribution to Clement of Alexandria's Refutation of Gnosticism,* Texts and
Studies in Religion (New York: The Edwin Mellen Press, 1977), pp. 13-
14.

[36]Lilla, pp. 71, 109-10, 227-32. Clement relied not only on his
Middle Platonist schooling, but also on his great Alexandrian prede-
cessor, Philo.

[37]Epictetus, *Diss.* 3.22. Rüdiger Vischer, *Das einfache Leben:
Wort- und motivgeschichtliche Untersuchungen zu einem Wertbegriff der
antiken Literatur* (Göttingen: Vandenhoeck & Ruprecht, 1965), pp. 85-
86. Ramsay MacMullen, *Enemies of the Roman Order: Treason, Unrest,
and Alienation in the Empire* (Cambridge: Harvard University Press,
1966), pp. 49-50. One degenerate Cynic was the Crescens who was responsible for the martyrdom of Justin and whom Tatian accused of
greed (*Orat.* 19).

CHAPTER TWO

EARLY CHRISTIAN ATTITUDES
TOWARD WEALTH

DETACHMENT

The heart of Clement's teaching about wealth was his
doctrine of detachment: it is permissible to possess riches,
but not to love them. This teaching had a philosophical
basis for Clement; but it was a significant theme in other
Christian authors, too (even in those with no philosophical
pretensions), so that we cannot dismiss it lightly as a
relic of Clement's pagan education. It was Paul who first
struck this note of detachment clearly:

> ...the appointed time has grown very short;
> from now on, let those who have wives live as
> though they had none, and those who mourn as
> though they were not mourning, and those who
> rejoice as though they were not rejoicing, and
> those who buy as though they had no goods, and
> those who deal with the world as though they
> had no dealing with it. For the form of this
> world is passing away (I Cor. 7:29-31).

We know, from this same chapter of I Corinthians, that Paul
did not encourage abandonment of existing marriages, but
rather an inner detachment from the all-absorbing claims of
marriage. In the same way, he asks here for detachment
from property, not abandonment of it.[1]

Paul offered an eschatological, not a philosophical
rationale for this detachment. Yet, he could express himself in philosophical terms, too. He said of himself on
one occasion, "I have learned in whatever state I am, to be
content (*autarkēs*). I know how to be abased, and I know
how to abound; in any and all circumstances, I have learned

the secret of facing plenty and hunger, abundance and want"
(Phil. 4:11-12). This "contentment" (*autarkeia*, "self-sufficiency") was a primary goal of the Cynic-Stoic philosophers; they sought it partly by practicing spare living,
partly by cultivating the doctrine that all external, material things are *adiaphora*. While Paul was no Stoic
philosopher himself, he found that their terminology expressed his own ideal of Christian behavior in this connection.[2]

The author of I John made a similar point in telling
his readers not to "love the world or the things in the
world" (2:15)——a warning directed not against material
things as such, but rather against one's attachment to
these things. "For all that is in the world, the lust of
the flesh and the lust of the eyes and the pride of life,
is not of the Father but is of the world" (2:16). Thus it
is not the object of lust, but the lust itself that is sinful. There is no reason to attribute John's teaching, any
more than Paul's, to a philosophical training.

The rhetorician Tertullian varied his argument with
his audiences, and had no personal commitment to philosophy.
When arguing against the Marcionites, he even defended the
right of the Old Testament God to bestow wealth on men because "by the help of riches even rich men are comforted
and assisted; moreover, by them many a work of justice and
charity is carried out." Yet, he, too, emphasized the necessity of using riches with detachment, relying on Paul as
his authority.[3]

The more philosophical authors differ only in that
the theme of detachment is more prominent and is phrased in
more philosophical terms. Thus, the author of the *Sentences
of Sextus* urged his readers to "practice *autarkeia*" (334),
to take losses lightly (91b), and to consider nothing as of
value that can be taken away (130).[4] And the premier Chris-

tian philosopher, Origen, also made detachment one of his
themes. Unfortunately, it is difficult to be sure what he
really thought, since he took no care to make his scattered comments on the subject consistent: he was capable
of urging extreme asceticism and the doctrine of wealth as
adiaphoron in the same work. Thus, in his treatise on the
Lord's Prayer, he refused to admit that even the necessities of material life were a worthy topic of prayer and
maintained that the petition for bread must not be taken
literally. Yet, elsewhere in the same work, he argued that
neither wealth nor poverty had any ethical significance in
itself; each offered its own set of temptations. [5]

Origen refused to consider wealth a good, reserving
that honored title for "the first cause" and "virtue." But
neither was it an evil. The rich whom Jesus condemned were,
according to Origen, not the rich as such, but either those
"distracted by wealth" or those who are "rich in false-
hoods." He even considered the possibility that to abandon
wealth might not lead to the desired detachment from it,
but rather to regret and a longing for one's lost property.
Ultimately, however, the spirit that is fully united to God
will have no more earthly dealings, for it is only the person "who had money or possessions or any sort of business
in the world" that is subject to the authority of this
world. Origen thus leaned toward a complete renunciation of
wealth as the ideal for the advanced Christian; but he did
not condemn wealth as such. [6]

We have already noted, in the works of Clement, that
detachment from wealth should rule out further acquisition
of it. We can cite a number of Early Christian authors who
attacked the acquisitive temperament. The author of the
Pastorals, for example, wrote, "The love of money is the
root of all evil." The author of *II Clement* warned that
"when we desire to obtain [the things of this world], we

fall from the right way" (5.7); and Hermas held that a
Christian should have only one business (*praxis*), so as to
keep him from excessive involvement in the world and from
sin. Athenagoras declared that all acquisition came from
passion, while Origen equated avarice and idolatry.[7]

Tertullian branded avarice as a gentile vice, as-
serting that "there is nothing which damnation [itself]
would fear that they hesitate to essay" for the sake of
profit. He blamed avarice when Christians engaged in the
incense trade despite its idolatrous connections. On one
occasion, he went much further and laid the blame not on
greed, but on riches as such: "for we all know that money
is the author of unrighteousness and the master of the
whole world." Still, it does not appear that Tertullian
thought money could be abolished, or even that Christians
should give up the use of it. In fact, some time later in
life, he bragged to a Roman governor of Africa that the
Christians' reputation for probity was based on their reliability in handling other people's deposits, which suggests that Christians had made a mark in the banking business.[8]

Even if acquisition was condemned, it was thought
permissible to keep whatever fortune one already had.
Irenaeus, for example, who argued that all fortunes were
built up on the basis of deception and fraud, did not suggest that Christians should therefore abandon such wealth
as they had inherited or earned before becoming Christians
—only that they should give alms from it. He defended
Christian wealth by implication when he compared it to the
spoils that the Israelites brought out of Egypt by divine
command.[9]

There is a great deal of material in our sources on
this question of avarice and acquisition. But most of it
would be little to our point here, for it deals not with

the Christian rich in general, but with the multitude of
temptations that beset the Christian clergy. The early
church was plagued—so the literary remains suggest—by
greedy ministers, wandering prophets who would milk one
church and move on to another, confessors who lived luxuri-
ously in prison, local elders who helped themselves from
the church treasury. This is an interesting topic in itself, but it falls outside our present purview. It is
enough to say here that Early Christian attacks on avarice
were directed more often at the clergy than at the rich
laymen.[10]

In sum, the ideal of detachment from wealth is one
which occurs frequently in the writings of our period. It
is most highly developed in those authors of a philosophical bent; but they do not have a monopoly on it. The normal attitude of the Christian authorities seems to have
been close to that of Clement of Alexandria. It was all
right for Christians to retain whatever wealth they might
have; but for them to accumulate more raised the spectre
of avarice. Such acquisition was not unlawful (at least,
no one was expelled from the church for becoming rich);
but it contradicted the ideal of detachment, by which alone
our authors could justify the continued possession of
wealth.[11]

SIMPLICITY

Clement's theme of simplicity of life is also well
represented in other writings, beginning with the Pastorals,
whose author urged Timothy to be content with the necessities of life. This teaching is to be distinguished from
that of asceticism, which tended to reject even the necessities as far as possible. The Q material in Matthew and
Luke drew a sharp contrast between the asceticism practiced
by John the Baptist and the more relaxed manner of life

pursued by Jesus who "came eating and drinking." Yet,
Jesus' own existence was one of great simplicity, and he
himself attacked luxury in the parable of "The Rich Man
and Lazarus."[12]

        In some of the later, more philosophically inclined
Christian authors, it is difficult to distinguish sharply
between simplicity and asceticism, no doubt because contemporary philosophers were merging the one into the other.
"Sextus," for example, taught that one should adhere to
the standard of simplicity because it is the necessities
of life alone that God freely supplies to all (117). He
forbade tormenting the body for the sake of the soul (411).
Yet, he also exalted "self-control" (*enkrateia*) as an in-
dispensable Christian virtue (438), so that already his
thinking was oriented toward asceticism as a means to grace
rather than simplicity as the natural style of Christian
living.[13]

        This tendency was still more pronounced in Origen.
He interpreted the "twisted flax" which went into the
making of the tabernacle as a sign of the offering of the
Christian's flesh. "Therefore God does not want flesh offered that is running with luxury and unstrung by delica-
cies, but rather he orders that it be twisted (*or* tortured)
and compressed...by abstinence, watches and the work of
meditations." On the other hand, Origen also taught that
one must give the body what is necessary to it; and he attacked those who forbade rendering this "tribute to Caesar."
When he defended Christian life and teaching against the
attacks of the pagan Celsus, he emphasized not asceticism,
but the ideal of moderation.[14]

        Origen's teaching varied with his audience and pur-
pose. And that was true for other Christian authors, as
well. Apologists, writing for pagans, were apt to give a
glowing report of the Christians' unswerving devotion to

the simple life. Minucius Felix, for example. portrayed
Christians as practitioners of a philosophical *frugalitas*—
what Seneca had called "voluntary poverty."[15] His fellow
Roman Hermas, who was addressing a Christian audience, not
a pagan one, drew quite a different picture. He spoke of
Christians who ate too much and made themselves sick,
warning them that luxury was amongst the very worst of
sins, right alongside adultery. When he urged Christians
to be content with a "modest competency" in this world and
to refrain from "evil luxury" and "much eating," he did
not intend to utter platitudes.[16]

In Tertullian, we have a single author who addressed
himself to both audiences, pagan and Christian, at different times. Speaking to pagans, he bragged about the faithful as models of simplicity and moderation; he even cast
them as the true heirs of the old Romans, who had practiced these same virtues. When he turned to a Christian
audience, he found it necessary to remind them of their
standards and to denounce them for failure to live up to
them.[17]

Thus, the prevailing Christian attitude was that
all the rich are tempted to extravagance in their manner of
life, while the proper Christian style was one of moderation. The teaching of simplicity must have received some
acceptance within the church, for apologists expected pagans to believe them when they claimed that Christians
lived by this ideal. But the rich layman did not always
embrace it with enthusiasm; and other writers (or the same
writer, when addressing himself to a Christian audience)
found it necessary to rebuke the same people whom the apologists had portrayed as exemplars of virtue. It was in
theory, more than in practice, that the early church up-
held its ideal of simplicity.

COMMUNISM[18]

Clement of Alexandria thus proves to have been representative of Early Christian thinking about wealth insofar as his teaching on detachment and simplicity of life
is concerned. What of the communist language that he occasionally used? There were instances of this among other
Christian writers as well; and we must attempt to decide
whether these other authors, like Clement, were simply
using communist premises to reach non-communist conclusions or whether there were some who actually saw community
of property as a characteristic of Christian religion and
ethics. It is this issue of Early Christian communism,
more than any other, that has inspired the modern discussion of our subject, and it therefore holds a special interest for us. At the same time, we must remember that the
relevant passages are few and scattered and that this is
not the most characteristic theme of Early Christian writings on wealth.[19]

Some authors made use of communist language for the
same purpose that Clement himself had used it—to form the
basis for an *a fortiori* argument for almsgiving. Thus, the
early "Two Ways" document exhorted:

> Thou shalt not turn away the needy, but
> shalt share everything with thy brother,
> and shalt not say that it is thine own,
> for if you are sharers in the imperishable,
> how much more in the things which perish?

Yet, there is no suggestion of a functioning community of
goods in either of the works derived from the "Two Ways"
document, the *Didache* and the *Epistle of Barnabas*. We find
no regulations for receiving property from new converts, no
penalties for false accounting, no method of allotting necessities. *Barnabas,* to be sure, is little interested in
any sort of regulations; but the many regulations in the
Didache concentrate rather on almsgiving and the payment of

dues to the clergy. Here, as in the case of Clement, the
language of communism is simply part of an argument for
almsgiving.[20]

     Apologists also were inclined to apply communist
language to Christian almsgiving, though with a different
purpose. Their object was to impress a pagan audience,
accustomed to the fact that some philosophers advocated
communism, with the philosophical character of Christianity. Thus Justin reported that Christians brought their
property "into a common fund (*koinon*)" for distribution to
those in need.[21] The author of the *Epistle to Diognetus*
claimed that Christians kept a "common table"; but, conscious that community of property was usually associated
by the philosophers with community of wives and families,
he hastened to add that Christians did *not* have a common
bed.[22] Tertullian embodied the same claim and the same
disclaimer in one sentence: "All things are without distinction [of ownership] among us except wives."[23] But
there is nothing else in the works of these authors to bear
out such claims; and there is a great deal in Tertullian
(for example, his attack on the luxury of rich Christians)
to disprove them. The claims were meant strictly for consumption by the pagan public; the reality behind them was
not true communism, but the Christian practice of almsgiving.[24]

     This is not to say that no Early Christian author
took his own language about communism seriously. Clement
himself no doubt believed what he said about the wrongful
nature of private property, even if he did not think that
it was possible to abolish it in practice. The author of
the *Sentences of Sextus* was quite serious about the matter:
"For those who have God in common—and as father at that—
it is impious for their property not to be common" (228).
Since the *Sentences* are replete with neo-Pythagorean ele-

ments and the Pythagoreans had an ideal of communal property within their small associations, this author may even
have conceived of communism as a practical goal.[25]

Origen, who regarded the *Sentences of Sextus* highly,
appealed to the example of Greek philosophy. He insisted
that a complete abandonment of goods was possible, since
the Cynic Crates of Thebes had done it. He felt that the
common fund of the church could serve to maintain those
who made this sacrifice. But he admitted that it was not
usual, even for Christian clergy.[26]

In sum, none of the Early Christian authors we have
examined thus far can be said truly to have advocated community of goods, with the probable exception of Sextus.[27]
The rest toyed with the idea——some as a way of enhancing
their arguments for almsgiving, others as a way of making
the church appear like a community of philosophers in the
eyes of the pagan reader. Origen could resort to communist
language for reasons as trivial as exegetical expediency,
when it helped him dismiss the literal sense of a passage
and get on to the allegorical one.[28]

There remains, however, one Early Christian author
whose thinking is of critical importance and whom we have
not yet considered——Luke. Luke described the earliest
Christian community in Jerusalem as practicing communism:
"the company of those who believed were of one heart and
soul, and no one said that any of the things which he possessed was his own, but they had everything in common"
(Acts 4:32). All who owned real estate sold it and brought
the proceeds to the apostles, who then distributed it according to need. One such man was Joseph Barnabas who sold
a field and handed the money over to the apostles (4:36-37).
Ananias and Sapphira, however, two other members of the
church, brought divine judgment on themselves by their
fraudulent mishandling of a similar sale.[29]

Luke's account of primitive Christian communism may
be intelligible on the literary level,[30] but it is difficult to reconcile all that he tells us historically. Luke
at first makes it sound as though it was a universal rule
that the rich should sell their property and hand the proceeds over to the church authorities. Yet, Peter assured
Ananias that he had been free *not* to sell and that, having
done so, he could have disposed of the money as he himself
determined. The fatal charge against him and his wife was
not that they had withheld the money, but rather that they
had "lied...to God" (5:4). Ananias and Sapphira aimed at
joining the heady ranks of those who had sacrificed heroic-
ally, but without making the actual sacrifice. If we had
only their story to go on, we should deduce that the primitive church at Jerusalem practiced not communism, but rather an extravagant form of almsgiving which entailed complete abandonment of goods. In the absence of other information about the matter, it is difficult to know which was
in fact the case.[31]

Either community of property or almsgiving seems
possible in terms of contemporary Judaism. Complete dissi-
pation of one's property through almsgiving was not unknown;
in fact, later rabbis sought to limit almsgiving to a fixed
percentage of income in order to prevent it. Neither was
communism unfamiliar, for the Essenes of the time practiced
community of goods. The historical context of the early
Jerusalem church is thus of no help to us.[32]

Ultimately, the question is whether Luke's summary
(4:32) or the story of Ananias and Sapphira is more apt to
reflect the actual life of the primitive church. I should
favor the latter, for a concrete narrative is likely to
have a foundation in oral tradition, while the summary is
apt to come from a redactor, as he interprets the traditional material he has received. We should conclude, then,

with the story of Ananias and Sapphira that the primitive
church practiced not true communism, but what Troeltsch
has called "love-communism," in which there was strong religious pressure for the rich to sacrifice their goods for
the community, but no formal requirement that they do so.
Luke then built on this foundation of fact by insisting
that, even though the abandonment of property was an act of
free will, it was nonetheless universal, so that the Jerusalem church had practiced a kind of voluntary communism.[33]

Luke's reason for presenting the earliest Christian
community in this light was apologetic, like that of some
later Christian authors who made use of communist themes.
He characterized the primitive communism with key phrases
borrowed from the social ideals of Greek philosophy and
Mosaic Law. In accordance with the philosophical ideal of
friendship, the Christians were of "one heart and soul";
like Israel when it is obedient to the Law, "there was not
a needy person among them."[34] In this way, Luke suggested
to his readers that the church was the fulfillment of all
the social ideals of antiquity. Like his successors among
the Christian apologists, he was probably guilty of a certain exaggeration.[35]

It thus appears that we can point to no one time or
place (before the rise of coenobitic monasticism, at any
rate) when Christians actually practiced communism as their
rule of life. While the primitive church at Jerusalem must
have come close, its arrangements remained voluntary, and
it did not require abandonment of property from every rich
convert.[36] Why then, did Early Christian authors, from
Luke onwards, resort repeatedly to the language of communism when describing Christianity to the pagan world or
when exhorting the Christian rich to give alms more generously? Some current within Christian life and thought
urged them in this direction, while some other influence

restrained them from trying to enforce communist practice
within the church. The task of defining these conflicting
currents, we must leave to a subsequent chapter.

RIGHTEOUS POOR AND WICKED RICH

Now that we have surveyed other authors in addition
to Clement of Alexandria, we can say that there was a
broad consensus throughout our period that wealth was permissible for Christians but suspect. While individual authors differ in the degree of their animosity toward wealth,
none is totally antagonistic, nor is any altogether friendly toward it. All join in recognizing wealth as a possibility for the Christian, while at the same time hedging
it about with certain restrictions and obligations. Clement's thinking has thus far proven to be representative in
general tenor.[37]

There remains, however, another attitude toward
wealth, hitherto passed over in our survey because it was
not represented in Clement's works. In a limited number of
Early Christian writings we find the motif of the "righteous poor," which assumes that it is the poor who are truly
pious and pleasing in God's sight, while the rich are
wicked. As we have seen, this motif has become common in
Jewish sectarian literature of the first centuries B.C. and
A.D., where the "poor" are often identical with the
"saints."[38]

The primitive Jewish-Christian community in Jerusalem was itself a Jewish sect—and under the particular
suspicion of the rich Sadducees. It would not be surprising if it had adopted this manner of speaking of itself;
and there is some evidence that it did. Paul referred once
to the "poor" (Gal. 2:10) and again to the "poor among the
saints at Jerusalem" (Rom. 15:26) in a way that has caused
some to believe that this was in fact the normal title of

the primitive Christian community.[39]

   The Epistle of James, which derives from early
Palestinian Christianity, draws the sharpest contrast of
any New Testament book between rich and poor.[40]   In discussing the attitude of James, however, one must distinguish between passages that deal with the Christian rich
and those that deal with non-Christians——something that has
not always been done.[41]   Within the church itself, James
knew that there were both rich and poor, whom he saw as ex-
periencing a reversal of their worldly fortune: the humble
brother had been exalted and the rich one humbled, and
both were to rejoice in this turn of events (1:9-10).   For
the rich, in particular, it was their "humiliation" now
that would save them from the wrath to come (1:10-11).   Unfortunately, James did not explain in what this humiliation
consists.[42]

   Toward the non-Christian rich, on the other hand,
James was bitterly antagonistic.   He accused them of de-
frauding their laborers, while they themselves lived in
luxury; and he promised them misery in the future.   He thus
considered the rich as such to be sinners and deserving of
the worst retribution——a fate from which the Christian rich
are saved only by their humiliation within the church.   Who
were these non-Christian rich?   They were persecutors of
the church, indeed, the very people who killed "the righteous man"——in other words, the Sadduces who inspired the
hatred of all contemporary Jewish sectarians.   If one of
them paid a visit to the church, he might be received, but
only on the same terms as a poor man.   It was, after all,
the poor whom God called and chose.[43]

   It will not do, in reading James' epistle, to give
the words "rich" and "poor" simply their social-economic
significance and to leave it at that.[44]   After all, if the
rich are by nature condemned to punishment, why are there

rich members within the church? For James, the primary
meaning of these words was their sectarian reference: Sadducees (the rich) are wicked and the opponents of the
church; non-Sadducees (the poor), pre-eminently the Christians themselves, are presumed to be righteous.[45]

Language so closely tied to the political and social
realities of a particular place and era could not have much
meaning outside those original, narrow boundaries. In
Revelation, one finds a few traces of an equation between
wealth (or, more precisely, trade) and sin; but the motif
has been softened drastically.[46] Elsewhere, one scarcely
meets with this theme in Early Christian writings—with one
great exception, where it was preserved permanently to act
as an influence on subsequent Christian thought, the Gospel
of Luke.

One turn-of-the-century scholar described Luke as
the "socialist evangelist"—a designation founded on Luke's
apparent interest in the poor.[47] He strikes this characteristic note early in his gospel, when Mary celebrates the beginning of the age of redemption by singing:

> He has shown strength with his arm,
> he has scattered the proud in the imagination of their hearts,
> he has put down the mighty from their thrones,
> and exalted those of low degree;
> he has filled the hungry with good things,
> and the rich he has sent empty away (1:51-53).

The glad tidings of Christ's birth are brought first to
poor shepherds (2:8-9); and the poverty of Mary and Joseph
themselves appears when they take their son to the temple
to redeem him in accordance with the Law—and present the
poor-man's offering (2:24).[48] Jesus opens his own ministry
with a quotation from Isaiah about preaching "good news to
the poor" (4:18).[49] And Jesus' opponents are later characterized as "lovers of money" (16:14).

Luke's most striking opposition between righteous
poor and evil rich occurs in the Sermon on the Plain:

> Blessed are you poor, for yours is the
> kingdom of God.
>
> . . . .
>
> But woe to you that are rich, for you
> have received your consolation (6:20b, 24).

Here we find the theme of the righteous poor in absolute
form. Poverty in itself is a virtue and will earn its reward; wealth in itself is a vice and will be punished in
the world to come with a reversal of fortune. The same
point is made again in the parable of "The Rich Man and
Lazarus" (16:19-31). There Abraham explains that the fate
of each soul after death is the exact opposite of the lot
it enjoyed in this life. Once again, poverty and wealth
are, in themselves, virtuous and vicious respectively.[50]

Most of this material which we have summarized here
is peculiar to Luke among the synoptic evangelists. Much
of it probably came to him from sources in the Palestinian church, where the motif of the righteous poor was,
as we have already seen, very much at home.[51] Was Luke,
then, acting merely as recorder and transmitter of this material, or did he actually have an active interest in per-
petuating the motif of the righteous poor? On the whole,
it is more likely that he was simply recorder and transmitter, and this for two reasons: (1) the motif disappears
entirely from Acts, the second volume of Luke's historical
work, unless one regards the account of the primitive communism as a continuation of this theme; (2) Luke displays
a particular interest throughout both volumes of his work
in distinguished or wealthy converts to Christianity and
correspondingly little interest in poor ones. Both these
observations suggest that Luke did not himself have a burning interest in the poor.[52]

There are, however, two passages, which pose the
question whether Luke may have actively extended and en-
hanced the motif of the righteous poor in his gospel. One

is the incident of Jesus' first sermon, at Nazareth, where
Luke probably inserted the long quotation from Isaiah, including the reference to preaching "good news to the poor"
(4:16-30).[53]   Luke was principally interested in the quotation, however, for its reference to miracles of healing,
which form the substance of the discussion that follows
(vss. 23-27).   The other passage is the Sermon on the Plain,
already noted, where Luke's version of the Beatitude and
his addition of woes against the rich and prosperous serve
to emphasize the sociological dimension of Jesus' message.

In the latter case, it is particularly difficult to
determine how far Luke's own editorial work has extended.
In the past, most scholars have held that the original of
the first Beatitude ran "Blessed are the poor...," altered
by Matthew to read "Blessed are the poor in spirit..." and
by Luke to read "Blessed are you poor...."   If this is correct, what Matthew did was to "explain" the sectarian, non-
literal sense of Jesus' words for a non-Palestinian audience, while Luke retained the original form of expression,
which would now be understood as referring to the literally poor.

More recently, it has been suggested that Matthew's
phrase "poor in spirit" was original.   If so, Luke actively
altered the sectarian language of the Beatitude, when he
omitted "in spirit."   The evidence for the originality of
Matthew's version, however, is not commanding.   More probably, Matthew understood the simple reference to the poor
in a sectarian sense and, feeling that he must explain this
for his audience, added the phrase "in spirit."   Thus, non-
Palestinians could understand what was already obvious to
Palestinians—that Jesus was blessing not the poor as such,
but rather the faithful under the title "poor."   Luke, then,
acted simply as transmitter of the tradition.[54]

What of the Lukan woes, which are absent from Matthew?

Why did Luke add them? It is unlikely, for a variety of
reasons, that these woes were associated with the Beatitudes from the beginning; they probably had a separate history in the oral tradition. It is improbable that Luke
composed them himself, since elsewhere he evinced no sustained antagonism toward the rich, except where he was re-
peating traditional material. Most likely, Luke found the
woes in the tradition that came down to him for they are
quite in line with the teaching of James about the non-
Christian rich. If they were not already combined with the
Beatitudes, he juxtaposed the two and reworked both to make
the parallelism more exact. In so doing, Luke acted in accordance with the Palestinian traditions that he followed;
but unlike Matthew, he did not seek to interpret or explain
the sectarian motif of the righteous poor for his non-
Palestinian audience—he simply recorded it for posterity.[55]

    In sum, Luke's seeming advocacy of the poor against
the rich was primarily a result of his preserving materials
shaped in the primitive Palestinian church, though he en-
hanced them to a degree by his own activity in arranging
and editing. Luke did not create the motif, nor even particularly champion it; for it appears in his works only in
the Gospel (and, indirectly, in the first few chapters of
Acts); in other words, in materials which came to Luke out
of the tradition of the Palestinian church.[56]

    But where did these materials have their origin? In
the primitive church itself, or in the ministry of Jesus?
Some of the materials must go back to Jesus—for example,
the parable of The Rich Man and Lazarus. Yet, the theme of
the righteous poor plays only a secondary role in this peri
cope; the main point is rather the uselessness of miracles
in inducing conversion.[57] Again, the first Beatitude must
surely go back to Jesus himself. Beyond these, it is impossible to be sure.

There is little in Mark's Gospel and nothing in the special material of Matthew to support the emphasis on the poor in Luke's special source or sources, though the three Gospels agree that Jesus promised a reversal of fortunes in the Kingdom of God: the first shall be last and the last first.[58] This reversal is *within* the kingdom; in other words, the rich are not here excluded from the kingdom as inherently sinful. Mark also reports the famous saying, repeated in Matthew and Luke, that "It is easier for a camel to go through the eye of a needle than for a rich man to enter the kingdom of God" (Mk. 10:25). There follows the related saying, "With men it is impossible, but not with God; for all things are possible with God" (10:27). Thus, there will be rich men in the Kingdom, despite their inherent handicap.[59]

It seems likely, then, that Jesus used the sectarian language of the righteous poor. He expected that the rich would enter the Kingdom only with difficulty and that they would there be transformed from "first" to "last."[60] This kind of teaching continued in the primitive Palestinian church. As the first Christians themselves developed sectarian patterns comparable to those of Pharisees and Essenes, they exaggerated Jesus' use of the theme. Thus James went considerably beyond Jesus in animosity toward the rich, and the Palestinian traditions known to Luke took a special interest in preserving this element of Jesus' teaching.

Whatever the relative roles of Jesus and the primitive Palestinian church in formulating the motif of the righteous poor, early Christians outside Palestine found it barely intelligible. Later Christian authors did not regard poverty as a good. Hermas, to be sure, thought it a virtue "to be poorer than all men"; but he included this in a list of expensive virtues, meant for the *rich*. In another

passage, he characterized poverty as an unmitigated evil
that drives men to despair. Origen even went so far as to
say that the poor are more likely to be vicious than virtuous, even if it is true (as he argued elsewhere) that the
righteous usually wind up poor.[61]

Tertullian was the only author outside the context
of the primitive Palestinian church for whom the motif of
the righteous poor had much importance. He used it much
the way he used the language of communism—as the foundation for *a fortiori* arguments. God "always justifies the
poor, always condemns the rich in advance"; therefore Christians should not worry about the loss of their property.
The kingdom of heaven will belong to the poor; therefore
Christian women should marry only Christian husbands, even
if they are poor. Tertullian had no personal attachment to
this theme; it was merely a rhetorical convenience for
him.[62]

Only those Christian writers, therefore, who had a
close connection with the primitive Palestinian church
treated wealth as culpable in itself. Among other Christian writers, we find varying degrees of hostility toward
riches and the rich; but nothing to match what we have seen
in James or the special materials of Luke's Gospel.[63] This
observation confirms our original classification of these
passages as a development of the Jewish sectarian theme of
the "righteous poor." This language was never meant literally, either in Judaism or in Christianity; each sect saw
itself as "the poor" and the oppressed in comparison with
the rich and powerful Sadduccees, whose paramount religious
position within Judaism was an affront to all other Jewish
groups. Since this political rivalry meant little to non-
Palestinian Jews and nothing at all to gentiles, the language that was born out of it could not but fade away. The
theme of the righteous poor survived in but one form, the

the doctrine that the prayers of the poor were of particular value, as we shall see in the following chapter.

CONCLUSIONS

The study of Early Christian attitudes toward wealth is hampered by the fragmentary nature of the materials and the desultory manner of the writers. Consistency was, for some of them, a matter of no concern whatever. Hermas, for example, was capable of declaring that wealth has its source in "the lord of this city" (i.e., the ruler of this world) and then, in the same breath, attributing it to "the Master."[64] Tertullian the apologist was capable of making statements which Tertullian the moralist would at once proceed to discredit. This difficulty inherent in the materials has been magnified by the tendency of some modern students of the subject to belabor congenial proof-texts without any reference to the overall context of the author's thought, where that can be determined.

By beginning with Clement of Alexandria, the one Early Christian author to give us something like a rounded view of his attitude toward wealth, I have attempted to avoid these difficulties. Clement gives us a fixed point of reference with which the other writings can be compared. In the process of making this comparison, it has emerged that Clement's thought, with its emphasis on detachment and simplicity, is indeed generally representative of Early Christian thought on the subject of wealth except for that of the primitive Palestinian church. In the latter, the theme of the righteous poor dominated to such an extent that there could be little discussion of the meaning of Christian wealth—even though James reveals to us that there were rich members of the church. Outside Palestine, the prevailing trend was to allow possession of wealth, so long as the rich man practiced detachment and lived in a simple style.

The themes and language of communism (in the sense
of a mandatory pooling of goods) were widespread among the
Early Christian writers, some of whom may well have believed that private property was contrary to God's will.
And yet, none of our authors except Sextus seriously urged
his readers to the practice of communism; nor is there any
firm evidence that community of goods was ever normal within the church, even in the primitive church of Jerusalem.
Apologists described Christian almsgiving in communist
terms in order to appeal to philosophically-minded pagans;
moralists cast doubt on the validity of private property
in order to encourage almsgiving. That is all.

It remains true, however, that the Early Christian
authors generally spoke negatively of wealth, even if they
were not prepared to rule it out altogether for Christians.
Clement's treatise *Who is the Rich Man that is Saved?* is
much the friendliest toward the rich of all the documents
we have; indeed, it was written to reassure them that salvation was possible for them. But even in that work, Clement imposed serious restrictions on the acquisition and use
of wealth. In his other writings, he was stricter still.

All our sources, then, except for the early Palestinian ones, take up much the same position. Though there
are differences of tone between the most rigorist of them
(Hermas and Tertullian) and the most tolerant (Clement),
these are of slight importance in comparison with the overall consistency. This general unity of thought did not
arise because later writers echoed a principle established
in the earliest authorities. Indeed, the leadership of the
primitive church was soon set aside; and no other author
before Clement (who was himself never an "authority" on the
subject) dealt with the question in a manner calculated to
set precedent. It seems likely, therefore, that the nega-

tive, but cautious attitude of the Early Christian writers
toward wealth resulted from social impulses active in the
church's life throughout the Greco-Roman world, influencing
each author independently.

This conclusion is confirmed by the remarkable consistency of Early Christian teaching on the related topic
of almsgiving, to which we now turn. Once we have analyzed this material, we shall be in a position to determine
what were the social realities which gave rise and lent
substance to Early Christian attitudes toward the rich
within the church.

[1]G. Uhlhorn argued that the teaching of detachment can be traced
to Jesus; Eng., pp. 65-69. But the case is unprovable.

Paul's "as if" ethic was viable only so long as the End was conceived as imminent, since one cannot live permanently in this world
by ignoring its character; see Jack T. Sanders, *Ethics in the New
Testament: Change and Development* (Philadelphia: Fortress Press, 1975)
p. 61 and n. 33. Consequently, it disappeared early from Christian
literature, except for an echo in a Christian addition to II Esdras
(16:41-42). On the whole, Paul has disappointingly little to say of
wealth; see Werner Georg Kümmel, p. 276. Indeed, it is difficult to
extract any kind of active social ethics from Paul; see Cone, pp. 159-
75, and Amos Niven Wilder, *Kerygma, Eschatology, and Social Ethics*
(Philadelphia: Fortress Press, Facet Books, 1966), pp. 18-19.

[2]*RAC,* s.v. "Autarkie," where Wilpert noted the difference in
Paul's ethical motive. See also J. L. Houlden, *Ethics and the New
Testament* (Harmondsworth, Eng.: Penguin Books, 1973), pp. 27-29. One
should not force Paul to be perfectly consistent in his ethics (pp.
25-34). Morton Scott Enslin, *The Ethics of Paul* (New York: Abingdon
Press, paperback edition, 1957), pp. 14-16, and William D. Davies,
Paul and Rabbinic Judaism: Some Rabbinic Elements in Pauline Theology
(New York: Harper & Row, Torchbook edition, 1967), pp. 111-46, are
right to emphasize the Jewish ancestry of Paul's ethics. But this did
not make it impossible for him to absorb and reuse popular Stoic ideas
see Charles Harold Dodd, *New Testament Studies* (Manchester: University
Press, 1953), pp. 131-32, and William Edward Chadwick, pp. 23-28. This
would happen with particular ease whenever Paul was dealing with a
subject, such as wealth, which lay at the periphery of his concern.
Jan Nicolaas Sevenster, *Paul and Seneca* (Leiden: E. J. Brill, 1961),
pp. 208-11, has shown conclusively that Paul was no Stoic, but this
does not disprove that Paul sometimes adopted Stoic language. The
same point may be made with regard to the studies of Douglas S. Sharp,
Epictetus and the New Testament (London: Charles H. Kelly, 1914), and
Wolfgang Schrage, "Die Stellung zur Welt bei Paulus, Epiktet und in
der Apokalyptik. Ein Beitrag zu 1Kor 7,29-31," *ZTK* 61 (1964):125-54.

[3]*Adv. Marc.* 4.15.8. (Translations of Tertullian are based on
ANF, often heavily revised.) *De cultu fem.* 2.9.6, quoting I Cor.
7:29-30. Tertullian was not a poor man himself; Timothy David Barnes,
Tertullian: A Historical and Literary Study (Oxford: Clarendon Press,
1971), pp. 137-38.

[4]This author advocated not only inner detachment, but actual rejection of private property; Henry Chadwick, *The Sentences of Sextus,
A Contribution to the History of Early Christian Ethics, TS,* n.s.,
vol. 5 (Cambridge: University Press, 1959), pp. 102-3. (Translations
of Sextus are my own.)

[5]*Orat.* 21.1; cf. 29.5-6. On Origen's ascetic tendencies, see

Henry Chadwick, *Early Christian Thought,* pp. 90-91. Origen's own
manner of life was that of a philosophical ascetic, according to
Eusebius, *H.E.* 6.3.9-12.

[6]*Cels.* 1.24 (wealth not a good); 7.23, cf. 7.21 (Jesus' sayings
understood allegorically); *Comm. in Mt.* 15.16 (abandonment); *Comm. in
Rom.* 9.25 (subjection to earthly authorities). Schilling, pp. 51-52,
goes too far when he characterizes the thinking of Origen as "ganz
und gar die Ideen des Klemens!"; but for all his ascetic tendencies,
Origen was unable to liberate himself from the moderating influences
within the church.

[7]I Tim. 6:10; cf. Heb. 13:5, ἀφιλάργυρος ὁ τρόπος· ἀρκούμενοι
τοῖς παροῦσιν. Hermas, *Sim.* 4.5-8. Athenagoras, *Res.* 21.4. Origen,
Hom. in Ex. 8.4; *Hom. in Jud.* 2.3. It is interesting that this argument does *not* seem to have been used in attacks on usury; Robert P.
Maloney, "The Teaching of the Fathers on Usury: An Historical Study on
the Development of Christian Thinking," *VC* 27 (1973):241-65.
   Although it goes beyond anything to be found in ancient writers
in clarity and definition, there are grounds for Seipel's comment (p.
120): "Die zwei Momente, welche den irdischen Besitz aus dem Bereiche
des Indifferenten herausheben und zu etwas sittlich Gutem order
sittlich Bösem machen können, sind der Erwerb und der Gebrauch."

[8]*De pat.* 7.5, 11-12; *De idol.* 11.1-2; *Adv. Marc.* 4.33.2; *Ad Scap.*
4.7.

[9]*Adv. haer.* 4.46.1-3 (4.30.1-3). (Citations from Irenaeus are
given first according to Harvey's numbering, then according to that of
Massuet, which is used in *ANF.*) The defense of Christian wealth is
implicit only.
   Just after our period, the author of *De aleatoribus* (6) took an
entirely positive attitude toward wealth—but only to dissuade his
readers from wasting it at the gaming table, so that they might be
able to give it to the church instead.

[10]Jn. 12:6 portrays Judas as the first of their line. Other examples may be found in Paul (II Cor. 2:17), the Pastorals (Tit. 1:11),
Did. 11.12, Polycarp (*Ep.* 11.1), and Lucian (*Peregrinus* 11-13).

[11]Erwin R. Goodenough, *An Introduction to Philo Judaeus,* 2d ed.
(Oxford: Basil Blackwell, 1962), p. 133 (cf. pp. 120-30), saw the
Christians' emphasis on detachment and other "inner" virtues as an in-
dex of their increasing responsiveness "to the ethical ideals of the
hellenistic world." This may be true, so long as we do not confine
this process to philosophically-minded writers. The idea that virtue
is essentially inward was a feature of Christian thinking throughout
the period, from Jesus to Augustine; see Frederick C. Grant, *Economic
Background of the Gospels,* p. 139, and Elizabeth Allo Isichei, *Political Thinking and Social Experience: Some Christian Interpretations of
the Roman Empire from Tertullian to Salvian* (Christchurch, N.Z.:

University of Canterbury, 1964), p. 75. Detachment continued to be a
key element in Christian thinking about wealth long after our period;
Giet, pp. 84-91.

[12]I Tim. 6:7-8. Mt. 11:18-19//Lk. 7:33-35 (John and Jesus). Lk.
16:19-31 (Dives and Lazarus); Irenaeus, *Adv. haer.* 4.3.2 (4.2.2), interpreted the parable as an attack on luxury and a warning that no
one "servire suis voluptatibus et oblivisci Deum."

[13]See also *Sent. Sex.* 294: πιστοῦ πλοῦτος ἐγκράτεια. At other
moments, the author seems closer to Clement, e.g., τρέφε σου τὴν μὲν
ψυχὴν λόγῳ θείῳ, τὸ δὲ σῶμα σιτίοις λιτοῖς (413). The development toward asceticism in the second century was important, but hardly enough
so for Haller, pp. 492-506, to claim that the concept of *enkrateia*
dominated the post-apostolic period.

[14]*Hom. in Ex.* 13.5; *Comm. in Mt.* 17.27 (on Mt. 22:15-22); *Cels.*
7.24, cf. 8.30.

[15]*Oct.* 36.3-4: "Ceterum quod plerique pauperes dicimur, non est
infamia nostra, sed gloria: animus enim ut luxu solvitur, ita
frugalitate firmatur. Et tamen quis potest pauper esse qui non eget
...?" Cf. Seneca, *Ep.* 17.5.
     Minucius was an African, but wrote in Rome, if one may judge by
the setting of his work.

[16]*Vis.* 3.9.3; *Mand.* 9.2.1; *Sim.* 1.6; *Mand.* 8.3. Hermas wrote in
the first part of the second century; and his example should warn us
against the common assumption (e.g., Seipel, pp. 195-203) that wealth
became a feature of church life only in the latter part of the century.

[17]To pagans: *Apol.* 39.17. To Christians: *De orat.* 6.3-4. Rich
women formed the particular object of Tertullian's ire; see *De cultu
fem.* 1.1.1, 2.5.1 et passim; *Ad uxor.* 1.4.6, 2.8.3 In this he followed the example of I Pet. 3:3-4 and I Tim. 2:9-10—and also that of
Stoic philosophy (cf. Seneca, *Ad Helv.* 16.3; *Ep.* 95.21). None of
these works stem from Tertullian's Montanist period; Barnes, p. 128.

[18]"Communism" in the nineteenth or twentieth century sense was,
of course, unknown in antiquity, when the state of economic thinking
was too rudimentary to make it possible. I include under this rubric
passages which attack the principle of private property, advocate
pooling of property, and/or hold up an ideal of equality as the natural state of man. See Wolf-Dieter Hauschild, pp. 34-35.

[19]For a survey of the early German discussion of the subject
(which represents the largest portion of the whole literature on the
topic), see Bigelmair, pp. 73-76.

[20]*Did.* 4.8; cf. *Barn.* 19.8. The close similarity of these parallel passages shows that the concept was an original part of the "Two

Ways" tradition. It may, therefore, be Hellenistic-Jewish in origin
rather than Christian; Robert M. Grant, ed., *The Apostolic Fathers:
A New Translation and Commentary,* 6 vols. (New York: Thomas Nelson &
Sons, 1965-68), vol. 3: *Barnabas and the Didache,* by Robert A. Kraft,
pp. 4-5, 7-9.

[21]*I Apol.* 14.2; cf. 15.10-17. *Koinon* was also a term for the
treasury of the Greek club (see below, p. 163), or even for the club
itself; see Marcus N. Tod, *Sidelights on Greek History: Three Lectures
on the Light Thrown by Greek Inscriptions on the Life and Thought of
the Ancient World* (Oxford: Basil Blackwell, 1932), p. 76.

[22]*Diog.* 5.7.

[23]*Apol.* 39.11: "Omnia indiscreta sunt apud nos praeter uxores."
Elsewhere, Tertullian did not deny the justice of private property
(*Adv. Herm.* 9.3). He even found it opportune to make use of the principle of private ownership to vindicate the exclusive right of the
orthodox to the use of scripture (*De praescr.* 37). Hauschild, pp. 35-
36, ignores this aspect of Tertullian.

[24]Troeltsch, pp. 115-18, makes this same observation.

[25]On Sextus, see Henry Chadwick, *Sentences,* pp. 102-3. The
larger question is, How far are we justified in making one or two incidental comments determinative of an author's overall attitude? When
we compare the minimal number of "communist" texts from Early Christian authors with the overwhelming evidence from the same authors for
an interest in almsgiving, it is difficult to justify a proof-text
method. But that is what any scholar who wishes to turn the early
Christians into socialists (or theoretical capitalists, for that matter) must do—and does, as recently as Hauschild. For a comparison of
Sextus with Clement of Alexandria, see Osborn, pp. 80-81.

[26]*Comm. in Mt.* 15.15 (Crates; maintenance from *koinon*). In *Hom.
in Gen.* 16.5, Origen accused the clergy in general and himself in particular (Meus enim primo omnium, meus, inquam, ipse accusator exsisto)
of failure to fulfill the Lord's command to divest themselves of property.

[27]R. M. Grant has caught the patristic attitude well; while the
Fathers did not rule private property out, they were not defenders of
it "as such, any more than most of them were defenders of the Roman
Empire. They took it for granted" (*Early Christianity,* p. 119).

[28]In *Hom. in Lev.* 15.2, Origen spoke as if Christians did not in
fact own any property. But this was simply a device to prove that the
legal provisions about sale and redemption of houses could not have
any literal meaning for Christians and thus to permit Origen to get on
directly to the allegorical interpretation.
   At a later date, Lactantius argued that justice demands equality,

but he was no revolutionary.   He held that Christians fulfilled this demand by recognizing a spiritual equality in each other; Schilling, pp. 70-78.

^{29}For detailed modern discussions of the passages in question, see F. J. Foakes Jackson and Kirsopp Lake, eds., *The Beginnings of Christianity,* 5 vols. (London: Macmillan & Co., 1922-30), 5:140-51, and Ernst Haenchen, *The Acts of the Apostles: A Commentary,* trans. Bernard Noble and Gerald Shinn (Philadelphia: Westminster Press, 1971), ad loc.

^{30}Luke T. Johnson, *The Literary Function of Possessions in Luke-Acts,* SBL Dissertation Series, No. 39 (Missoula, Mont.: Scholars Press, 1977), pp. 173-222.

^{31}The controversy is an old one, as witness the work of Mosheim (see above, p. 1).   The basic arguments on both sides have not varied much over the centuries, and they remain inconclusive. Most of them were already known to Chastel (Eng.), pp. 53-57. Haller, pp. 552-55, added the argument that the case of Barnabas must have been unique, for Luke would have used more than one example had he known them. This feeble claim was easily refuted by Kautsky (Eng.), pp. 284-92; but it is still to be met with in the literature, e.g., Johannes Leipoldt, pp. 110-12. J. Duncan M. Derrett made an effort to resolve the conflict over the story of Ananias and Sapphira by blaming Sapphira, who prevented her husband from fulfilling *his* duty to the church with *her* money, "Ananias, Sapphira, and the Right of Property," *Downside Review* 89 (1971):225-32. The article is largely an exercise of imagination, though based on interesting concepts of Jewish law.

^{32}On limitation of almsgiving, see Claude G. Montefiore and Herbert Loewe, eds., *A Rabbinic Anthology,* with a prolegomenon by Raphael Loewe (New York: Schocken Books, paperback edition, 1974), p. 419, citing *Ket.* 67b. On the Essenes, see above, pp. 27-28.

^{33}Lake (Foakes Jackson and Lake, 5:140-46) argued that Luke himself introduced the motif of the lie into the story of Ananias and Sapphira, while he reproduced the summary in a form already available to him from a Jerusalem source. But it is probable that Luke had no historical "thread" in the first part of Acts, only isolated stories; Martin Dibelius, *Studies in the Acts of the Apostles,* ed. Heinrich Greeven, trans. Mary Ling and Paul Schubert (London: SCM Press, 1956), pp. 102-8. The sources of Acts, whatever they were, have not yet been successfully isolated; Haenchen, pp. 81-90. Schuyler Brown, *Apostasy and Perseverance in the Theology of Luke,* Analecta Biblica, no. 36 (Rome: Pontifical Biblical Institute, 1969), regards the motif of the lie as pre-Lucan.

We cannot rule out the possibility that Luke reproduced a summary from a Jerusalem source, for we know that he treated the Markan summaries with respect; Henry J. Cadbury, *The Style and Literary Method of Luke,* Harvard University Press, 1920; reprint ed., New York:

Kraus Reprint Co., 1969), pp. 108-11. But there are internal signs
that, at the very least, he rewrote it (Haenchen, pp. 232-35), whereas
the story of Ananias and Sapphira appears to display characteristics
of oral style, except for the verses dealing with the death of Sapphira (pp. 239-41). For what it is worth, both summary and story
show some signs of having been composed first in Greek; Raymond A.
Martin, *Syntactical Evidence of Semitic Sources in Greek Documents,*
Septuagint and Cognate Studies, no. 3 ([Missoula, Mont.]: Society of
Biblical Literature, 1974), pp. 93-94.

[34]Aristotle, *Eth. Nic.* 9.8.1168b5-10 (the theme is also found in
later Stoic and Academic writings and was particularly associated
with the Pythagoreans). Deut. 15:4.
   Some late nineteenth-century scholars emphasized the element of
philosophical apologetic here to the point where they saw no historical reality behind Luke's account at all; e.g., H. Holtzmann, pp. 25-
60. Cf. Schilling, pp. 13-17.

[35]Leipoldt, pp. 147-50, argued that Luke deliberately suppressed
Paul's great collection so that it would not appear that the communist
experiment at Jerusalem had failed. For Luke as apologist, see David
L. Mealand, "Community of Goods and Utopian Allusions in Acts II-IV,"
JTS, n.s., 28 (1977):96-99.

[36]George Wesley Buchanan's attempt to find an allusion to community of goods in the ἁρπαγὴ τῶν ὑπαρχόντων of Heb. 10:34 is unconvinc-
ing; *To the Hebrews: Translation, Comment and Conclusions,* Anchor
Bible, vol. 36 (Garden City, N.Y.: Doubleday & Co., 1972), p. 174, cf.
p. 276. Ephrem Baumgartner, pp. 625-45, argued that communism did indeed continue within the early church, but on a strictly voluntary basis and in accordance with *Rerum novarum* of Leo XIII. He failed, however, to take the context of his proof-texts seriously.
   In any event, ancient communism was purely a communism of "the
means of consumption" and therefore could not assume any permanent
form, according to Kautsky (Eng.), pp. 351-54. Troeltsch (Eng.), pp.
62-63, says much the same thing.

[37]This synthesis does not represent an ethical consensus. Indeed,
it is inappropriate to speak of an Early Christian ethic, since the
term "connotes philosophic reflection upon human conduct" and only a
few of our authors were interested in such reflections; William D.
Davies, "The Moral Teaching of the Early Church," in *The Use of the
Old Testament in the New and Other Essays: Studies in Honor of William
Franklin Stinespring,* ed. James M. Efird (Durham, N.C.: Duke University
Press, 1972), pp. 310-32, especially p. 310. We are dealing rather
with a consistent moral *attitude.*

[38]See above, pp. 30-32.

[39]E.g., Dieter Georgi, *Die Geschichte der Kollekte des Paulus für
Jerusalem,* Theologische Forschung, no. 38 (Hamburg: Herbert Reich-

Evangelischer Verlag, 1965), pp. 22-30, where Georgi rejects "eine rein soziologische Bedeutung" for the expression and reviews the discussion to his time of writing.

[40]The origin of James is a difficult problem. Martin Dibelius, *James,* rev. Heinrich Greeven, trans. Michael A. Williams, ed. Helmut Koester (Philadelphia: Fortress Press, 1976), pp. 21-24, concluded that it was not possible to pin down the place of writing, since the work reflects a type of Hellenistic Jewish paraenesis of wide currency. (Authorship by James, brother of Jesus, however, is excluded.) Dibelius, pp. 45-46, relied heavily on comparison of James's attitude toward the rich with that of Hermas to suggest that the work is late; but the comparison is ill-founded. Hermas is quite different in the degree of animosity he expresses and in the kind of complaint he makes —one directed against the Christian rich, not outsiders (see below, pp. 135-36, 154). It is striking that Dibelius must resort to James's "archanizing dependence" on earlier literature to explain the vehemence of his treatment of the rich (p. 44). We might better look for an origin at a time and place where we know that this theme was current, i.e., Palestine before A.D. 66.

Even if it seems best to place the work slightly later, its origin should be sought among the Ebionites, who revered the memory of James and had a less than Pharisaic regard for the Torah, along with a strong distaste for Paul's theology. This would explain the work's ethical characteristics as discussed by Sanders, pp. 115-28. Such an origin would also help explain the work's late and uncertain entry into the catholic canon; cf. Dibelius, *James,* pp. 51-52.

[41]E.g., Paul, p. 515; Cone, pp. 184-87; Kautsky, pp. 276-79; Martin Dibelius, "Das soziale Motiv," pp. 201-2; Leipoldt, pp. 138-40.

[42]Despite Dibelius, *James,* pp. 85-87, it is only with violence that Jas. 1:9-10 can be made to contrast "the lowly brother" with "the rich" outsider. The Greek (ὁ ἀδελφὸς ὁ ταπεινός...ὁ δὲ πλούσιος) calls for the same noun to be applied again, just as the verb καυχάσθω must be repeated. The verb is, of course, ironic on any interpretation, for James refers to some kind of real humiliation within the church. He seems to say that the rich have only one choice—to suffer now in the church or later in the judgment.

The discussion of rich visitors (2:1-5) implies the possibility of rich enquirers and therefore of rich members of the church. Even if it was a fictional example, introduced to enliven the paraenesis (so Dibelius, *James,* p. 129; but cf. 134-35), was it therefore inappropriate or unrepresentative? One can ask this question without falling into Bo Reicke's extravagance of implicating these Christians in the politics of the Roman aristocracy, *The Epistles of James, Peter, and Jude,* Anchor Bible, vol. 37 (Garden City, N.Y.: Doubleday & Co., 1964), p. 27.

[43]Jas. 2:1-12; 5:1-6. Dibelius, *James,* pp. 138-39, correctly concludes that this is not a case of wholesale persecution by the rich.

It fits with the sporadic attacks made on the church's leaders by the Sadducees, as pictured by Luke (Acts 4:1-22; 5:17-42; perhaps 12:1-3) and Josephus (*Ant.* 20.9.1; cf. Dibelius, *James,* pp. 14-15). The reference to "the righteous man" (5:6) is probably general for "the pious poor" (Dibelius, *James,* pp. 239-40); but there is nothing to exclude Cassiodorus' interpretation of the verse as an allusion to the crucifixion. The statement that "he does not resist you" would then be an allusion (not verbal) to the Suffering Servant of Isa. 53.

⁴⁴Nonetheless, Charles Harold Dodd, *More New Testament Studies* (Grand Rapids, Mich.: William B. Eerdmans Publishing Co., 1968), pp. 4-5, saw Jas. as "characterized by an acute sense of the miseries of an oppressed class." Dibelius, *James,* wavered between emphasizing the traditional and metaphorical character of James's language (e.g., pp. 44-45) and arguing, with Nietzsche, that Jas. expresses a piety of the literally poor (pp. 48-50). Frederick C. Grant, p. 122, was correct in saying that "the thought of the author springs from a traditional magnification of poverty—as a virtue in itself."

⁴⁵James would presumably have differed from contemporary Essenes or Pharisees by including the *am ha-arets* in his definition of "poor."

⁴⁶Rev. 13:16-17 (mark of the beast as condition of trade); 18:11-19 (lament of the merchants over fallen Babylon). On the other hand, there are passages which emphasize that damnation will fall on all classes alike (6:15; 19:18).

⁴⁷Peabody, pp. 69-70. Ireanaeus, *Adv. haer.* 3.14.3, had already noted the importance of the attack on wealth in Luke's gospel.

⁴⁸The significance of this would be apparent only to a reader versed in the Torah.

⁴⁹The context here is Markan; Luke has introduced the citation from Isa. 61:1-2.

⁵⁰Dodd, *More New Testament Studies,* pp. 4-5, compares Luke and James, both of whom he sees as having adopted the Hellenistic motif of a περιπέτεια, in which all earthly distinctions would be reversed; Luke is distinguished from James by the fact that his version of the peripety is "etherealized," not revolutionary. (The motif was Jewish, as well; see Israel Abrahams, *Studies in Pharisaism and the Gospels, First Series* [Cambridge: University Press, 1917], pp. 116-17.) Troeltsch (Eng.), pp. 170-71, n. 17, on the other hand, saw James as glorifying the worth of the soul in itself, which rendered "quite remote any idea of a value in poverty in itself"; Luke corrupted this idealism. Joachim Jeremias, *The Parables of Jesus,* 2d rev. ed. (New York: Charles Scribner's Sons, 1972), pp. 184-86, denied that Luke could have intended an actual peripety of wealth and poverty in Dives and Lazarus, because such a doctrine is not to be found elsewhere; but he ignored the example of the Beatitudes and Woes.

[51]It has often been argued that some of Luke's special material
came from Palestinian Jewish-Christian (even Ebionite) sources; e.g.,
Cone, pp. 62-67. For the difficulties of this question, see the lin-
guistic arguments in Paul Winter, "Some Observations on the Language
of the Birth and Infancy Stories of the Third Gospel," *NTS* 1 (1954-55):
111-21, and Nigel Turner, "The Relation of Luke 1 and 2 to the Hebraic
Sources and to the Rest of Luke-Acts," *NTS* 2 (1955-56), 100-109.

[52]Cone, pp. 145-46, argued that the communism of Acts belonged in
the same context as Luke's interest in the poor in his gospel; so,
too, Johannes Behm, pp. 275-97. But Luke actually stresses the case
of the rich giver in Acts (Barnabas, Ananias), not that of the poor
receiver.

[53]Rudolf Bultmann, *The History of the Synoptic Tradition,* trans.
John Marsh, rev. ed. (New York: Harper & Row, paperback ed., 1976),
pp. 30-31.

[54]For the originality of Luke's "poor," see ibid., pp. 109-10.
David Flusser has argued from comparable expressions in the Qumran
literature that Matthew's "poor in spirit" was original; "Blessed Are
the Poor in Spirit," *Israel Exploration Journal* 10 (1960):1-13.
Jacques Dupont considered the question impossible to resolve, since
what is primitive is not necessarily original; *Les Béatitudes: Le
problème littéraire-Les deux versions du Sermon sur la montagne et des
Béatitudes,* rev. ed. (Bruges: Abbaye de Saint-André, 1958), pp. 214-
16. So, too, Dodd, *More New Testament Studies,* pp. 9-10. Hans-
Joachim Degenhardt, pp. 50-51, argued that Luke was trying to retain
a sociological reference for "poor" while at the same time altering
the formula of the Beatitudes from third person to second in order to
limit the sense of "poor" to "disciples," those whom Jesus was addressing at the moment; this explanation, however, falls apart when
one considers that the Woes are also couched in the second person.
    On the secondary character of Luke's use of the second person,
see Dupont, pp. 272-98.

[55]Ibid., pp. 299-321, argues that the Woes are a Lukan composition. At the other extreme, Dodd, *More New Testament Studies,* pp.
3-4, claims that the combination of Beatitudes and Woes was a well-
established literary pattern and possibly original. Bultmann, pp.
111-12, and Percy, pp. 105-6, are willing to see them as pre-Lukan,
but call attention to the awkwardness of their present setting.

[56]Degenhardt, p. 76, claims that Luke's interest in material possessions was inspired by his concern for the peculiarly gentile vice
of πλεονεξία; but this is a racial slur elevated to the status of a
historical argument. Houlden, pp. 55-60, 90, is correct in saying
that Luke's own concern was less for poverty than for generosity.
Luke's attitude "betokens a concern for the oppressor rather than
pity for the oppressed"; Henry J. Cadbury, *The Making of Luke-Acts*
(London: S.P.C.K., 1961), p. 263. Sanders, pp. 35-40, argues that

Luke's ethic is confused and has not yet attained the consistency of his theology.

We must beware of overemphasizing Luke's own concern for the theme of poverty; such materials on the subject as he derived from Mark and Q, he altered only stylistically, according to Degenhardt, pp. 208-9. Luke did, however, make use of the language of "rich and poor" metaphorically, so that in his Gospel, "rich" means roughly "belonging to the Jewish leadership that rejected Jesus"; Johnson, pp. 138-44.

[57]Jeremias, *Parables,* pp. 186-87; Percy, pp. 104-5. The parable does, however, carry the motif of the pious poor further than Jesus' contemporaries would have found convenient, since the beggar who is found in Abraham's bosom is necessarily an *am ha-arets.*

[58]Mk. 10:31 and parallels; see also Mt. 20:16 and Lk. 13:30. The logion does not exclude the rich, but acts as a warning to them. See the study of this and related logia in Norman Perrin, *Rediscovering the Teachings of Jesus* (New York:Harper & Row, paperback ed., 1976), pp. 142-46. For a summary of the "Theology of Reversal," see Batey, pp. 18-22.

[59]The whole narrative (Mk. 10:17-31) continues to be as important to our topic now as it was when Clement used it as the text for *Quis div.* (see above, p. 49). It receives more detailed treatment below, pp. 115-17.

[60]It is so difficult to disentangle Jesus' teaching on the topic from the developments of the tradition and from the evangelists' own work that one cannot hope for any unanimity among scholars. It is clear that Jesus viewed wealth with suspicion and that he blessed the poor (Dibelius, "Das soziale Motiv," pp. 189-90, 193). On the other hand, he continued to assume the existence of private property (Degenhardt, pp. 210-11). It may be that some of our uncertainty about his teaching arises from distinctions which Jesus himself made between a stricter standard which he imposed on his closest followers and the more relaxed one which he laid on the rest; Kümmel, "Begriff," pp. 271-74; Rudolf Schnackenburg, *The Moral Teaching of the New Testament,* trans. J. Holland-Smith and W. J. O'Hara (New York: Herder & Herder, 1965), pp. 121-32. Percy's claim, pp. 89-91, 104-5, that Jesus demanded an absolute choice between property and the Kingdom can be maintained only at the cost of ignoring much of the data.

The metaphorical character of Jesus' speech is another source of uncertainty in our interpretation of his message. The logia are often allusive and imprecise. Cone, p. 71, observed, with regard to a related problem: "...while the message is distinctly declared to be 'good tidings' to the poor and unfortunate, it does not very clearly appear how these classes of people are to be relieved." And Dupont, pp. 322-23, observed with regard to the variants of the first Beatitude in Matthew and Luke that the two interpretations could only have arisen from an ambiguous source, which had a messianic interest in the poor rather than a practical one.

⁶¹Hermas, *Mand.* 8.10; *Sim.* 10.4.3. (Justin, *I Apol.* 13.4, agreed
that poverty was not naturally desirable.) Origen, *Cels.* 6.16, 7.18
(cf. 2.41 on poverty of philosophers). Athenagoras, *Res.* 13.1
(*contra* Cadoux, p. 284) is purely metaphorical and has nothing to do
with literal poverty.

In later times, it was primarily those authors who were intimately connected with monasticism who argued that poverty was a virtue in
itself; Seipel, p. 70.

⁶²*De pat.* 7.1-4; *Ad uxor.* 2.8.5. Tertullian emphasized the Lukan
attack on wealth, *Adv. Marc.* 4.14.1-2; but this was part of a process
of showing the consistency of the Marcionite Jesus with the Creator,
not an expression of Tertullian's own moral doctrine.

⁶³A partial exception is formed by the Christian apocrypha, e.g.,
II Esdras 16:41-42. The origin and audience of most such works is ob-
scure; but some (at least the Clementine cycle) originated among the
Ebionites—cf. κτήματα ἁμαρτήματα, *Hom.* 15.9.

⁶⁴*Sim.* 1. Seipel, p. 53, ignored the fact that *two* theories of
wealth are given here.

CHAPTER THREE

ALMSGIVING: THE RELIGIOUS
VALUE OF WEALTH

ALMSGIVING IN JUDAISM
AND THE GRECO-ROMAN WORLD

Clement's principal recommendation to the rich who feared for their salvation was that they should give alms liberally, for almsgiving could atone for sin. In this, Clement agreed with a great many other Early Christian authors, who differed from him only in that they made little effort to present a rationale for this teaching but rather counted on their audiences to accept it without a murmur. This doctrine of redemptive almsgiving is of importance to us because it ascribes to wealth a positive role in the religious life of its possessor.

The doctrine of redemptive almsgiving came to the church out of Judaism (where it was undergoing a parallel development during our period). The teaching of the Christian authors followed Jewish precedent in several areas where pagan practice was decidedly different. Above all, Christians agreed with Jews concerning the *recipients* of alms and the *motives* for giving. We shall first consider Jewish attitudes, then examine the ways in which Greco-Roman philanthropy differed.

The Torah prescribed for Jews an organized system of relief directed specifically to the welfare of the poor and financed by the mandatory payment of poor tithes every third year (Deut. 14:28-29). This system was supplemented by provisions designed to benefit those whose impoverishment went too far to be relieved by a dole; for example, if

anyone had been forced to part with his inheritance, he
could reclaim it in the Year of Jubilee (Lev. 25:8-24).
Since usury was forbidden between Israelites, the poor were
to borrow at no cost (25:35-38). At the very worst, an impoverished Israelite could sell himself into slavery on
more favorable terms than the non-Israelite; and he had the
right to go free in the Jubilee (25:39-55).

To obey these laws was not, of course, a work of
special merit on the part of the rich. But almsgiving
(which went beyond the requirements of the Law) followed
the same pattern in being directed to the relief of the
poor only. The author of Proverbs had recommended giving
to the poor, and the later rabbis assumed that alms were
always directed to the poor specifically. Since there are
degrees of poverty, the rabbis were not strict in excluding
people from the receiving of alms. In fact, they allowed
that different qualities of recipients were entitled to
different degrees of support, so that distressed gentlefolk
could lay claim to a style of life that would seem unthinkable luxury in the case of the ordinary beggar. Still, it
was only the "poor" who were properly eligible for alms,
even though there were always some who received alms under
false pretenses.[1]

There was little that the poor could do in return for
the alms bestowed on them. The Jewish authorities encouraged the giver to expect his reward from God rather than
from the one benefited:

> He who is kind to the poor lends to the Lord,
>   and he will repay him for his deed (Prov. 19:17)

The payment God gives consists of prosperity in this world;
therefore, a personal catastrophe implies that the person
who suffers it has been deficient in almsgiving. (Job himself suffered for this reason—because his philanthropy did
not equal that of Abraham.) The power of almsgiving extend

also to the world to come: it hastens the redemption of
Israel and ensures the welfare of the donor after death.[2]

Almsgiving was the good work par excellence; indeed,
it was often called simply "righteousness" (s͟edaqah).   Before the destruction of the Temple in A.D. 70, the rabbis
reckoned it along with the Torah and the Temple service as
one of three "pillars of the world."[3]   After A.D. 70, it
virtually replaced the Temple service; Johanan ben Zakkai
consoled the bereaved people by saying, "Grieve not, we
have an atonement equal to the Temple, the doing of loving
deeds, as it is said, 'I desire love, and not sacrifice.'"[4]

Jewish almsgiving was thus a religious act, exercised
exclusively toward the poor, which looked for a reward from
God.

The philanthropy of Greco-Roman society differed in
both respects.   To begin with, it was directed not to the
poor as such, but to one's friends and fellow-citizens,
whatever their economic status.   State philanthropy was
given to the citizen as citizen, and not to any one group
singled out because of need.   (Occasionally, the city state
might extend its benefactions to all residents, citizen and
non-citizen alike.)   Private persons might make gifts to
their fellow-citizens; or they might exercise their philanthropy on a more intimate circle.   Pliny listed their op-
tions as "hometown, neighbors, relations, and friends."
The claim on the giver consisted not in need, but in some
pre-existing personal relationship.[5]

The attitude of Greeks and Romans in this matter thus
differed markedly from that of Jews and Christians (and of
modern Western society)——so much so that modern writers
have sometimes condemned classical antiquity for hardness
of heart.[6]   This is mistaken.   Public benefactions such as
grain doles and banquets benefited the poor more than the
rich, since the poor must always spend a larger proportion

of their income on food than the rich. Philosophically
minded writers agreed that the giver of private benefactions should take the recipient's need into consideration
as well as his relationship to the giver. The difference
was that the Hellenic world was reluctant to single the
poor out for special treatment.[7]

Classical philanthropy also differed from Jewish as
to reward. The Jew gave to the poor but expected his reward from God; the pagan expected his return from the persons benefited in a tangible and immediate form. The rich
who gave gifts received honors in return. Indeed, the
whole fiscal system of the ancient city was based on this
arrangement; and taxation was left at a level so low as to
provide for no more than the barest necessities of government. Everything else came from the *philia* ("friendship")
of the rich; and to the benefactor, the public gave in return titles of honor, inscriptions (for which the benefactor himself sometimes paid), statues, and other privileges.
It is not surprising, under the circumstances, that the
fundamental motive for philanthropy was *philotimia,* "love
of public recognition."[8]

Private benefactions were also given with an eye to
personal gain, even if the philosophically minded did not
approve. Pliny the Younger objected to people "who give
particularly to those that give most [in return]." And
Juvenal complained about the way the rich took care of
their peers and let the poor struggle along as best they
could. It had been different, to be sure, in the days of
the Republic. But those were the days when a mob of poor
clients might further a man's career; and those days were
long past by the late first century A.D. Now that the
poor had little to give the rich, the rich had no motive
to benefit them.[9]

Greco-Roman philanthropy, then, differed from Jewish in
being directed not to the poor as such, but to relatives,
friends, fellow-citizens, or clients. And where the Jewish almsgiver expected his reward from the hand of God,
Greek or Roman looked for a direct return from those benefited.

This is not to suggest that there was a hard and fast
distinction between Jews and the other inhabitants of the
Roman world. There was much overlap and interchange of
customs and attitudes, and Jews adopted some Hellenistic
practices in this regard. Founders of synagogues were com-
memorated in inscriptions. And we read in Matthew 6:12 of
rich men who gave their alms with a public flourish—even
sounding trumpets to announce themselves. But the differences remain important for us because they represent basic
differences in social expectations. The early Christians'
choice of the Jewish pattern in this particular matter had
major social consequences, as we shall see in the following chapter. But, for the present, we must examine the
teaching about alms which the Christians founded on their
Jewish models.[10]

ALMS FOR THE POOR

We begin with the question of who was to receive alms.
Christian alms, like Jewish, were destined for the poor
only—or rather, to be precise, *not* for the poor in the
classical sense of the term, but for the destitute, those
totally unable to support themselves. Paul ordered able-
bodied men not to rely on the church's charity; he even
excommunicated those who were "living in idleness." The
author of the Pastorals insisted that believers should support their aged relatives and that only truly destitute
widows should be enrolled as the church's responsibility.
The point is one so familiar to the reader of Early Chris-

tian literature that there is no need to cite a great many
passages: the object of almsgiving was to share, in the
words of Justin, "with everyone *in need*."[11]

Nonetheless, our authors, like the rabbis, were not
eager to draw sharp lines. Many urged indiscriminate almsgiving, so that the worthy would not lose out because of
the unworthy who took alms without being in need. Thus we
saw Clement of Alexandria warn the rich not to try to distinguish the worthy from the unworthy, for fear that they
might overlook some deserving poor in the process. Others
took the same position. The *Didache,* for example, tells
us: "Give to every one that asks thee, and do not refuse,
for the Father's will is that we give to all from the gifts
we have received" (1.5). Hermas made the same point, ad-
ding that the burden of guilt lies upon the conscience of
the receiver, not the giver.[12]

Occasionally, an author might recommend caution; but
to most, it seemed better to give indiscriminately, even
if the giver suspected fraud. This seems odd, in the light
of our authors' insistence that alms were meant to benefit the
poor only. But the reason lay in the other aspect of almsgiving—the promise of reward. Clement held that the almsgiver would even be *punished* if he overlooked a worthy poor
person. To hold back out of fear of fraud could deprive
the giver of his reward. The advantage to the giver concerned our authors even more than the need of the recipient.[13]

THE REDEMPTIVE POWER OF ALMSGIVING

This concern for the giver of alms, a constant feature of Early Christian writings on the subject, was partic
ularly apparent in the arguments that our authors used to
encourage almsgiving. The principal motive for almsgiving
was the reward which the benefactor could count on

receiving from God. Paul argued that we should not "grow
weary in well-doing, for in due season we shall reap" (Gal.
6:9). Jesus is presented in the synoptic Gospels as saying
that alms given in this world win treasure in heaven.[14]
Luke pressed the point further: those who give alms can
count on an exact and corresponding reward in the world to
come (6:37-38); and those who feed the poor will be "re-
paid at the resurrection of the just" (14:13-14). Indeed,
it was the almsgiving of Cornelius the centurion, along
with his prayers, that secured for him the honor of becoming the first Gentile Christian (Acts 10:4).[15]

Authors as diverse as the prophet Hermas and the
philosopher "Sextus" agreed that almsgiving wins favor with
God. The author of *II Clement* warned that there would be
no one at the Last Day to plead the cause of those who do
not give alms. Tertullian argued for almsgiving as a way
of laying down "money for soul, not soul for money."[16] It
was hardly necessary to explain how this could be, for no
Early Christian ever denied that it was so. God himself
had said it through the mouths of his servants: Jesus, the
prophets of Israel, and the prophets of the church. To put
the matter another way, almsgiving is a form of obedience
to God—and therefore, as Samuel decreed, better than sacrifice. How could one doubt its effectiveness?[17]

Some writers did, however, attempt to explain the way
in which almsgiving worked its miracles. Irenaeus was particularly fertile and original in this regard. The argument, noted above, that almsgiving is better than sacrifice
was his. In another passage he argued that almsgiving
erased the effects of past avarice, citing the example of
Zacchaeus, who was saved when he gave half his goods to the
poor. Elsewhere, he argued that almsgiving worked a kind
of purification or sanctification of heathen wealth. Just
as the Israelites had spoiled the Egyptians and devoted the

proceeds to the building of the Tabernacle, so Christians
might erect a Tabernacle of God within themselves by correct use of their pre-Christian fortunes.[18]

     Most arguments, however, fell under one or the other
of two headings: the equation of almsgiving with sacrifice
(which possessed a generally accepted atoning power), or
the belief that the poor who receive alms have particular
influence with God.

     The first of these, the equation of almsgiving with
sacrifice is to be found in Early Christian writings
throughout our period, beginning with the New Testament.
James regarded the care of widows and orphans as an essential element in true *thrēskeia* or worship (1:27); and the
author of Hebrews referred to almsgiving as a sacrifice
"pleasing to God" (13:16). At a later date, Justin held
that almsgiving was *the* Christian sacrifice, superior to
those offerings that are consumed in flames (*I Apol*. 13).
And the *Sentences of Sextus* pronounced all other sacrifices
unacceptable to God. This is parallel with the contemporary development in Judaism.[19]

     Origen elaborated the concept at some length in his
discussion of the Levitical sacrifices. He compared these
sacrifices unfavorably with that of Jesus on the ground that
they were many, while his was unique and all-sufficient. But
then he feared that this would discourage some Christians,
who might suppose that the uniqueness of Jesus' atoning sacrifice left no remedy for post-baptismal sins. Not so,
Origen said: the Gospel, too, knows many "remissions of sin.
The first is baptism, the second martyrdom, the third almsgiving, and so on through a series of seven (listed in order
of declining importance). Thus, "whenever you give alms and
bring forth an attitude of mercy toward the needy from your
earnest devotion, you have loaded the sacred altar with fat
kids." Alms are the Christian sacrifice.[20]

Even authors who did not specifically link almsgiving with sacrifice still stressed its atoning power in
comparable terms. Thus the *Didache* prescribed, "Of whatso-
ever thou hast gained by thy hands thou shalt give a ran-
som for thy sins" (4.6). And the author of *II Clement*
wrote, in words that are apt to startle the modern reader:
"Almsgiving is...good even as penitence for sin; fasting
is better than prayer, but the giving of alms is better
than both.... Blessed is the man who is found full of these
things; for almsgiving lightens sin" (16.4). The phrasing
is unusually blunt, but the doctrine is not essentially
different from that of James, Hebrews, the *Didache,* or
Origen.[21]

The other major explanation of the atoning power of
alms was that which relied on the belief that poor Christians have particular influence with God. This may well
be a survival of the Jewish sectarian motif of the poor as
the righteous, though it also had roots in the Wisdom literature of the Old Testament, where the beggar's prayer or
curse is powerful. We have already come across the idea
in Clement's treatise on *The Rich Man,* but it was much
older than Clement. Indeed, it was present in the teaching
of Jesus himself, who emphasized the identity between himself and his followers when they received alms: "Truly, I
say to you, as you did it to one of the least of these my
brethren, you did it to me" (Mt. 25:40). Or, again, "whoever gives you a cup of water to drink because you bear the
name of Christ will by no means lose his reward" (Mk. 9:
41).[22]

How do the poor exercise their influence with God?
Through their prayers and thanksgivings, which they exchange for the alms of the rich. Paul promised the Corinthians that they would be "enriched" as a result of their
offering for the Jerusalem church, because their service

would "overflow" in thanksgiving. Clement of Rome offered
the same interpretation of the interchange between rich and
poor. Hermas compared it to the common practice of plant-
ing elms and vines together, so that the vine, being
trained on the tree, would give better fruit. The poor man
turns the rich man's sterile, earthly wealth into fruit
pleasing to God; and both are benefited by the relationship
Origen argued that, over a period of time, the prayers of
the poor would lead to the perfecting of their benefactor
(*Comm. in Mt.* 15.17).[23]

     This theory was turned into practice, for Christians
made conscious and deliberate efforts to facilitate the exchange of alms for prayers. According to Hippolytus, this
was the purpose of the Agape: "at each act of offering, the
offerer must remember his host, for he was invited to the
latter's home for that very purpose." (The poor were confident of their own worth in this regard; and sometimes
they neglected to show the proper social deference to their
hosts.)[24] The poor might even be paid outright for their
prayers, as when Marcellus, in the *Acts of Peter,* gave the
widows each a gold piece "for their services," that is, for
the prayers that they had offered in his newly re-purified
house.[25]

     In light of this business-like approach to the inter-
change of alms and prayers, we cannot be surprised that,
for some authors, the poor became almost commodities.
Hermas advised the rich to "purchase afflicted souls,"
rather than lands or houses, as a security for the future.[26]
The *Epistle of Barnabas* gave this advice:

>   I beseech those who are in high positions, if
>   you will receive any counsel of my good will,
>   have among yourselves those to whom you may
>   do good; fail not (21.2).

It is critical for the salvation of the rich that they
should bestow alms on the poor; and they must ensure

that they have a supply of suitable persons for this purpose.[27]

It is remarkable that in all our literature, there
is no clear attack on this calculus of good works. It is
difficult to find even a few dubious notes of dissatisfac-
tion. In I Peter one reads, "you were ransomed...not with
perishable things such as silver or gold, but with the
precious blood of Christ" (1:18-19). This might be a protest against the doctrine of atoning alms, but, then again,
it may be no more than rhetorical heightening of the value
of Jesus' sacrifice. Again, Luke has Jesus speak of giving
alms from "those things which are within" (11:41). Does he
mean to "spiritualize" almsgiving by turning it into a
strictly interior virtue? Unfortunately, the meaning of
the phrase is almost totally obscure; and we cannot say.[28]
The subject of atoning alms did not even enter into the
conflict over faith and works between Paul and James, for
Paul supported the doctrine as enthusiastically as James.
There was no voice of protest among the Early Christian
writers.[29]

I do not mean to suggest that Early Christian writers never appealed to more disinterested motives for almsgiving. Paul used a variety of arguments to promote his
collection for the church at Jerusalem, among them an appeal to *isotēs,* the Greek philosophical ideal of "equity."[30]
Paul and the Johannine tradition were alike in appealing to
love of the brethren as a motive for almsgiving; and later
authors such as Clement of Alexandria and the anonymous
writer of *II Clement* made use of the same theme.[31] A number of teachers, beginning with Jesus himself, treated almsgiving as an imitation of God's own beneficence.[32] The
point is not to suggest that such ideas were absent from
Early Christian literature, but to say that they were of
secondary importance. The principal reason urged by our

authors for the giving of alms was that almsgiving would
work for the salvation of the donor.[33]

ALMS FROM THE RICH: ABANDONMENT

The donors benefited in this way were primarily rich
Christians, since they could best afford to give generously. The obligation of giving was not, to be sure, limited
to them. Several authors encouraged fasting as a means
whereby the poorer Christian could obtain something to give
as alms; and Athenagoras even claimed that this was a common custom among them.[34] But Paul considered it a matter of
remark when the relatively poor churches of Macedonia gave
generously to his collection for Jerusalem; and he asked
the Corinthians to give rather from their "abundance"
(*perisseuma*) (II Cor. 8:2-4, 13-15).

The normal almsgiver was thus the rich believer.
Paul treated such a person's ability to give alms as a
gift of the Spirit; and Hermas described almsgiving as the
diakonia of the rich. The author of the Pastorals held
that the business of rich Christians was "to do good, to
be rich in good deeds, liberal and generous"; and he promised them the appropriate reward for doing so. In the same
way, Clement of Rome saw the rich as obligated to "bestow
help" on the poor. According to Hermas, God allowed the
Christian rich to keep some portion of their wealth just so
that they might give alms from it.[35]

The rich, then, were the prime almsgivers of the
Early Church. They were expected to give lavishly, both
for the sake of the poor and for the furtherance of their
own salvation. There was even some suggestion that they
ought to divest themselves entirely of their property by
distributing it to the needy. We have already alluded to
this question more than once, but we must now examine the
origins of the problem, asking whether Jesus himself really

demanded abandonment of property from those who would follow him. If not, why did the evangelists preserve such a
demand among his teachings? If he did, why did the later
church show no sign of following his command?[36]

The principal passage is the story of the rich man
who came to Jesus to ask what he must do to be saved—the
very narrative which formed the text for Clement's discourse on *The Rich Man*. We must now consider its original
meaning, in the context of the gospels. Jesus told the
man to keep the commandments; but he protested that he had
always done so. (Apparently, he still felt that he fell
short of salvation.) Jesus then told him, "You lack one
thing; go, sell what you have, and give to the poor, and
you will have treasure in heaven; and come, follow me."
This seemed too much for the man, who went away sorrowful.
With this story, Mark combined the (originally independent)
saying of Jesus that "It is easier for a camel to go
through the eye of a needle than for a rich man to enter
the kingdom of God" (10:25). This addition had the effect
of generalizing the story of the rich enquirer to apply to
all rich persons.[37]

Mark's point in combining these elements was to
warn his readers that wealth posed a danger to the Christian in time of persecution (10:30). He stressed that it
would be difficult for them to be saved and that the world
to come would represent a reversal of the present social
order. The other two synoptic evangelists followed his
lead, but revised his narrative to suit their own purposes
—Matthew, in particular, treated abandonment as a goal of
Christian perfection.[38]

But what did Jesus himself mean by requiring surrender of property from this man as a prelude to discipleship?
If we take the story by itself, we shall see that there is
a fundamental contrast being painted between two kinds or

degrees of piety: that of the Law and that of discipleship.
There is nothing to suggest that Jesus' original answer
was a false one—the man *could* be saved by keeping the Law.
Nor is there any reason within the story to suppose that
the man was wrong when he claimed that he had already done
so. (If we claim that he cannot have kept the Law because
no one can do so, we are importing Pauline assumptions into the Synoptic text.)[39] What was important was that the
man was not satisfied with keeping the Law; he still felt
the need for some more decisive relationship with God.
Jesus offered him this by giving him the chance to join
his own inner circle of disciples.[40]

This was the original meaning of the command to
abandon property. The Synoptic Gospels agree that when
Jesus sent the members of his inner circle out on mission,
he sent them out in absolute poverty—even lacking necessities of life. Indeed, it would have been impossible to
practice Jesus' own wandering life, if one had property to
maintain or a business to look after. Apostles were supposed to travel light, and they enjoyed the right to live
off the benevolence of the people among whom they worked.
It was such a role that Jesus offered to the rich enquirer,
who proved unable to rise to the occasion; but there is no
suggestion that Jesus expected this surrender from followers outside his inner circle.[41]

Only in Luke is it made to appear that Jesus demanded complete renunciation of property on the part of all
Christians. There Jesus says, "Whoever of you does not re-
nounce all that he has cannot be my disciple" (14:33). But
the language of that statement, like that of the discourse
in which it is embedded, is hyperbolic. It is possible to
take literally the command to "hate" father, mother, wife,
children, brothers, and sisters? Did Luke mean anything
more by these words than Matthew in his more modest paralle

version: "He who loves father or mother more than me is not
worthy of me"?   Luke cannot have understood this discourse
(14:25-35) literally.   Nor can he have intended to teach
any general obligation of abandonment; for he alone of the
synoptic evangelists had Jesus countermand the Early Christian custom of missionary poverty.   Again, in the story of
Zacchaeus, he held that the price of salvation was scrupul-
ous justice and lavish almsgiving, not abandonment.[42]

　　None of the synoptic evangelists, then, maintained
that abandonment of wealth was a norm for the average
Christian.   At most, they held that it was an ideal goal
("If you would be perfect...")or a norm for those who wished
to embark on missionary work of the wandering, apostolic
type.   But even for this latter purpose, abandonment was
rare in the church after the first century.[43]   The difficulty of controlling wandering prophets encouraged the ra-
pid development of settled ministries; and even a wanderer
such as Paul quickly found that he must not rely on new
converts for his livelihood because of the risk that he
would appear to be a mercenary or charlatan.   Eusebius, to
be sure, tells us that it was common custom for missionar-
ies of the post-apostolic generation to abandon their goods,
but he gives no substantiating details.   Apart from Gregory
Thaumaturgus in the third century, there seem to be no concrete instances recorded.[44]

　　Gregory's teacher, Origen, does not seem to have regarded abandonment as an ideal for Christians of his day,
even though he understood the story of the rich enquirer
as commanding it—at least on the literal level.   In his
Commentary on Matthew, he argued that it is possible to
abandon property, after the example of the Greek philosophers, and that Jesus could have understood such an act as
the ultimate demonstration of love of neighbor (15.14-15).
He found fault, however, with the idea that such an act

could lead directly to perfection or salvation, for the
person who dispersed his wealth would not automatically
take leave of his passions and vices (15.16). It is better to allegorize the passage, explaining wealth as the
spirits we "acquire" which prompt us to sin, while the
giving of this wealth to the poor means the return of
these spiritual possessions to "the beggarly source of
sins."[45] This curiously far-fetched argument suggests
that Origen wished to avoid what he thought to be the literal sense of the gospel story as irrelevant or misleading.
He concludes that the rich are not debarred from heaven.[46]

        Abandonment of property was thus never a norm for
the lay Christian during the period of our study. Even
for the clergy, it was common only among wandering mission-
aries of the apostolic generation. Jesus demanded it only
of his inner circle. The practice virtually ceased with
the introduction of a settled, local ministry.[47]

ALMS AS THE CEMENT OF THE CHURCHES

        The great emphasis on almsgiving in Early Christian
writings undoubtedly owed something to a genuine concern
for the poorer brethren. But our authors made it quite
explicit that they were also concerned about the souls of
the rich and what almsgiving could contribute toward their
salvation. In addition to these two motives for the stress
they laid on almsgiving, we can at least surmise a third—
the institutional requirements of the churches. Alms were
the cement of unity that bound people together within the
individual congregation and bound congregations together
within the ecumenical church. The constant flow of alms
was therefore a principal concern for all responsible
clergymen.

        Some alms were no doubt given privately from one
Christian to another; but our authors wrote principally

of alms which passed through the treasury of the church.
This was already the norm in the primitive church of Jerusalem whose rich members brought their gifts and laid them
at the apostles' feet. The clergy then distributed the
alms to the local poor and to Christian travelers.[48] The
number of these varied with the size and location of the
congregation; and the treatment they received varied with
their social status, for, as Origen insisted, "One must
not deal the same with those who have been brought up from
infancy in harsh and narrow circumstances and those who
were nourished generously and delicately and afterwards
fell into poverty." The demand on church's treasury could
be considerable. But there were advantages to be gained,
for so long as the almsgiving apparatus remained function-
al, rich and poor were tied together into a single body by
their mutual interdependence.[49]

Gifts from one church to another were also important
in that they helped maintain ties of communion throughout
the world. Thus, the church at Antioch in the first century sent alms to the church at Jerusalem, despite their
differences of practice and theology (Acts 11:27-30). And
Paul's great collection for Jerusalem was intended to cement relations between his new churches and the present
church, as well as to meet actual need. The custom did
not disappear with the first century, for we find Dionysius
of Corinth, late in the second, writing of the historic
obligation which his church owed to the church of Rome for
its benefactions. (Walter Bauer was no doubt right in
thinking that the theological influence of Rome was reinforced by this characteristic generosity.) Almsgiving
thus took on an institutional as well as a theological importance for our authors.[50]

CONCLUSIONS

The early church, then, elected unanimously to follow the Jewish tradition of almsgiving rather than Greco-
Roman ideas of philanthropy. Like both, it linked almsgiving with reward; but like the former, it made God the
agent of this reward, not those benefited. It is this
promise of reward which particularly interests us here,
for it implies a positive evaluation of wealth which contrasts strongly with the attitudes studied in the preceding chapter. There we saw that Early Christian authors
viewed wealth with suspicion; they regarded it as something from which the Christian must separate himself spiritually, if not physically. How, then could they perform
an about-face when they came to speak of almsgiving and
offer to the rich an opportunity for salvation that was
scarcely available to the poor?

One may object that the contradiction is more apparent than real, for almsgiving does, after all, represent a
kind of separation from wealth, as the almsgiver hands his
goods over to the needy. Our authors did not, however,
ask anyone to separate himself entirely from his property.
The assumption was that the rich man would retain control
of his wealth, while devoting some substantial portion of
his income to almsgiving. In doing this, he would guarantee his salvation. The power and authority of wealth continued to be his; the religious authorities asked only
that he use it for his own religious benefit.

This combination of positive and negative attitudes
toward wealth demands some explanation. No doubt our authors felt some need to balance their attack on wealth by
showing that the rich could be saved despite their initial
disadvantage. Clement of Alexandria makes it clear that
this was his object in writing *The Rich Man*. But why this

necessity? Why not simply write the rich off as a loss?
Part of the answer must lie in the churches' need to maintain their welfare apparatus. Our writers promoted almsgiving for the sake of the church as well as for the eternal salvation of the giver. The social importance of the
rich within the church was as fundamental in determining
attitudes toward wealth as was any preconceived doctrinal
position.

  The social role of the rich believer is obscure,
since Early Christian writers have left us little explicit
information about it. Nonetheless, there are certain passages which reflect concrete events within the life of the
church and which therefore give us a clue to how the rich
actually functioned within the congregation. We turn now
to these materials, in the hope that we may discern the
social background against which the religious authorities
of the early church evolved their equivocal attitudes toward wealth and almsgiving.

FOOTNOTES

[1]For the teaching of Proverbs on almsgiving, see, for example,
11:24-25; 19:17; 21:13; 22:9, 22-23; 28:27. For rabbinic teaching on
fraudulent receipt of alms, see Montefiore and Loewe, pp. 418, 429; on
distinctions in charity, pp. 425-28.

[2]Job's distress at his suffering was intensified by recollection
of his faithfulness in giving alms (29:11-12). Sirach 4:3-6 warns that
failure to give will call down a curse. Tobit 4:10 credits almsgiving
with the power to prolong life.
  For the rabbinic teaching, see Montefiore and Loewe, pp. 412-19.
Failure to pay the poor-tithe could cause pestilence, *Aboth* 5.13.

[3]*Aboth* 1.2, cf. 2.8.

[4]Montefiore and Loewe, pp. 430-31, cf. p. 414. Johanan referred
to all charitable works, not only almsgiving. See also Neusner, pp.
168-72.

[5]Pliny, *Ep.* 9.30.1. On the recipients of benevolences, see
Hendrik Bolkestein, *Wohltätigkeit und Armenpflege im vorchristlichen
Altertum: Ein Beitrag zum Problem "Moral und Gesellschaft"* (Utrecht:
A. Oosthoek, 1939), pp. 95-100, 114-15, 297-99, 337-39. Uhlhorn, pp.
99-100, erred in assuming that Augustus' bounty was directed to those
"who could not live without relief."
  It was on religious occasions that non-citizens were most likely
to be included in benefactions; A. R. Hands, *Charities and Social Aid
in Greece and Rome* (Ithaca, N.Y.: Cornell University Press, 1968), pp.
90-91.

[6]Schilling, p. 37, for example, held that "Selbsucht war der
Grundzug des römischen Wesens...." But William Stearns Davis, *The
Influence of Wealth in Imperial Rome* (New York: Macmillan Co., 1910),
pp. 248-53, observed that the problem was largely one of terminology
and that, with the ancient Romans, one must speak of "liberality," not
"charity." Bolkestein, pp. vii-viii, cited the modern confusion between *Wohltätigkeit* and *Liebestätigkeit* as leading to a neglect of the
study of classical methods of relief.

[7]Aristotle, *Rhet.* 2.7.2; Pliny, *Ep.* 9.30. On the ideal of giving
among the Stoics, see Eberhard F. Bruck, "Ethics vs. Law: St. Paul,
the Fathers of the Church, and the 'Cheerful Giver' in Roman Law,"
Traditio 2 (1944):97-121. Gifts for "charitable" purposes in the
modern sense were not distinguished from other sorts of gifts (e.g.,
for public shows, repair of walls, or prosecution of a war); Hands,
pp. 42-43.

[8]Hands, pp. 37-39; Finley, pp. 150-76. Benefactors of cities

might even be treated as divine; see Dieter Georgi, "Socioeconomic Reasons for the 'Divine Man' as a Propagandistic Pattern," in *Aspects of Religious Propaganda in Judaism and Early Christianity,* ed. Elizabeth Schüssler Fiorenza (Notre Dame, Ind.: Notre Dame University Press, 1976), pp. 27-42, especially pp. 31-33.

On *philotimia,* see Hands, pp. 43, 77-78. Christians were not immune to its attractions, as we learn from a fourth-century dedicatory inscription, taken from a Christian chapel near Hebron and now embedded in the cloister wall of the Chicago Theological Seminary:

+ Ҟ ΤΟΥΤΟ ΤΟ ΝΕΟΝ ΕΡ
ΓΟΝ ΓΕΓΟΝΕΝ ΕΚ ΤΗϹ
ΑΥΤΗϹ ΦΙΛΟΤΙΜΙΑϹ
ϹΤΕΦΑΝΟΥ ΤΟΥ ϹΟΦΟ
ΤΑΤΟΥ Ҟ ΕΝΔΟҲ ΑΡΧΙ
ΑΤΡΟΥ ΤΟΥ ΘΕΙΟΥ ΠΑΛΑΤ
ΙΟΥ ⟶ ☩

⁹Pliny, *Ep.* 9.30.1-2; Juvenal, *Sat.* 1.95-126 (on the aristocracy receiving *sportulae*), 3.190-231 (on the relief afforded the rich after fires).

Tertullian, *Adv. Marc.* 4.31.1, contrasted the superior morality of Christians, who postpone the reward of their almsgiving to the resurrection, to that of pagans who expect a reward here and now.

¹⁰Philo's teaching on liberality was thoroughly Greek in spirit; Goodenough, *Philo,* pp. 130-31. For synagogue inscriptions, see C. K. Barrett, ed., *The New Testament Background: Selected Documents* (London: S.P.C.K., 1958), pp. 50-52. Jesus contrasts the two types of benevolence in Lk. 14:12-14, where he advises hosts to invite the indigent to dinner instead of those who can repay.

¹¹II Thes. 3:6, 9-10. I Tim. 5:3-8. Justin, *I Apol.* 14.2. The normal objects of Christian charity were the Christian poor; but outsiders were not dogmatically excluded. Thus Paul urged Christians to "do good to all men," but gave priority to those "who are of the household of faith" (Gal. 6:10).

¹²Hermas, *Mand.* 2.4-6. This passage is closely related to the one in *Did.* and may derive from the same "Two Ways" tradition; Robert McQueen Grant, ed., *Apostolic Fathers,* vol. 6: *Hermas,* by Graydon F. Snyder, pp. 65-66. The concept is already found in Mt. 5:42, "Give to him who asks...." The "Two Ways" tradition also warned against unworthy reception of alms (*Did.* 4.5 // *Barn.* 19.9; *Did.* 1.5).

The advice of "Sextus" not to let "an ungrateful man deter you from doing good" (*Sent.* 328) is somewhat different; it is related rather to the Stoic concept of duty (cf. Marcus Aurelius, 2.1, on not being deterred by ingratitude).

¹³The lack of consistency is most clearly visible in the *Didache,*

which commands indiscriminate almsgiving in 1.5 and then reverses itself in 1.6: ἀλλὰ καὶ περὶ τούτου δὲ εἴρηται· ʿΙδρωσάτω ἡ ἐλεημοσύνη
σου εἰς τὰς χεῖράς σου, μέχρις ἂν γνῷς, τίνι δῷς.

[14]Mt. 19:21 // Mk. 10:21 // Lk. 18:22. Cf. the contrast between
earthly and heavenly treasure in Mt. 6:19-21 // Lk. 12:33-34, where it
is not clear, however, how the heavenly treasure is acquired.

[15]The passage from Luke 6 is paralleled in Mt. 7:1-2, but the
explicit reference to almsgiving is found only in Luke. Lk. 14:13-14
is related to Mt. 6:1-4. Here both evangelists emphasize the importance of secrecy in almsgiving, for a reward in this world might in-
validate that in the next. Similarly, the rabbis were suspicious of
any element of self-glorification; see Montefiore and Loewe, p. 420.
The same thought appears in *Sent. Sex.* 341: ᾧ ἂν ὑπουργήσῃς ἕνεκα
δόξης, μισθοῦ ὑπούργησας.

[16]Hermas, *Sim.* 10.4 (Do good works benefiting the destitute, before the Tower is finished without you). *Sent. Sex.* 52 ("If you were
good to the needy, you would be great with God"), cf. 379. *II Clem.*
6.9, cf. 4.2-3. Tertullian, *De pat.* 7.13.

[17]For Jesus as authority for almsgiving see Acts 20:35 (Paul's
farewell address to the Ephesian elders); cf. Justin, *I Apol.* 15, a
pastiche of sayings of Jesus. *Barn.* 3.3-5 invoked the authority of the
Hebrew prophets; Hermas, *Mand.* 2.4, appealed to his own prophetic authority.
    The argument based on I Sam. 15:22 comes from Irenaeus, *Adv. haer.*
4.29.1-4 (4.17.1-3).

[18]*Adv. haer.* 12.5, on Zacchaeus; 4.46.3 (4.30.4), on erecting of
"Tabernacle." The principal purpose of the latter passage was the
refutation of Gnostic objections to the spoiling of the Egyptians. We
should not force it as a key expression of Irenaeus' own thinking
about alms.

[19]*Sent. Sex.* 47: θυσία θεῷ μόνη καὶ προσηνὴς ἡ ἀνθρώποις εὐεργεσία
διὰ θεόν. Haller, pp. 545-46, described this development as a response
to Jewish and gentile criticism of the Christians as having no real
sacrifices; but we have seen that the development was not limited to
Christianity. Haller also points out the connection between the sacrificial interpretation of alms and that of the Eucharist at which they
were offered.
    To the explicit descriptions of alms as sacrifices, we must add
two passages which clearly imply this theology: Phil. 4:18, where
Paul describes the Philippians' gift to him in sacrificial terms, and
Polycarp, *Ep.* 4.3, where the widows and orphans are the church's
θυσιαστήριον.
    Sanders, pp. 125-27, ignores the sacrificial motif in James.

[20]Origen, *Hom. in Lev.* 2.4.

[21]On *II Clem.*, see R. M. Grant, ed., *Apostolic Fathers*, vol. 2: *First and Second Clement*, by R. M. Grant and Holt H. Graham, p. 129, where Graham has recognized the relationship with Old Testament, with Jewish thought, and with Mt. The date and place of origin of *II Clem.* are obscure, perhaps Rome c. 136-40 (Grant, 2:109) or Corinth c. 100 (Karl Paul Donfried, *The Setting of Second Clement in Early Christianity*, Novum Testamentum, Suppl. 38 [Leiden: E. J. Brill, 1974], pp. 1-15).

Given that the doctrine of the atoning power of alms was widely accepted, it is surprising that there is little evidence of almsgiving as a regular part of penitential discipline before the time of Cyprian. Tertullian in his *De paenitentia* does not mention it at all, although he defends other, apparently existing disciplines of fasting, wearing poor clothes, and refraining from entertainments (11).

[22]Bultmann regarded these sayings as Jewish material reworked in the early church, *Synoptic Tradition*, pp. 123-24, 142-43. Jeremias, however, has argued that they must go back to Jesus himself, *Parables of Jesus*, pp. 205-10.

Clement of Alexandria (see above, p. 32) believed that the same point was made in the parable of the Unfaithful Steward (Lk. 16:1-9), where one makes friends, through almsgiving, who will subsequently receive one into heaven. According to Jeremias, *Parables of Jesus*, pp. 45-46, it is the angels who will receive one, not the "friends." Jeremias, p. 47, doubted that the parable had any bearing on almsgiving, since he regarded vs. 9 as an isolated logion originally unrelated to the parable. For the opposite point of view, see Francis E. Williams, "Is Almsgiving the Point of 'The Unjust Steward'?" *JBL* 83 (1964):293-97. For an older, but similar treatment, see Cone, p. 133, n. 1.

[23]II Cor. 9:12-14; Paul added his own thanksgiving (vs. 15) as a guarantee of the result. Seipel, pp. 12-13, saw the same concept in II Cor. 8:14 ("...your abundance at the present time should supply their want, so that their abundance may supply your want"), reasoning that the abundance of the poor can only be spiritual. In this he followed the interpretation of Origen, *Comm. in Mt.* 15.17. *I Clem.* 38.2 treats the thanksgiving as the poor man's religious duty, parallel to the rich man's duty to give alms.

Hermas, *Sim.* 2.5-6; cf. *Sim.* 5.2.10, where the same relationship is presented under the parable of a steward and his underlings.

[24]Hippolytus, *Ap. Trad.* 26. This work was written c. 217, at the time of the schism between Hippolytus and Callistus, but it had a conservative purpose and probably reflected the usage of perhaps thirty to fifty years earlier. See Burton Scott Easton, trans. and ed., *The Apostolic Tradition of Hippolytus* (Cambridge: University Press, 1954; reprint edition [Hamden, Conn.]: Archon Books, 1962), p. 25. Uhlhorn, pp. 89-90, held that the *agapae* were purely a means of aiding the poor from the very beginning, but this is unlikely (cf. Easton, p. 97). The

agape originated in common meals of the whole church, even though it
had become practically a dole by the time of Hippolytus. See Gregory
Dix, *The Shape of the Liturgy*, 2d ed. (London: Dacre Press, 1945), pp.
82-87.

[25]*Actus Vercellenses* 19. Cf. *Acts of Paul (Pap. Heidsieck*, p.
33), where Hermocrates gives alms to the widows as part of his cam-
paign to gain healing for his son. The poor had to be warned against
presuming on this relationship. Thus, Clement of Rome instructed the
weak to "reverence the strong" (*I Clem.* 38.2), and an anonymous post-
Cyprianic author listed the *pauper superbus* as one of his "Twelve
Abuses of the Age" (*De duodecim abusivis saeculi*, 8, cited by Schilling, pp. 66-68).

[26]*Sim.* 1.8.

[27]Tertullian, *Ad uxor.* 2.8.4-5, held that it would be profitable
for rich women to marry poor Christian men, since the kingdom of heaven
has been promised to the poor.

[28]For the literature on Lk. 11:41, see Dupont, p. 318, n. 4. The
phrase was already a problem for Jerome; see the discussion of the
early history of its interpretation in Uhlhorn, pp. 401-2.

[29]Paul, I Cor. 13:3, insisted on the importance of correct motive,
but he did not deny the power of almsgiving. *Gospel of Thomas* 6, however, does appear to reject almsgiving as a Christian practice. The
disciples ask, "Shall we give alms?" And they receive only this reply:
"Do not lie; and that which you hate do not do." *Thos.* 14 is even
stronger. Edgar Hennecke, ed., *New Testament Apocrypha*, new ed. Wilhelm Schneemelcher, English trans. ed. R. McL. Wilson, 2 vols. (Philadelphia: Westminster Press, 1963), 1:511-22.

[30]II Cor. 8:13-14. *Isotēs* can mean "equality"; but the Greek
philosophers generally shunned the idea of a numerical equality among
men, and the Greek word did not often carry that connotation. See,
for example, Plato, *Lg.* 6.757, and Aristotle, *Pol.* 5.1302a7. Georgi,
Geschichte der Kollekte, argued that Paul's usage was based on Jewish
speculation which took *isotēs* as a name for Sophia. This would explain the peculiar phrase ἐξ ἰσότητος (8:13), but seems to ignore
ὅπως γένηται ἰσότης (8:14).
    Paul's argument might best be characterized as an appeal to the
vague ideal of "fairness." As such, it does reappear once in our literature—Hermas, *Vis.* 3.9.2.

[31]I Thes. 4:9-10; Rom. 12:10-13; I Jn. 3:17; *II Clem.* 4:1-3. On
Clement of Alexandria, see above, pp. 34-35. "Love" in the context of
Early Christian literature partakes "more of active good will than of
emotion; it can be commanded as emotions cannot" (Davies, "Moral
Teaching," p. 329). Insofar as there is any single key to Early
Christian ethics, it is surely the "Love Commandment"; see for example,

Sanders, pp. 50-66, on the relation between Matthew and Paul. This makes it still more surprising that love is not often given as the principal reason for almsgiving.

[32]Mt. 5:42, cf. 45. Paul transforms the idea into an imitation of Jesus, who "was rich, yet for your sake...became poor" (II Cor. 8:9). This is an extension of the theme of imitating God's benevolence, not a reference to Jesus' earthly condition, contra George Wesley Buchanan, "Jesus and the Upper Class," *Novum Testamentum* 7 (1964-65):195-209.

Later uses of the theme may be found in *I Clem.* 33.1-34.8 (where the topic is not limited to almsgiving) and *Diog.* 10.6.

[33]This has long been recognized, usually with some embarrassment, by modern scholars. Since most approached our subject from the point of view of ethical theory, they have then ignored this aspect of early Christianity and proceeded to turn their attention to more acceptable ethical motives. See, for example, Chastel (Eng.), pp. 38, 45; Uhlhorn, p. 120; Cone, pp. 92-117; Troeltsch (Eng.), pp. 133-37. Despite efforts to stigmatize the doctrine of rewards as a development of the post-apostolic church (e.g., Haller, pp. 525-34), it was in fact intrinsic to the ethical teaching of Jesus according to Amos Niven Wilder, *Eschatology and Ethics,* pp. 78-83.

[34]Hermas, *Sim.* 5.3.7; *Sent. Sex.* 267; Origen, *Hom. in Lev.* 10.2 (a quotation, perhaps from Sextus); Athenagoras, *Leg.* 11.4; Tertullian, *De ieiun.* 13.3, seems to suggest that this was a community practice as well as an individual one.

[35]Rom. 12:8; the reference is to contributors, not church officials who distribute alms; see William Sanday and Arthur C. Headlam, *A Critical and Exegetical Commentary on the Epistle to the Romans, ICC,* 5th ed. (Edinburgh: T. & T. Clark, 1902), p. 357; Hermas, *Mand.* 2.6; I Tim. 6:17-19; *I Clem.* 38.2; Hermas, *Sim.* 9.30.5, which modifies *Vis.* 3.6.6, where the rich had been threatened with total loss of property. These two passages belong to the latest and earliest parts, respectively, of Hermas' work; indeed, *Sim.* 9 is a reinterpretation of *Vis.* 3 (see R. M. Grant, *Apostolic Fathers,* 6:3-6).

Tertullian, *Apol.* 39.4-6 (on the *modica stips* paid voluntarily by Christians), does not contradict our theory. Tertullian has nothing to say here about the role of the rich laity; he is only concerned to show that the Christian clergy do not pay for the privilege of holding office—there are no *summae honorariae* in the church.

[36]See above, pp. 35-36, for Clement of Alexandria's rejection of the ideal of abandonment, and pp. 53-55, for abandonment in connection with communism.

[37]Mk. 10:17-22 // Mt. 19:16-22 // Lk. 18:18-23. Mark's combination of materials is not perfectly smooth, for the disciples (vss. 23-27) express fear whether anyone (not just the rich) can be saved and

Peter (vss. 28-31) calls attention to their own situation and conduct,
even though they were not rich. On the oral and redaction history of
the logia here, see S. Légasse, pp. 64-83.

    Percy, pp. 91-93, also noted the difficulties in Mk. 10:23-27, as
did Bultmann, pp. 21-22. Dibelius, "Das soziale Motiv," p. 190, saw
the narrative as originally a challenge to an individual, not as a
general law.

    [38]Légasse, pp. 86-92 (Mk.), 100-103 (Lk.), 113-46, 202-7 (Mt.).
But William D. Davies, *The Setting of the Sermon on the Mount* (Cambridge: University Press, 1966), pp. 208-14, denies that Matthew set
up any distinct status of Christian perfection; he demanded perfection
of all Christians.

    [39]Percy, p. 104. But Paul Sevier Minear, *Commands of Christ*
(Nashville: Abingdon Press, 1972), pp. 98-112, considers the motif of
obedience to the commandments unoriginal here; and Bultmann, p. 41,
implies that it belongs in the milieu of the early Palestinian church.
The later tendency of the Jewish Christians, however, as evident in
the treatment of this story in *Gospel of the Hebrews,* was to understand the Torah itself as requiring complete abandonment of property,
thus denying that the man had fulfilled the Law. Would they, at an
earlier date, have created the suggestion in Mark that the Law can be
surpassed? That Jesus did teach that obedience to the Law was possible
and even possessed the power to save is evident from the parables of
the Rich Man and Lazarus and of the Good Samaritan (Lk. 16:19-31; 10:
25-37).

    [40]Irenaeus, *Adv. haer.* 4.23.2 (4.12.5), had already seen that
this was the implication of the command to abandon property.

    [41]Gerd Theissen, "Wanderradikalismus." An English
translation by Antoinette Wire, without complete notes, can be found
as "Itinerant Radicalism: The Tradition of Jesus Sayings from the Perspective of the Sociology of Literature," in *The Bible and Liberation:
Political and Social Hermeneutics,* ed. Norman K. Gottwald and
Antoinette Wire (Berkeley, Calif.: Community for Religious Research
and Education, 1976), pp. 84-93. See also Theissen, *Sociology;* cf.
above, p. 40, n. 43.
    The distinction between two grades of discipleship had already
been noted by Seipel, pp. 249-59, Schilling, p. 6, and Troeltsch, pp.
59-61. There is a useful study of the similarities between wandering
preachers in early Christianity and their Cynic contemporaries in Leo
Leslie Tait, "Stoic and Christian Preaching" (M.A. thesis, University
of Chicago, 1917), pp. 43-55.

    [42]Lk. 22:35-38; 10:1-10. Degenhardt, pp. 36-41, attempts to re-
solve the inconsistency by arguing that the *mathētai* in Luke's gospel
are always surrogates for the church's ministers in Luke's own day;
but Luke's usage is far from consistent in this regard. Behm, p. 281,
noted that the passage commands abandonment of both property and

family—and that the disciples still had both (Mk. 1:29).

⁴³There were already violations within the first century. Jesus
had commanded the missionary to abandon property and family alike; but
Peter still had both in Mk. 1:29, and John 21 even portrays the disciples as returning to their Galilean fishing business after the
crucifixion. Cf. Behm, pp. 281-82. Perhaps the ideal of abandonment
applied only while the disciple was actively on mission; but in that
case, the prohibition of family had lapsed by Paul's time (I Cor. 9:5),
that of property by Luke's.

⁴⁴I Cor. 9:1-18; Eusebius, *H.E.* 3.37.2. On Gregory Thaumaturgus,
see Chastel, p. 93, citing Gregory of Nyssa, *De vit. Greg. Thaum.*
Origen, for all his talk about clerical poverty, did not observe it
himself (*Hom. in Gen.* 16.5); cf. Charles Stanley Phillips, pp. 92-93.

⁴⁵...τοὺς αἰτίους τῶν ἁμαρτημάτων πτωχούς (15.18).

⁴⁶In his treatment of the story of the Rich Enquirer, Origen may
have been influenced by Clement's interpretation of it in *Quis div.*,
which comes to similar conclusions. But there do not seem to be any
clear references to *Quis div.* in Origen's commentary. If a relation
does exist, Origen has reworked Clement's ideas extensively in terms
of his own method of Biblical interpretation and made them distinctive-
ly his own.

⁴⁷The question whether asceticism was the correct mode of discipleship for all, for the clergy only, or for an elite was never finally settled within our period; see Georg Kretschmar, "Ein Beitrag zur
Frage nach dem Ursprung der frühchristlichen Askese," *ZTK* 61 (1964):
27-67.
    Paul was so far from advocating complete abandonment of property
that he promised earthly rewards for almsgiving: "he who sows bountifully will reap bountifully" (II Cor. 9:6). For Tertullian, total loss
of property was simply a disaster which the Christian should prepare to
face bravely—never an ideal of voluntary conduct, *De pat.* 7.

⁴⁸Acts 4:35. On early Christian organization for charity, see
below, pp. 160-62. On the significance of "laying at the feet," see
Luke Johnson, pp. 200-203.

⁴⁹Origen, *Comm. in Mt.* 6.1. Modern authors have often stressed
that the Christian welfare apparatus could provide a great sense of
security for the poor person of antiquity; see, for example, Case, p.
246, and Kautsky (Eng.), pp. 357-59, who compared the system to "the
insurance aspects of a modern trade union." Reuben Christian Schellhase, "Social Aspects of Early Christian Charity" (Ph.D. dissertation,
University of Chicago, 1952), pp. 342-43, suggested that the opportunity to give alms was also a route to increased social prestige for women. But it was Chastel, the counterrevolutionary, who realized that

the social security of the poor is also the means by which the authorities can control them, (Eng.), pp. 64-69. Of more recent authors, only
Donald Wayne Riddle, *The Martyrs,* pp. 89-91, seems to have discerned
the importance of this aspect of the church's charities.

[50]A large literature has accumulated on the subject of Paul's
collection for the church at Jerusalem; surveys of it will be found in
Keith Fullerton Nickle, *The Collection: A Study in Paul's Strategy,*
Studies in Biblical Theology, no. 48 (Naperville, Ill.: Alec R. Allenson, 1966), passim, and Georgi, *Geschichte der Kollekte,* pp. 9-11.
Nickle argues that Paul aimed at hastening the Parousia by bringing
gentiles to Jerusalem, pp. 133-39; but he admits that Paul's motives
were mixed, including charitable concerns along with a hope of cement-
ing relationships between his new churches and the mother church of
Jerusalem, pp. 100-129.

For the letter of Dionysius of Corinth, see Eusebius, *H.E.* 4.23.
10.

Walter Bauer, *Orthodoxy and Heresy in Earliest Christianity,* with
appendixes by Georg Strecker, trans. Philadelphia Seminar on Christian
Origins, ed. Robert A. Kraft and Gerhard Krodel (Philadelphia: Fortress Press, 1971), pp. 121-24.

CHAPTER FOUR

THE DANGER OF RICHES
TO THEIR POSSESSOR

THE WEAKNESS OF THE RICH

It is striking that when our authors spoke of the
rich themselves (as distinct from the more abstract topic
of riches), it was almost always by way of warning or rebuke. We have already observed that Clement of Alexandria
spoke of them as particularly subject to temptation, though
he did not specify what sins threatened them most.[1] From
other authors, we learn that possessions tie the rich to
the life of this world, involve them with pagan society,
distract them from the enthusiastic exercise of their
faith and, above all, lure them into apostasy in time of
persecution. In brief, the rich are portrayed as marginal
Christians—lukewarm in time of peace and prone to lapse at
the slightest hint of trouble.

We meet this characterization of the rich already in
the Gospel of Luke, in a discourse on possessions and the
Judgment which Luke himself assembled from his sources (12:
1-13:9). Here we find diverse materials, some peculiar to
this gospel, some common to Matthew as well, welded together
by Luke's own complex scene-setting. The structure of the
discourse is determined by a double audience, one consist-
ing of disciples, the other of "the multitude." Luke has
Jesus address himself now to one group now to the other,
thus distinguishing between two types of messages addressed
to two different classes of hearers.[2]

Jesus first addresses himself to the disciples with

a warning of God's impending Judgment (vss. 2-10). This
Judgment is far more to be feared than earthly persecution:
"...my friends, do not fear those who kill the body, and
after that have no more that they can do.... Fear him who,
after he has killed, has power to cast into hell" (vss. 4-
5). With these words, Luke sets the theme of the entire
discourse: that earthly goods are incommensurate with
heavenly.[3]

        In light of these related threats of persecution and
Judgment, Jesus admonishes his disciples to be detached
from earthly goods: "Do not be anxious about your life,
what you shall eat, nor your body what you shall put on.
For life is more than food, and the body more than clothing" (vss. 22-23). God knows the needs of his people and
will supply all necessities (vss. 24-30). To the disciples
of Jesus, he will give heavenly goods as well—goods so
superior to the earthly that one must even surrender the
earthly for the sake of the heavenly.[4]

        This message of total abandonment is not meant for
all Jesus' hearers, but only for a narrower circle—the
servants whom the master has left waiting for him, above
all the steward who is in charge. It has been suggested
that the inner audience of the disciples in this particular
discourse represented for Luke the clergy of the church of
his own day. But this can scarcely be right, for Luke regarded the institution of apostolic poverty as anachronistic. The inner circle of disciples here stand only for
themselves. It is their unique closeness to Jesus which
imposes the obligation to abandon all else: "Everyone to
whom much is given, of him will much be required" (12-48).
Thus far, Jesus' message to the disciples.[5]

        The message to the multitude is broken into two
units, interspersed with the speeches to the disciples. Th
first of these units (12:13-21) is devoted to the subject o
property: a man from the crowd asks Jesus to adjudicate a disputed ir

heritance between him and his brother. Jesus refuses
peremptorily with the words, "Man, who made me a judge or
a divider over you?" He follows this refusal up with a
denunciation of "covetousness" and with the parable of the
Rich Fool. There is an interesting series of non sequiturs here, for the man has not, strictly speaking, co-
veted his brother's property, but has asked for help in
recovering what he believes to be his legal and moral
right. Neither does the parable of the Rich Fool have
anything to do with "covetousness": what the Fool proposes
to enjoy is his own property.

These non sequiturs show that the three units of
tradition here (vss. 13-14, 15, and 16-21) were originally
independent of each other.[6] But Luke wished them to be
understood as mutually interpretive; for him, the pivot
was the logion about covetousness. By placing it between
the other two elements, he brought all three units under
that one rubric. To seek to recover one's rightful possessions, unjustly withheld by others, is "covetousness";
to rely on one's own hoarded wealth, as though it were
central to one's life, is "covetousness." There remains,
therefore, no *legitimate* form of concern about wealth for
anyone, even the multitudes.

Jesus' second speech to the multitude (12:54-13:9)
centers on the theme of Judgment. He warns them that they
should be aware of what is coming and should prepare for
the crisis at once, before it is too late (12:54-59).
Violent death in this world is already a manifestation of
Judgment to come; and there is not a soul in the audience
who does not deserve such a fate (13:1-5). For the moment,
God is giving people a respite for repentance; but it is
only a short respite (one year, vs. 8).

The content of Jesus' message is thus much the same
for both audiences, but it is given in two different forms.

In the simpler form of the message, addressed to the multitude, Jesus says, "All concern for or confidence in possessions is covetousness, a violation of the fundamental
moral code; beware of it, for the Judgment is imminent."
For the disciples, the connection between the two themes
is more complex. "Persecution is coming. The test [perse-
cution] touches upon the material things of this world,
but the kingdom is of heaven and is immeasurably more
precious than the goods of earth. Therefore, sacrifice
here in order to be rich there." Luke saw in wealth a
danger for the rich——the danger that they will fail God's
ultimate judgment because "covetousness" will tempt them
to denial of Christ in time of persecution.[7]

The theme of the weakness of the rich did not origi-
nate with Luke. It was present in his sources, and he
merely emphasized it by the way in which he arranged them.
The tradition behind Mark shows signs of the same concern.
In the allegorical explanation of the Parable of the Sower,
Jesus is made to explain that the seeds sown among thorns
represent people who hear the Word, "and the cares of the
age and the deceit of riches and the desires for other
things" choke the word (Mk. 4:19). Here, wealth is presented as a distraction, leading people to ignore the
saving message, rather than as a temptation to apostasy.
But it is equally a danger to Christian life. Matthew and
Luke abbreviate Mark at this point, but preserve the essential point about riches (Mt. 13:22; Lk. 8:14).[8]

Mark, then, did not associate the danger of wealth
so intimately with the time of persecution as did Luke.
Wealth simply contributes to a kind of spiritual lethargy
that "chokes out" Christian faith in the way that weeds
choke a garden. Thus, we may speak of a two-fold danger
which the Evangelists identified as arising from the possession of wealth: in time of persecution, wealth tempts

a Christian to deny Jesus; in time of peace, it tempts
him to grow lax in his faith.[9]

In a passage of the Revelation of John, the glori-
fied Christ addresses both dangers (3:14-22). He de-
nounces the Laodiceans because their wealth has led to a
sense of self-satisfaction and thence to a neglect of the
Lord's business; they have become "lukewarm." The remedy
for their condition is to buy of Christ "gold refined by
fire...and white garments" (3:18). Here, as often in
Revelation, "fire" is a symbol of suffering, while the
white robe is a symbol of martyrdom. Thus, the remedy
for the laxness of the rich is the successful completion
of the ordeal of persecution; and the rich are summoned
to overcome both dangers at once.[10]

THE RICH AS POTENTIAL APOSTATES

Early in the second century, the prophet Hermas
drew a similar portrait of the rich:

> These are those who have faith, but also
> have the riches of this world. When perse-
> cution comes, because of their wealth and
> because of business they deny their lord....

Hermas' objective was that the rich Christians should
again become "useful," and this can happen only if "their
wealth be cut away from them." After this, they may be
prepared for martyrdom or, like Hermas himself, for an
active and enthusiastic role in the life of the congregation. Otherwise, the rich Christians move on a lower
spiritual plane than their brethren, with little concern
for understanding the truths of their religion.[11]

Hermas blamed the failures of the rich on the fact
that they moved in wider social circles than their poorer
fellow-Christians: they "are mixed up with business and
riches, and heathen friendships, and many other occupations of this world." Hermas was undoubtedly correct in

observing that any given social group has most power to
constrain those of its members who have no other social
validation for their lives. Association with pagans,
along with the demands of business, probably did serve to
free many of the rich from complete dependence on the
Christian community and its approval or disapproval. In
Hermas' own case, the loss of wealth had reversed this tendency; and it was therefore associated with an increase in
his religious fervor. He saw no reason why the same cause
should not produce the same effect in others; God in his
mercy would strip the rich of their property only in order
to save them.[12]

Tertullian, at the very end of the second century,
also spoke of the way in which wealth interfered with the
will to martyrdom. In one of his earliest works, he set
himself the task of cheering and encouraging a group of
Christians imprisoned for their faith. He expressed a
fear that those who long for the "fruit of this age" will
find it hard to put up with their present sufferings (*Ad
mart.* 2.5). He thought it appropriate to encourage the
rich among them with the crass argument that "Even if you
have lost some of the joys of life, [remember] 'It is good
business to let something go in order to make larger prof-
its'" (2.6). Let them substitute heavenly for earthly
goods as objects of their acquisitiveness.

In another work, addressed to women, he again voiced
fear that earthly luxury would impede the will to martyrdom: "I fear the neck, beset with pearl and emerald nooses,
will give no room to the broadsword!" The rich must,
therefore, cast away ornament and subject the body to
fasting and mortification to prepare for the rigors of im-
prisonment and torture.[13]

Like Hermas, Tertullian was aware that the problem
of wealth was not confined to the moment of decision

during persecution. Even in time of peace, material goods
tempt the rich into a compromise with paganism. Much business was transacted in and around pagan temples; and while
Tertullian was forced to tolerate the practice, he warned
that such places posed a danger of religious contamination
(*De spect.* 8.8-10). There were also elements of pagan religion in the normal contract forms. Christians generally
agreed that a man separated himself from the church if he
actually took an oath by the pagan gods; but what if his
creditor were liberal enough to allow him to sign a contract claiming that he had taken the oath, even though he
had not? Some Christian businessmen were arguing that
there could be no harm in this; but Tertullian saw in
their complacency a betrayal as serious as the actual
oath-taking (*De idol.* 23).

Tertullian expressed, even more sharply than Hermas,
the social tension that prevailed between the rich person's
role in society and his membership in the church. The
rich of antiquity were expected to take upon themselves
the burdens of public office, of those very magistracies
by which Jesus had been condemned and God's servants were
still being attacked. These magistracies, moreover, were
intimately associated with the civic religion of antiquity.
Rich Christians pointed out that their birth and wealth
made it difficult for them to resist this "idolatry." Tertullian replied:

> For avoiding it, remedies cannot be lack-
> ing; since, even if they be lacking, there
> remains that one by which you will be made
> a happier magistrate, not in the earth, but
> in the heavens (*De idol.* 18).

It comes down to a choice of social position with idolatry
on the one hand, or of Christian faith with martydom on
the other.

Toward the end of his life, Tertullian's views on

the rich developed a certain intransigence, as evidenced
by the treatise *De fuga in persecutione*. This work is concerned not only, as its title suggests, with the question
of flight in time of persecution, but with the larger question of the use of money to avoid martyrdom. By the early
third century, public officials had come to recognize the
opportunities for extortion that lay in the illegal status
of the church; and Tertullian himself declared in an open
letter to Scapula, governor of Africa, that the Christians
of the province were paying out enormous sums for protection from the law (*Ad Scap*. 5.1-3). Bribery and flight
became twin methods for avoiding persecution.

Tertullian argued against both on the practical
ground that they are money wasted: if you flee, they will
catch you sooner or later, just as they did the "most holy
martyr Rutilius" (*De fuga* 5.3); if you succeed in buying
off the local officials, a bribe will not save you from
the mob (14). Tertullian also argued theologically: to
escape martyrdom by means of money is itself a kind of
apostasy, a denial of God's power and goodness:

> He has fallen, therefore, who only hoped
> to escape: refusal of martyrdom is in
> fact a denial. A Christian is saved by
> money and has it for this purpose—not to
> suffer, while [he claims] he will 'be rich
> toward God!' But Christ was rich in *blood*
> for *him*. 'Happy accordingly are the poor,'
> it says, 'because the kingdom of heaven
> is theirs who have only their soul in
> pocket' (*De fuga* 12.5).

To be saved from the crown of martyrdom by money is a contradiction; even if one's wealth preserves one from a public lapse, the very use of it proves one's private weakness—dependence on things of this world.[14]

On this point, however, Tertullian was isolated.
The treatise *De fuga* was written after he became a Montanist; and it was easier for him to criticize the long-

standing practice of the catholics after he had ceased to
be one of them himself. More orthodox authors never criticized the custom of flight in time of persecution; and
they never mentioned the custom of paying bribes, though
one must believe that they knew it. Tertullian's absolute
antithesis between money and martyrdom remains uniquely
his own.[15]

Origen, writing later in the third century, represented a more typical attitude. He doubted whether the
person who is "distracted by wealth and, as it were, lamed
by its thorn" will enter heaven.[16] Yet, it can be done;
and for the person who succeeds in doing it, the reward
will be great. When Origen's wealthy patron Ambrose was
imprisoned for his faith, Origen addressed to him a work
of exhortation which placed an astonishing value on wealth.
The author maintained that Ambrose, as a rich confessor,
had before him the opportunity to achieve such a blessed-
ness as few or none had achieved before him; for Jesus
promised that "whoever has left brothers or sisters or
parents or children or fields or houses for the sake of my
name will receive many times as much." Origen even avowed
that if he himself were to become a martyr, he should like
to be rich and the father of many children so that he
might receive still more in return (*Exhort. ad mart.* 14).[17]

It is unlikely that Origen meant these observations
materially; he understood the promised reward rather in
terms of divine favor or of merit with God. Even so, he
sensed that this teaching would seem objectionable to some,
since it exalted the rich martyr over the poor one; and he
justified it by comparing the case of the martyr who undergoes torture with that of the martyr who enjoys a relatively painless death. The former enjoys "a brighter virtue
in martyrdom"; in the same way, a man who undergoes the
torment of parting with great possessions deserves added

credit (*Exhort. ad mart.* 15).

However distasteful the tone of this passage may be to modern democratic sensibilities, Origen was not saying anything radically different from what earlier Christians said. His point was that riches constitute a danger to those who possess them; in particular, they are an added temptation in times of persecution, encouraging the rich Christian to deny his Lord. Therefore, to triumph over them is supremely meritorious.

What all these authors have in common is their identification of wealth as a threat to the eternal welfare of its possessor. In time of peace, say some, it causes laxness in faith; in time of persecution, they all say, it tempts Christians to lapse. That these statements represent a firsthand assessment of the early Christian rich, not just a literary tradition, is implied in two ways by the nature of our sources. In the first place, several of the works in question were addressed to specific situations: Origen and Tertullian were writing to rich Christians imprisoned for their faith and threatened with death; Hermas' attitude arose out of his own experience; John was assessing the character of a specific congregation. Second, our sources are independent of each other: except for an occasional allusion to Mark's story of the Rich Man in the Synoptic Gospels, each of these authors seems to have relied on his own resources to address needs that he himself confronted—the laxness and weakness of the rich.

We may compare a graphic description of how rich Christians behaved under stress at the very end of our period—the Decian persecution of A.D. 251, as it was felt in Alexandria:

> ...all cowered with fear. And of many of
> the more eminent persons, some came forward
> immediately through fear, others in public
> positions were compelled to do so by their

> business, and others were dragged by those
> around them. Called by name they approached
> the impure and unholy sacrifices, some pale
> and trembling, as if they were not for sacri-
> ficing but rather to be themselves the sacri-
> fices.....But others ran eagerly towards the
> altars, affirming by their forwardness that
> they had not been Christians even formerly;
> concerning whom the Lord very truly predict-
> ed that they shall hardly be saved (Eusebius,
> *H.E.* 6.41.11-12).

The account comes from a letter of Dionysius, the contemporary Bishop of Alexandria, to Fabius of Antioch.[18]

This is not to say, of course, that the rich Christians always and everywhere lapsed at the first breath of
persecution. We can assemble a fair list of martyrs and
confessors who were propertied people or people of standing. Already in the era of the New Testament we find an
author commending his readers for rising above attachment
to wealth: "you joyfully accepted the plundering of your
property, since you knew that you yourselves had a better
possession and an abiding one" (Heb. 10:34).[19] In the
second century, the respectful treatment that Polycarp of
Smyrna received at the time of his arrest suggests that he
was from the upper orders of society.[20] In Lyons, where
there was a fierce local persecution under Marcus Aurelius,
the martyrs included all sorts of people from a slave-wo-
man up to Vettius Epagathus "a man of position" (*episēmos*).[21]
In Africa, a little later, we meet a group of martyrs that
included one Vibia Perpetua, *honeste nata, liberaliter
instituta*.[22] The rich did not invariably lapse.[23]

We can understand, however, why they may have been
more prone to do so. To begin with, they were often marginal Christians already, as Hermas and Tertullian saw.
Again, they were more exposed to attack during persecution,
since they were known in public to a degree that the average, poorer Christian could avoid.[24] As Dionysius observed

not unsympathetically in the passage quoted above, those
"in public positions were compelled to [sacrifice] by
their business." Finally, the very fact of their wealth
gave government officials an added weapon against the rich
Christian, for confiscation of property was a normal part
of any capital sentence in Roman law, even if the offender
were subsequently let off alive.[25] For these reasons, it
is quite credible that rich Christians were more prone to
lapse than poor ones. But over and above that, their
lapses were bound to have made a particularly deep impression on the Christian community—an impression certain to
promote special concern over them, as we shall see.

IMPLICATIONS OF APOSTASY

        Any lapse at all was a dreadful psychological blow
to an embattled congregation. Theologically, it meant the
damnation of a brother's soul; sociologically, it chal-
lenged the validity of that group for which the rest were
being asked to give their lives. The letter in which the
church at Lyons recounted its sufferings makes the anxiety
explicit:

> The first martyrs were obviously ready,
> and they fulfilled the confession of martyr-
> dom with all readiness, but some others ap-
> peared not to be ready, and failed in train-
> ing and in strength, unable to endure the
> strain of a great conflict, and about ten in
> number failed, as those born out of due time.
> *They caused us great grief and immeasurable*
> *mourning, and hindered the zeal of the others*
> *who had not been arrested.* Yet they, al-
> though suffering all the terrors, neverthe-
> less remained with the martyrs and did not
> desert them. But at that point we were all
> greatly terrified by uncertainty as to their
> confession, not fearing the threatened pun-
> ishment but looking towards the end and
> *afraid lest someone should fall away*
> (Eusebius, *H.E.* 5.1.11).

Thus, the lapse of even the lowliest member of a congregation was a source of anxiety.[26]

But the loss of a rich member created practical, as well as psychological problems for the church. The late second or early third century *Acts of Peter (Actus Vercellenses)* gives us a picture of the troubles which such a loss could inflict on a small Christian community. The situation, in this case, is not one of violent persecution; but Marcellus, a rich member of the church of Rome, yields to political pressure and leaves the church to attach himself to a heretical teacher—Simon Magus. Like the rich Alexandrians of whom Dionysius spoke, he does not wait until force is applied.

When Peter arrives in Rome, he finds the whole Christian community in disarray; and the lesser members agree in blaming the problem on Marcellus' defection. Before, Marcellus had been a model of what the rich Christian should be: he was lavishly generous to the Christian poor and host to the church. But after Simon Magus converted him, Marcellus called a halt to his former open-handedness, and the ensuing disruption of the church at Rome was total.[27]

The lapse of a rich member thus created practical problems for the church as well as problems of morale, particularly in a small congregation. If the church had been meeting in the rich man's house, where was it to meet now? If he had been supporting the widows and the other poor, who would feed them now? If he had provided hospitality for visiting Christians, where would they go now? If the church could no longer meet, or if it could not maintain its poor members, it lost influence among the population at large and found its own bonds of community badly weakened. If it could not receive and accommodate Christian visitors, it lost touch with churches elsewhere in the Empire.[28]

     It is not surprising, therefore, that the danger of
the rich Christian's lapsing was of some concern to our
authors.   Whether it was of frequent occurrence or not
(and our evidence on this score is ambiguous), it had serious consequences.   Thus, the concern that our authors expressed was inspired by anxiety for the congregation as
well as a pastoral care for the rich, for the danger affected both.   If wealth tempted a believer first to become
a marginal Christian, then to fall away altogether, the
consequences were disastrous both for the rich individual
and for the community of believers.

FOOTNOTES

[1] See above, p. 51.

[2] Hans-Werner Bartsch, *Wachet aber zu jeder Zeit! Entwurf einer Auslegung des Lukasevangeliums* (Hamburg: Herbert Reich, 1963), pp. 114-15, characterized the "whole complex" of 12:1-13:9 as a chance assemblage of traditional materials which Luke has taken over whole and which says nothing about Luke's own concept of the subject matter. But the careful craftsmanship and the varied nature of the materials make this improbable. The unity of the scene, which is set in 12:1 and not altered until 13:10, signals the unity of the material in Luke's conception.

[3] Luke is particularly concerned, in this chapter, with the subject of persecution, as he indicates by his inclusion of the logion about those who confess or deny Jesus "before men" and his reference to the disciples' being hailed before "the synagogues and the rulers and the authorities" (12:8-11).

[4] The surrender takes the form of almsgiving: "sell your possessions and give alms" (12:33). See the interesting attack by Franz Meffert (pp. 25-28) on the refusal of Protestant scholars to see alms as *Rettungsmittel gegen diese Gefahren.*

[5] For the disciples as representing the clergy of Luke's day, see Degenhardt, p. 93, who does not, however, explain how the verses on almsgiving could apply to them. Schuyler Brown, p. 101, n. 419, is correct in emphasizing the difference between the command to abandonment in Luke's gospel, which was relevant only in time of Jesus, and the behavior that Luke expected of church officials in his own day.

[6] Jeremias, *Parables of Jesus,* pp. 100, 164-65. Neither was vs. 21 an original part of the parable, pp. 110-12.

[7] It is impossible, then, to accept Degenhardt's claim that Luke did not emphasize the danger of wealth to salvation (pp. 221-22). Nor can we agree that fear of Judgment and hope of reward play no part in Luke's discussion of riches (p. 213). For a better treatment of the meaning of persecution for Luke and the relationship of wealth to apostasy, see Schuyler Brown, pp. 98-130. Of particular interest are pp. 106-7, where Brown points to the role of wealth in the downfall of both Judas and Ananias and Sapphira.

[8] The allegorical interpretation of the Sower originated in the church, before the time when Mark wrote; Jeremias, *Parables of Jesus,* pp. 77-79. I have substituted "deceit" as translation of ἀπάτη for the RSV's "delight." The latter translation has the merit of giving

us a consistent series of three subjective dangers (cares, delight,
desires); but it is the less natural use of ἀπάτη. Luke reworked
Mark's language rather thoroughly here, perhaps because he felt that
the list lacked parallelism in its Markan form.

[9]In Mk. 13:15, property is presented as an eschatological danger:
"let him who is on the housetop not go down, nor enter his house, to
take anything away." But the significance of the passage seems to
have been limited, for Mark, to the situation of the siege of Jerusalem. It is difficult, then, to extend it into a warning about persecution. Cf. Vincent Taylor, *The Gospel According to St. Mark* (London: Macmillan & Co., 1959), pp. 511-12.

[10]On fire, cf. Rev. 8:1-5, where the casting of fire on the
earth is prelude to the plagues of the Seventh Seal. On the white
robe, cf. 6:9-11, where white robes are given to the waiting souls of
martyrs, the robes have been "made white in the blood of the Lamb"
(7:14).

[11]*Vis*. 3.6.5-7; *Mand*. 10.1.4-6; *Sim*. 8.9.1. William Hugh Clifford Frend, *Martyrdom and Persecution in the Early Church: A Study of
a Conflict from the Maccabees to Donatus* (New York: New York University Press, 1967), pp. 149-50, says that Hermas "condemned wealth and
good living as symbols of apostasy." Actually, Hermas went rather
further than that; for him, these things were virtually the cause of
apostasy, since they loosened the ties of the rich to the church.
Phillips, pp. 82-85, was more nearly correct in saying that Hermas
"regarded the wealthier sort of Christians as the Church's 'soft
spot' in the time of persecution...."
    Case, pp. 181-82, doubted that there existed such rich Chris-
tians as Hermas speaks of; but there is no good reason for incredul-
ity.

[12]*Mand*. 10.1.4-6; *Vis*. 3.6.5-6. In these earlier stages of his
work, Hermas believed that God would strip the rich of all their possessions. Ultimately (*Sim*. 9.30.5), he allowed a partial reprieve
for purposes of almsgiving; see above, p. 127, n.35. It is thus a
mistake to say (with Schilling, pp. 22-23) that Hermas proceeded toward a deeper suspicion of wealth; he actually became milder toward
the rich. Martin Dibelius, *Der Hirt des Hermas,* Die apostolischen
Väter, vol. 4 (Tübingen: J. C. B. Mohr [Paul Siebeck], 1923), p. 599,
saw in this shift of attitude the kind of flattery toward the rich
which "James" rebuked in his epistle.
    On Hermas' own loss of wealth, see *Vis*. 3.6.7. Dibelius, *Hirt
des Hermas,* p. 469, was reluctant to grant that Hermas had ever really been rich. We need not, of course, place him on a par with Seneca;
but there is no difficulty in imagining him as a rich freedman (cf.
Vis. 1.1)—a common enough phenomenon in the Early Empire.

[13]*De cultu fem*. 2.13.3-5. This is but one of many arguments

against ostentation in this work.

[14]The peculiar quotation of Mt. 5:3 deserves notice; but perhaps Tertullian was paraphrasing rather than quoting an oral tradition. The italics are my own, a concession to the inflexibility of English word order.

[15]For Tertullian's change of heart on this question, see Barnes, pp. 176-77. E. Nöldechen, "Tertullians Verhältnis zu Klemens von Alexandrien," *Jahrbücher für protestantische Theologie* 12 (1886):278-301, especially p. 299, saw *De fuga* as an attack on Clement of Alexandria. But the evidence for a direct relationship between the writings of the two men, while intriguing, is too slender to afford certainty.

[16]*Cels*. 7.23. Origen was here explaining Jesus' saying on the difficulty of the rich man's entering heaven. He also offered an alternative explanation, which referred the statement to the case of "the person rich in false doctrines." Since he described the first interpretation as ἁπλούστερον, he probably preferred the second. But cf. the statement that tribulation can be light only for those "not weighed down by the things around them" (*Exhort. ad mart.* 2).

[17]On Ambrose as Origen's patron, see Eusebius, *H.E.* 6.23.1-2; on his confession under Maximin, see 6.28.1.

[18]The allusion in the last line of the quotation to the story of the Rich Man (Mt. 19:23) shows that Dionysius was still thinking primarily of eminent persons.

[19]The interpretation of this passage as a reference to community of property within the church is improbable; see above, p. 97, n. 36.

[20]*Mart. Pol.* 7-8. The kindness of Herod and Nicetas was, of course, intended to encourage apostasy; but the long delay for prayer granted by the police detachment that arrested Polycarp seems to express personal respect for him. The fact that Polycarp was burned probably indicates that he belonged to the broad legal classification of *humiliores* (Garnsey, p. 126); but this would follow in any case from the fact that he was born a Christian ("Eighty six years I have served him," 9.3) and therefore would have avoided public office. (Not all local wealth was included in the decurionate at this time in the East; Garnsey, p. 256.) We must also beware of assuming that local authorities always adhered to the letter of the law with respect to executions, particularly when they were pressed by a mob; cf. Garnsey, p. 274.

[21]Eusebius, *H.E.* 5.1.10.

[22]*Mart. Perp.* 2.

[23]Clement of Alexandria, *Strom.* 4, Chap. 8, denied that the

Christian philosophy and its resultant boldness in the face of death
were the property of any one class. But Edmond Le Blant, "La richesse et la christianisme," probably went too far in defending the
rich, basing his work as he did on some dubious martyr legends.

[24]In the persecution at Lyons, for example, the mob called for
Attalus by name because he was well-known; but he was found to be a
Roman citizen, unlike many of the martyrs, and remanded to custody.
Eusebius, *H.E.* 5.1.43.

[25]On exile as capital punishment for *honestiores*, see Crook, pp.
273-74, and Garnsey, p. 121. Most forms of *relegatio* involved confiscation of property; see *OCD,* s.v. "Relegatio," by Adolf Berger and
Barry Nicholas.

[26]The italics in the quotation from Eusebius are, of course, my
own.

[27]*Actus Vercellenses* 8. The *Acts of Peter* stem from the latter
part of the second century, and I would not suggest that they have
any historical bearing on events at Rome in the first century. What
we have in this case is a tale based on realities of church life at
the time when the work was written. Cf. Hennecke, 2:271-75.

[28]It might be objected that the martydom of a rich Christian
would be as great a financial blow to the church as his defection;
for confiscation accompanied any capital sentence. But what the
early church feared was that the rich would give way long before the
danger became serious. Marcellus (*Actus Vercellenses* 8) gave way to
political pressure, not threat of martyrdom.
It is possible that the danger of martyrdom and confiscation
could often be circumvented. We know all too little about the pro-
cedures of Roman persecution under the Early Empire. What we do know
is that it produced confessors (Christians who held firm in their
confession, yet were let off) as well as martyrs. The confessors may
have escaped capital punishment by bribery, or by the intercession of
influential friends or kinsmen; cf. the fear of Ignatius of Antioch
(*Rom.* 4) that the Christians at Rome might interfere with his expecta-
tion of martyrdom. Throughout our period, there was probably a reasonable chance for the rich Christian to escape both martyrdom and confiscation, with his fortune relatively intact; but many of the rich
did not wait to test this possibility.

CHAPTER FIVE

THE DANGER OF THE
RICH TO THE CHURCH

TENSION BETWEEN RICH AND POOR

Early Christian writers were concerned not only that
the rich might fail the church altogether under threat of
persecution, but also that they might disrupt the ordinary
life of the congregations. This latter tendency was manifested partly in a contemptuous attitude on the part of the rich
toward their social inferiors within the church, partly in
insubordination toward the established church authorities.

The problem of contemptuous behavior arose very early.
Paul complained that the more prosperous Christians of
Corinth formed self-serving cliques at the celebration of
the Lord's Supper and excluded the poor from their proper
share:

> ...when you assemble as a church, I hear
> that there are divisions among you; and I
> partly believe it, for there must be fac-
> tions among you in order that those who
> are genuine among you may be recognized.
> When you meet together, it is not the
> Lord's supper that you eat. For in eating,
> each one goes ahead with his own meal, and
> one is hungry and another is drunk. What!
> Do you not have houses to eat and drink in?
> Or do you despise the church of God and
> humiliate those who have nothing? (I Cor.
> 11:17-22).

In this instance, either the more prosperous were bringing
their own meals with them (and refusing to share with others), or else they were claiming a kind of superior right
to the communal supper that had been prepared for the
church-meeting (*ekklēsia*). In either case, it was the

indigent who were suffering.[1]

If Paul saw this kind of conflict between rich and
poor in places other than Corinth, he alluded to it only
indirectly, by discouraging all behavior that might suggest
exalted rank. Thus he wrote to the Romans:

> Live in harmony with one another; do not
> be haughty, but associate with the lowly;
> never be conceited.... Beloved, never
> avenge yourselves, but leave it to the
> wrath of God...(Rom. 12:16, 19).

Again, Paul or one of his early followers wrote to the
Ephesians:

> I, therefore, a prisoner for the Lord,
> beg you to lead a life worthy of the
> calling to which you have been called,
> with all lowliness and meekness, with
> patience, forbearing one another in
> love, eager to maintain the unity of
> the Spirit in the bond of peace (Eph.
> 4:1-3).

The key to unity within the church, from the Pauline point
of view, was voluntary self-abnegation on the part of the
rich and powerful.[2]

Concerns of this sort were not limited to Paul. James
as we have already seen, found occasion to denounce the
rich who hail Christians into court; but there it seems
likely that he had non-Christian rich men in mind. More to
our present point is his declaration that the rich brother
is "to rejoice in his humiliation" (1:10). James objected
to any formal recognition of social distinctions within the
church, and he admonished his readers to "show no partial-
ity as you hold the faith of our Lord Jesus Christ" (2:1).[3]

The same note was struck in the document of the "Two
Ways," which emphasized the importance of just and impart-
ial judgment and, like Paul, advised its audience to associ
ate with the poor rather than the haughty:

> ...be thou "meek, for the meek shall
> inherit the earth;" be thou long-

> suffering, and merciful and guileless,
> and quiet, and good, and ever fearing
> the words which thou hast heard. Thou
> shalt not exalt thyself, nor let thy
> soul be presumptuous. Thy soul shall
> not consort with the lofty, but thou
> shalt walk with righteous and humble
> men (*Did*. 3:7-9).

This is precisely the teaching of Paul and James.[4]

The signs of tension between rich and poor are less obvious after the early second century. Origen complained once of the person who "has a care for the poor, but not according to knowledge—precisely because he wants to be praised by men." But we are not sure whether he meant a rich almsgiver (so the analogy with the chaste and abstinent man in the same passage would suggest) or a church official (the words *curam pauperum* might be translated "charge of the poor"). Clear and explicit evidence of conflict between economic groups is limited to the first century of the church's life.[5] Probably the difficulties were resolved by insisting that the poor show respect to the rich—as we have seen Clement of Rome and Hippolytus urge.[6]

INSUBORDINATION OF THE RICH

The rich posed a more enduring threat, however, to church order by their attitude of insubordination toward the church's regularly constituted officers. This tension flared into open opposition on only a few occasions, so far as we know; but the broad distribution of these incidents indicates that the problem was one of no single place or time, but was inherent in the social structure of the early Christian community.

The earliest incident of this kind appeared in the relationship of the Apostle Paul to the congregation he founded at Corinth. It is notoriously difficult to recon-

struct the exact character of the opposition that confronted Paul at Corinth; but one element in it was an overween-
ing admiration for rhetorical education. Paul's opponents
prided themselves on being *sophoi*, "wise, educated" (I Cor.
3:18-20); some of them were partisans of Apollos, a man
whom Luke described as "eloquent" (Acts 18:24); they condemned Paul for his inability at public speaking (II Cor.
10:10). We cannot, of course, say that anyone who had acquired a rhetorical education in classical antiquity was
rich; for the sons of prosperous "poor" families could
learn rhetoric. But this education was expensive enough
that the lowest strata of society were definitely excluded
from it. Paul's opponents were not indigent.[7]

While there was an educational gap between Paul and
his opponents, the heart of the controversy between them
seems to have been less a matter of social status than of
the source of authority. Paul ruled the Corinthian church
from outside. Having once founded it, he gave some authority to certain early converts who had devoted themselves to
the service of the church; but, absent though he was, Paul
retained the right of supreme oversight for himself. This
meant that the local, Corinthian elite could acquire only
limited authority over their own church, unless they could
persuade the congregation as a whole to disregard Paul's
claims. Given the ancient tradition of Greek civic patriotism, there would be many in Corinth who saw no reason why
the Christian church of their great city should hang upon
the whims of an apostle currently resident in Ephesus.[8]

The same problem of resentment toward the outsider,
who does not really belong to the native social and power
structures, is evident in the Pastoral Epistles. These
three works take the form of letters of instruction to
apostolic delegates, each of them set over a large district
with responsibilities of oversight in several churches.

The delegate is particularly charged with the task of setting the ministry of the church in order in each place,
appointing and ordaining ministers from among the local
population. But his own authority comes from an outside
source, and he will, therefore, have difficulty in en-
forcing it on his flock. His youth and inexperience (the
common initial disadvantages of a professional minister)
will hamper him.[9]

Among his potential opponents will be the rich, as
witness one particular instance of disorder in the churches
—the practice of women teaching and leading prayer in the
church. The author of the Pastorals desires "that in every
place the *men* should pray," and he permits "no woman to
teach or to have authority over men; she is to keep silent"
(I Tim. 2:8,12). The women who have committed the offence
are specifically *rich* women as the intervening verses show:

> ...women should adorn themselves modestly
> and sensibly in seemly apparel, not with
> braided hair or gold or pearls or costly
> attire but by good deeds, as befits women
> who profess religion (I Tim. 2:9-10).

These verses are not an irrelevant intrusion, but complete
the author's mental picture of the rich women involved in
this breach of church order.[10]

The subject of the rich remained prominent in the
author's mind throughout I Timothy. He returned to them
at the end of that letter with a final exhortation, in
emphatic position just before his final salutation:

> As for the rich in this world, charge
> them not to be haughty, nor to set their
> hopes on uncertain riches but on God who
> richly furnishes us with everything to
> enjoy. They are to do good, to be rich
> in good deeds, liberal and generous, thus
> laying up for themselves a good founda-
> tion for the future, so that they may
> take hold of the life which is life in-
> deed (I Tim. 6:17-19).

Here the incident of insubordination is no longer in the
forefront of the author's concern (though he does attack
the arrogance of the rich); rather, he concentrates on
telling the rich Christians what their *proper* role is—to
support the church generously. Their office is to give
alms, not to compete with the properly constituted authorities.[11]

Hermas, too, in his *Shepherd,* saw the rich as trouble makers. He spoke of Christians who "became rich and
in honour among the heathen; then they put on great haughtiness and became high-minded." Some of them "were double-
minded, and made schisms among themselves" (*Sim.* 8.9). In
this way, Hermas blamed the rich for divisions afflicting
the church. They should spend their energies giving alms
and winning their salvation (*Sim.* 9.30.5); and yet, they
will not even associate with the clergy (the "servants of
God"), because they are afraid of being asked for something
(9.20.1-2).

We can identify one particular instance, in the period just before Hermas, of a schism that was fomented by
rich Christians. It took place in Corinth and is known to
us through the *First Epistle of Clement.* When the Corinthian church turned out its established ministers and replaced them with new men, the Roman Church, through this
letter, protested this revolution, maintaining that the
clergy hold office for life.[12]

It is difficult, at this distance, to discern the
origins of the trouble, since Clement's language is carefully veiled. But there is one helpful passage:

> All glory and enlargement was given
> to you and that which was written was
> fulfilled, "My Beloved ate and drank,
> and he was enlarged and waxed fat and
> kicked." From this arose jealousy and
> envy, strife and sedition, persecution
> and disorder, war and captivity. Thus

> "the worthless" rose up "against those
> who were in honor," those of no reputa-
> tion against the renowned, the foolish
> against the prudent, the "young against
> the old" (3.1-3).

Two points are important here, the first of which is that
Clement blames the rebellion on the increased prosperity
of the Corinthian church. But there is a problem in inter-
preting his meaning. Does he intend this "prosperity" to
be understood literally, of an increase in wealth or social
standing, or figuratively, of an increase in spiritual
riches or ecclesiastical prestige?[13]

It is unlikely, to begin with, that Clement meant the
words in a figurative sense, for he would hardly have considered an increase in spiritual well-being to be the prelude to spiritual disaster. Apart from that consideration,
there is evidence elsewhere in the letter which suggests
that Clement was thinking of literal economic prosperity
here. Formerly, Clement says, "you did all things without
respect of persons, and walked in the laws of God, obedient
to your rulers, and paying all fitting honour to the older
among you" (1.3); that was at the time when the Corinthians
had been "satisfied with the provision of Christ [or God]"
(2.1). In other words, the Corinthian church, in its earlier period of development, had been content with the necessities of a simple life and had maintained its order according to the tradition, honoring its older members and
the constituted authorities. Now, the rule of the day has
become "respect of persons," that is, attention to social
distinctions. Clement means us to understand that the increasing prosperity of the church at Corinth led directly
to the rebellion.[14]

The second point of importance in the passage from
Chapter 3 is Clement's treatment of the insurgents: they
are the worthless, those of no reputation, the foolish, the

young. Here, too, we must ask how Clement meant these
phrases: are they to be understood with reference to normal social judgments, or as reflecting a purely ecclesiastical sense? In other words, do the insurgents really belong to the lower orders of society? Are they ill-edu-
cated? Are they really young? If the overall state of
the Corinthian church was indeed, as I have just suggested,
one of social and economic prosperity, then it is unlikely
that the insurgents represented a social tendency directly
opposed to that of the congregation at large; and it is
correspondingly unlikely that Clement's words were meant
literally. Instead, they must refer to status *within the*
church: the insurgents were people of no proven virtue
(worthless), not well-known to other churches (of no reputation), and inexperienced in Christianity (foolish).
Probably they were also recent converts—*neoi* in the sense
of "new men" rather than "young."

This agrees with Clement's observation that the whole
rebellion was undertaken "on account of one or two persons"
(47.5-6). If the leaders were really few in number, they
must have been people of some prestige. It is unlikely
that this prestige was religious in origin, for there is
no reason to believe that the leaders of rebellion had any
distinctive teaching; the controversy was purely a rivalry
over office.[15] The prestige that fueled the insurgency,
therefore, is likely to have been social in origin, and
the movement was inaugurated to place a small number of
important new converts in positions of power within the
church that would comport with their social prestige. It
would have seemed small loss, to many people, if a few
relics of an earlier and less exalted stage in the life of
the Corinthian church were replaced in the process.

Another important instance of a clash between the
rich Christians and their clergy is to be found in the

writings of Cyprian, which we shall postpone to the following chapter. We may add here some incidental items of information that suggest a connection between the rich and
divisions in the church. One of the early leaders of Adop-
tionism was a banker, as Eusebius tells us.[16] Tertullian
claimed that the heretic Marcion was rich; and the Gnostic
teacher Valentinus was highly educated. Tertullian also
complained that the heretics would ordain anybody on an
instant's notice ("today he is a presbyter who was but a
layman yesterday"), and the ordinands included "neophytes,
people hindered by secular business, our own apostates."[17]
This suggests that the opportunity of dominating a small
Christian community, held a certain attraction for some
rich believers.[18]

The early church, then, was faced from time to time
with situations in which the rich refused to play the role
of docile contributors. Yet, the incidents we have discussed arose from a variety of proximate causes: the intrusion of ministers from outside on local social structures; male/female competition; secular pride; changing social status within the congregation. Were the various incidents, then, as unrelated as their apparent causes? Or
was there some deeper source of difficulty within the normal structures of the early church, creating a sense of
tension between church officers and rich laity which in
turn set the stage for these occasional outbreaks of open
animosity?

ROLES OF THE RICH LAYMAN
AND THE MINISTER

In order to answer this question, we must review the
functions of the rich and of the officers in the early
church as they relate to finances and to prestige within

the church. We have already observed in the preceding
chapter that the rich were expected to give alms generously in order to support the church's poor. They were also
expected to provide for the social life of the church with
substantial gifts of property: private places for the holding of church meetings and cemeteries for Christian burial.
Buildings were needed from the earliest times, even before
the Christians had definitively separated themselves from
the synagogue, for the observance of the exclusively Christian rites of Eucharist and Agape. The cemeteries, even
though of later origin, soon came to be considered essential.

The primitive church at Jerusalem already had at
least one house at its disposal for church purposes—that
of Mary, mother of John Mark (Acts 12:12).[19] Paul, too,
several times mentions churches that met in the house of
one or another person: Gaius (Rom. 16:23), Aquila and
Prisca (I Cor. 16:19; Rom. 16:3-5), Philemon (Phil. 2),
Nymphas (Col. 4:15). Public halls may have been suitable
in times of peace for public preaching and disputation, as
when Paul rented the lecture hall of Tyrannus at Ephesus
(Acts 19:9); but they do not seem to have been used for the
Christian assemblies.[20]

It is significant in this connection that the only
Christian church which has survived from our period—that
of Dura-Europos—was a private house converted into a
Christian meeting-place, without ever losing the external
appearance of a private house. We cannot know whether the
house was turned over to the church by its owner or pur-
chased by the congregation for the purpose of conversion;
but in either case, rich members will have been responsible.[21]

The use of private houses explains why, in the first
half of the third century, Minucius Felix could refer to

Christian *sacraria,* while denying that the Christians had
any real temples (*delubra et aras*). At the end of the
Valerian persecution (A.D. 260), the government issued an
order restoring confiscated Christian "worship places" to
the churches. By this time, the Christians may perhaps
have owned some buildings that had been built as churches;
but a congregation was no less dependent on its rich members if it had to beg from them the building site and the
money for construction than if it begged the building already built.[22]

The church was also dependent on its rich members for
gifts of land as cemeteries. We do not know where the
Christians of the first century buried their dead; but they
probably used family *areae,* when possible, for this would
have secured them a certain privacy for Christian rites.
Later on, the congregation took responsibility for some of
these *areae*. The oldest such cemetery seems to be the
Catacomb of Callistus at Rome, which probably passed under
church management in the latter half of the second century.
Other catacombs at Rome that had begun as family tombs
seem to have become church property about 230, when there
was an outburst of new excavation. By the middle of the
third century, church ownership of cemeteries must have
been widespread, for they were confiscated everywhere by
Valerian in 257 and returned to the churches, after he fell
captive to the Persians, by his son Gallienus.[23]

That individual families continued to have a particular interest in the catacombs is shown by the paintings to
be found in them, many of which are in private tombs or
family alcoves. But the cemeteries were now church property, operated for the benefit of the whole Christian community. Hippolytus directed that the charges must be modest:
"only the hire of the grave-digger and the cost of the tile
shall be asked. The wages of the caretakers are to be paid

by the bishop" (*Apostolic Tradition,* 34). Thus, the bishop
replaced the donor as administrator of the property, as
soon as it was handed over to the church.[24]

Taking this material together with the discussion of
alms in the preceding chapter, we see that the principal
function of the rich lay people of the early church was
financial. They provided buildings for the church's worship, cemeteries for the burial of the dead, food and
clothing and shelter for destitute believers, assistance
to those in prison, and subsistence for the clergy. They
provided all this, but they did not direct the disposition
of the funds which they gave. Once the gifts of the rich
had entered the church treasury, they became the sole responsibility of the officers, who dispensed these moneys
without any system of accountability to the church as a
whole. Despite the recurring problem of peculation, we
read of only one occasion in the whole of our literature
when steps were taken to ensure against it—Paul's insistence that representatives of more than one church should
accompany the funds that he had collected for the poor in
Jerusalem (I Cor. 6.3-4; II Cor. 8:16-24). It was otherwise accepted that ministers were solely responsible in
the matter of church funds.[25]

Even in the fairly simple variety of church life
represented by the *Didache,* the principle was that, where-
ever there was a resident prophet, the people were to give
their "first fruits" to him; only in places without such a
prophet, did people give them directly to the poor (13.3-4).
This role as dispenser of the church's wealth gave the
minister great power, both locally and ecumenically, for
by giving or withholding hospitality he determined with
whom his congregation was or was not in communion.[26]

Ambitious laymen were tempted to usurp this power.
Thus, in III John, a certain Diotrephes is blamed because

"he refuses himself to welcome the brethren, and also stops
those who want to welcome them and puts them out of the
church" (10). It is no accident that this same Diotrephes
"likes to put himself first," that is to say, "has usurped
the position of leadership.[27] This prerogative of giving
or withholding hospitality also played a part in the troubles at Corinth in the late first century; for the usurpers
naturally took this role upon themselves. The Romans,
therefore, included a number of pointed references to hospitality in their letter (*I Clem*. 1, 11, 12, 35).[28]

Throughout the second century, control of the church
treasury continued to be a source of clerical authority.
Ignatius of Antioch gave Polycarp, bishop of Smyrna, some
advice as to the handling of these responsibilities: he is
to take special care of widows ("Be their protector after
the Lord"); he must let nothing be done without his personal permission; and he must reject requests from Christian
slaves to buy their freedom from the common chest (*Ad Pol*.
4). Later in the century, Justin Martyr records that the
Sunday collection was fiven to the presiding officer of
the church, who was then directly responsible for the care
of orphans, widows, invalids, prisoners, foreign visitors
and, in general, "all who are in need" (*I Apol*. 77.6).

Thus, visitors, widows, orphans, the indigent—all
were directly dependent on the bishop of their church. The
same must have been true of the lower clergy, who would
have received their subsistence from the bishops. It was
an unusual circumstance when Origen, after being appointed
by Demetrius of Alexandria to conduct the catechetical
school, sold his classical library in order to provide himself with an independent income. The ordinary thing would
have been for him to receive his living from Demetrius; but
Origen acted thus so that "he might never be in need of
others' assistance," with the result that he was relatively

independent of his bishop from the beginning of his career.[29]

In summary, all good things flowed from the bishop. The finances of the church were thus divided between two groups of people: the role of the rich was to give, that of the ministers to spend. The rich could, of course, show their disapproval of the ministers by refusing to give or by giving only small amounts; and the ministers could encourage more liberal giving by their appeals for alms and by their theological interpretation of the value of alms. But in practice, the giving and the spending were the responsibilities of two distinct groups of people. In the best of times, this might be a workable arrangement; at all times, a certain tension was generated by the fact that the church did not operate, in this respect, in the way typical of voluntary societies in the context of Greco-Roman culture.

CHURCH AND CLUB

The church was a voluntary association for purposes of worship and fellowship. The ancient world knew many such associations, called by such names as *collegia, thiasoi,* and *hetairiai,* organized around the worship of a divinity or hero and providing occasions for festive gatherings and fellowship among their members. It has been argued (inconclusively, it seems) that there existed a legal analogy between the Christian communities and that class of clubs known to Roman law as *collegia tenuiorum,* "poor men's clubs." We shall not enter into that question here, but rather call attention to the clear *social* analogy between the church and the pagan club, both of which were voluntary associations, often embracing people of more than one social order and devoted to purposes of worship, fellowship, and, often as not, the proper burial of their members.[30]

The analogy extended even to details of club and
church life. Like the church, the clubs owned meeting
houses, places of worship, and burial places. And much of
the church's technical language for aspects of its own
life seems to have been borrowed from that of the clubs.
The assembly of the members is called *ekklēsia* or *sunagōgē*.
The handing on of office is expressed through the verb
cheirotonein. The treasury is called *to koinon*. One modern author has even claimed that early Christian communism
was borrowed from Greek club life; but, quite apart from
the difficulty of whether the early Christians were com-
munists, there is no epigraphic evidence of communal living
in ordinary Greek clubs—only the literary evidence concerned with philosophical foundations.[31]

One aspect of the church's life which may have been
atypical was the breadth of its membership. Greek clubs
were often somewhat exclusive. Outside Attica, women were
seldom admitted; and slaves and freedmen became members of
clubs only under Roman influence. But this simply means
that, in this one respect, the church approximated the Roman club more nearly than the Greek; for the Roman club
had always exhibited this breadth of membership.[32]

Given the major similarities between the church's organization and that of the clubs of the day, the rich
Christian of antiquity must have expected his role to be
similar to the one which his non-Christian peers played in
their *hetairiai* or *collegia*. To a great extent he will
have been correct, for the patrons of clubs, like the
Christian rich, were expected to meet the financial needs
of their associations. Repeatedly in inscriptions, we meet
with references to the gifts of patrons, most often in the
form of endowments for the celebration of one or another
feast. Greek clubs were, almost without exception, founded
and endowed by an individual benefactor, often in honor of

a deceased family member. The building of the club's temple, like the original founding of the club, was normally
the work of individuals, rarely of the collectivity. To
be sure, the ordinary members of the club also contributed
to its treasury through their monthly *stips;* but this contribution went into a special reserve for burial expenses.
The amenities of club life were paid for by the patrons.[33]

     Thus far, the roles of the rich in church and club
follow similar patterns; but here the resemblance stops.
In the club system, the patron gave designated gifts: the
inscriptions carefully record the terms of the gifts and
the limited freedom of the club's officers to alter these
terms. In the church system, by contrast, the exhortation
was simply that the rich should *give,* leaving the role of
administration entirely to the clergy. Except for the
gift of houses or cemeteries, the rich Christian had little control over the purpose of his donation; and even in
the case of real estate, it was the bishop who made the
rules about its use, not the donor.[34]

     Then, too, the patrons of clubs expected deference
and honors from the societies they benefited. If a rich
man contributed to a club, his beneficence would be recognized by the grant of a title—*patronus,* perhaps, or
euergetēs.[35] Rich women received corresponding titles.
Birthdays were celebrated and crowns bestowed. Inscriptions were set up in public places (sometimes on the
donor's house) to record both the gift and the honor.
Other inscriptions were set up at the donor's grave as a
permanent record of his generosity. Indeed, the publication of the honor came to be as important as the honor itself, being specified with equal exactitude in the resolu-
tion of the club and duly recorded in the inscription. In
the church, however, we hear of no such honors bestowed on
the rich, nor has a single example of such an inscription

come down to us from the Christians of our period.[36]

In sum, the rich Christian retained the financial
obligations of his pagan counterpart in club life, but he
lost most of the latter's privileges. The club patron
gave gifts earmarked for certain specific uses; the Christian was expected to give with no strings attached, so
that he lost control of his gift to the officers of the
society. Patrons of clubs enjoyed a position of superior-
ity, publicly acknowledged with honors and inscriptions.
The rich Christian not only had to make do with the same
status as any other layman in the church, but also had to
listen to the clergy admonish him of the dangers of wealth
and reprove him for his greediness.

The officers of church and club also differed from
each other in ways that complemented the differing roles
of the rich. The club followed the ancient traditions of
civic government in the Greco-Roman world, in which magi-
strates held office for a restricted period of time and
shared their prestige, if not their authority, with other
prominent citizens (members of the *ordo*). In Roman clubs,
the authority was often shared collegially by two chief
officers elected for one or five year terms. In Greek
clubs, there was more often a single chief officer, with
a priestly title. (In addition, there was a variety of
treasurers and secretaries; and some of these subordinate
officers may have enjoyed longer terms.) In the church,
by contrast, there was a tradition (as we have already
seen in discussing *I Clement*) that ministers held office
for life; and apart from the clergy there was no *ordo* to
share official prestige.[37]

In addition, the officers of the pagan club were
often people of means themselves—insofar as the club included such. They sometimes paid *summae honorariae* for
the privilege of holding office; and they often met some

portion of the club's expenses out of their own pockets.
In this way, they will have had a certain sympathy for the
principle that those who give more to the club deserve
more of it. In the church, however, the practice of pur-
chasing office was violently condemned, even as early as
Luke's story about Simon Magus (Acts 8). Tertullian explicitly denied that the church collected any *summae honorariae*. Thus, the church's officers will have had no personal interest in seeing that generosity had its reward.[38]

In this way, the stage was set for collisions between
the rich layman and the church's officers. The rich were
denied some of the satisfactions that made participation in
the pagan clubs worthwhile; and the clergy were less amen-
able than club officers to control by the rich (because of
their lifetime tenure) and less sympathetic (because their
positions were divorced from any financial qualifications).
The mere fact of these differences between club life and
church life was not enough to create open conflict between
the clergy and the rich; but it created a basic tension
within the church. For rich laymen, their expectations
based on the familiar rules of the clubs, would tend to
encroach on the prerogatives of the clergy, while the clergy had to keep the rich in their place of subordination
without alienating them altogether. Any one of a number
of circumstances could bring the latent conflict of interests into the open.[39]

OCCASIONS OF CONFLICT

One such occasion of conflict arose from the missionary origins of the church. Pagan clubs were strictly local in nature (the guilds of actors were an exception);
but the church had been created as a world-wide ("ecumenical") movement by the wide-ranging activities of apostles.

Thus the pagan club could work out problems of the relative
status of its members within the stable framework of its
own local social hierarchy. But a Christian congregation,
especially in the early days, was always liable to have officers intruded upon it by an authority outside its own
city. We have already noted the evidence (in I Corinthians
and I Timothy) that this practice created resentment among
local elites. It is not surprising that centralized "apostolic" oversight of local congregations ultimately gave way
to the typical pattern of early Catholic organization—an
independent church in every city. (Even when the bishop
himself, as sometimes happened, came from elsewhere, it was
the local congregation who chose him.)[40]

Paul and the author of the Pastorals show that one
way in which local elites might be reconciled to the ecumenical character of the church was by assigning them a
role within the church's hierarchy. In the undoubted Pauline epistles, this role is vague. For example, Paul com-
mends certain leading members of the Corinthian church to
their fellow believers with these words: "Now, brethren,
you know that the household of Stephanas were the first
converts in Achaia, and they have devoted themselves to the
service of the saints; I urge you to be subject to such men
and to every fellow-worker and laborer" (I Cor. 16:15-16).[41]
In the Pastorals, the intent was clearly to co-opt such men
into the clergy. The proper candidate for bishop is a
paterfamilias, a householder whose conduct is well-known to
be hospitable, sober and restrained and who has shown the
ability to keep a family under control (I Tim. 3:2-7; Tit.
1:5-9). When such men were ordained, the local elite and
the clergy would become identical.[42]

To some degree, then, it was possible to overcome the
tension between rich laymen and the ministry by merging the
two roles. One could make quite a list of bishops who show some evidence of wealth. We have already noted the case of Polycarp of Smyrna,

received, at the time of his arrest, the respectful treatment normally reserved for prominent citizens. Polycrates
of Ephesus came from a veritable dynasty of bishops (he
was the eighth in his family); and since "charisma" alone
is not usually inheritable, the family must have had some
more tangible distinction which led to this unusual record.
The Roman counter-bishop Hippolytus was of rich and/or
aristocratic background. Gregory Thaumaturgus and his
brother Athenodorus came from a notable Pontic family;
their sister was married to the governor of Palestine.
Cyprian of Carthage and Dionysius of Alexandria were both
rich and well educated. The church thus often drew its
bishops from among the rich.[43]

But even this solution of the problem was not permanent or effective everywhere. Two factors would undermine
it in the great metropolitan churches: either the social
hierarchy of the congregation might change with new con-
versions, or the whole church might grow so large that it
contained too many rich members. The former situation lay
behind the troubles at Corinth which called forth the letter of Clement. There, important recent converts felt
themselves excluded from their rightful role in the church
by the fact that the existing ministers enjoyed life tenure. These men may have represented some quite different
stage in that congregation's social development—the Jewish
stage as opposed to the Gentile, or a phase dominated by
rich plebians as opposed to decurions or equestrians (it is
too soon to think of Achaean senators in the church). When
people of greater prestige entered the congregation, it
seemed natural to many at Corinth to transfer leadership to
them. The appeal of the Roman church against this transfer
was successful only because of the deep-rooted tradition of
life tenure of the clergy.[44]

If a congregation grew too large, however, there was

no way in which *all* the rich members of the congregation
could possibly be given the kind of prerogatives that the
club analogy suggested. It is likely that the metropolitan churches reached this stage of growth early on. The
normal size of a Greek club was not much above thirty to
thirty-five; groups of one hundred or more were uncommon.
The same held true of Roman *collegia*. Yet, the churches
of major cities must have exceeded these limits in short
order. If the church at Rome was supporting 1,500 poor by
the middle of the third century, can it have numbered much
less than 1,000 members even at the end of the first century?[45]

By the same token, the normal club had only a very
small number of patrons. Where there was more than one,
they were frequently members of the same family. But a
church of 1,000 members might have included as many as 20
or 30 individuals of wealth, if it contained anything like
a fair assortment of social orders.[46] These cannot all
have fulfilled the role of patrons, even by becoming clergymen; for the church was tending more and more toward a
standardized monarchical episcopate, and there was now
room for only one supreme authority in each congregation.
In these large congregations, then, there were numbers of
rich members who were permanently consigned to a status
lower than that which they would have expected on the analogy of the clubs.

What, then, became of these "surplus" rich Christians? We have already noted that heresy may have had
special attractions for the rich. Heretical groups were
frequently smaller than the older churches from which they
pulled away. There was room for an energetic and enter-
prising patron to foster the organization and establishment of such a group. More than one anti-heretical writer
complained about heretical groups paying salaries to their

clergy. In the catholic churches, this was unnecessary,
since the clergy themselves controlled the church's treasury; therefore, the custom of paying salaries in heretical
groups suggests that the rich patrons kept control of
funds in their own hands. The services of the rich were
so essential to the organization of such groups, that their
domesticated clergy will scarcely have felt able to object
to these arrangements. If the rich patron also happened
to be a Christian teacher in his own right, like Tertullian, participation in a new, small congregation will have
offered not only an opportunity to reaffirm a traditional
social role, but also the chance to teach without opposition.[47]

   Other rich Christians no doubt remained within the
catholic churches. These must somehow have come to terms
with the fact that they could not hope to dominate their
congregations in the traditional manner of the patrons of
clubs. One way of doing this would be to loosen one's ties
of identification with the church, without breaking them
altogether. In this way, a rich Christian could, as it
were, withdraw from competition for control of the community without feeling that he had failed in a struggle for
dominance. This loosening of ties did, in fact, appear in
the large Roman church of the early second century, for
Hermas blamed the rich there for their indifference toward
the church's life. They shunned study of the Bible; they
avoided the clergy for fear of being asked for money; they
spent too much time on their businesses and their pagan
friendships. This same lack of identification with the
church, as we have seen, made it easy for the rich to
lapse in time of persecution. Thus, the sheer size of the
larger Christian congregations weakened the relationship
of the rich to the church.

   The very success of Christianity, then, created

problems for the rich within the church. The only analogous voluntary institutions in the ancient world were the
clubs; and their small size and strictly local character
fostered a dynamic in the relationship of the rich and the
club officers that could not be preserved in a rapidly
growing, ecumenical institution such as the church. Expectations of the rich regarding their role in the church
were bound to be disappointed insofar as they were based
on an inappropriate model; and the creation of a new model
was a long and difficult task. While that task was being
carried out, the tension between officers and would-be patrons within the church persisted and gave rise, from time
to time, to open conflict within the church. Since our
early Christian authors were almost all ministers themselves, they naturally placed the blame for these incidents on the rich and so created an image of the rich as
endangering the church by their divisiveness.

CONCLUSIONS

    The Christian rich, then, posed a danger to the
church itself, insofar as they could find no stable and
familiar role within it. In particular, the analogy of
church life with club life suggested to them expectations
that the church, with its tradition of tenured, religious-
ly authoritative officers, could not meet. Hence arose
incidents of insubordination directed toward the ministers.
If the rich layman did not accept his subordination, he
could seek to dominate the congregation by taking on the
role of its clergyman—by usurpation if the office was already filled. Or he might secede into a smaller, more
easily dominated heretical group. Or he might simply
loosen his ties with the church, without breaking them off
altogether. Our authors show the rich in all these roles;

Tertullian wrote bitterly of the faults that led them, as
he saw it, to usurpation, secession, or indifference—"I
mean their haughtiness and magnificence and love of the
world and lack of concern for God, whereby they deserve a
'woe' from the Creator." Ironically, he himself followed
the same path when he seceded into Montanism.[48]

At the same time, the officers of the church were
conscious how much the congregations depended on the rich
and their gifts. It was both these factors—on the one
hand, a consciousness of need; on the other, a living
rivalry—that shaped the early church's peculiar attitude
toward wealth in general. We have seen that the Early
Christian attitude toward wealth was compounded of two
contrary tendencies; we can now say that each of these was
a response to one element in the social role of the Christian rich. If our authors did not give wealth their unqualified blessing, if, indeed, they resorted periodically
to the language of communism, it was because they dared
not give their potential rivals for leadership any encour-
agement. If, on the other hand, they exalted the religious
value of almsgiving to a degree that no modern theologian
would consider acceptable, it was because they knew the
rich were indispensible in support of the church.

The pervading themes of Early Christian teaching on
the subject of wealth, therefore, were not a logical unity;
and they were derived neither from tradition nor from ethical principle, but from uniformities of social structure.
The teachings of the Greek philosophers and of the Hebrew
scriptures offered the church the choice of more than one
attitude toward wealth, ranging from unqualified approval
to total rejection. The church's rejection of these extremes was not predetermined by any clear-cut ethical principle; in most of our authors, philosophical ethics is
distinguished for its absence. Neither was the early

church's course in the matter predetermined by its own tradition. The roots of the Christian tradition lay in the
teachings of Jesus and of the primitive church at Jerusalem,
which employed a very negative rhetoric about wealth. Later
writers shifted away from this sectarian language about
wealth; yet, somehow they shifted in the same direction.

     The controlling factors, then, were not intellectual,
but social. If the fathers, at one moment, say that private property has no foundation in God's will and, at another, ascribe phenomenal merit to the correct disposition
of it, there lies behind these seeming contradictions the
necessity of the church's officers to keep the rich under
control, and yet to keep them attached to the church.

FOOTNOTES

¹For the possibility that the rich were bringing their own meals, see C. K. Barrett, *A Commentary on the First Epistle to the Corinthians* (New York: Harper & Row, Publishers, 1968), pp. 262-63. It was common practice, however, in antiquity to favor the more distinguished members of a community with extra portions at public distributions; Hands, pp. 90-93. The offenders at Corinth may have done no more than help themselves to what they regarded as a normal social prerogative. The author of the Pastorals sought to transfer this prerogative to the ministry: οἱ καλῶς προεστῶτες πρεσβύτεροι διπλῆς τιμῆς ἀξιούσθωσαν (I Tim. 5:17). On the material nature of this honor, see J. N. D. Kelly, *A Commentary on the Pastoral Epistles: I Timothy, II Timothy, Titus* (New York: Harper & Row, Publishers, 1963), pp. 124-25, and Martin Dibelius and Hans Conzelmann, *The Pastoral Epistles,* trans. Philip Buttolph and Adela Yarbro, ed. Helmut Koester (Philadelphia: Fortress Press, 1972), p. 78.

John G. Gager, pp. 33-34, sees I Cor. 10-13 as an attack on emerging status distinctions, foreign to a millenarian community.

²Enslin, pp. 254-66, characterizes this line of thought as Jewish in origin.

³See above, pp. 57-59.

⁴Cf. *Barn.* 19.3-4. *Didache* has reworked the material from the "Two Ways" and enlarged it with a reference to the tradition of Jesus' Beatitudes. *Barn.*, moreover, has the materials in a different, more miscellaneous order, which suggests that the author of the *Didache* both transposed and expanded on the elements of the passage just quoted, with a view to making the point against arrogant behavior in the church stronger than it was in the original.

⁵Origen, *Comm. in Rom.* 8.1. W. H. C. Frend, "Heresy and Schism as Social and National Movements," in *Schism, Heresy and Religious Protest,* ed. Derek Baker, Studies in Church History, vol. 9 (Cambridge: University Press, 1972), pp. 37-56, especially pp. 41-43, sees social divisions between rich/urban and rural/poor as determining the nature of the church in Carthage at the time of Cyprian, with the former more accommodating to pagan society and the latter more rigoristic and apocalyptic. But, as I argue in Chapter VI of the present work, I think Cyprian was principally concerned with the tension between the rich and himself as head of the church.

⁶See above, p. 112.   Similarly, tensions between slaves and masters or women and husbands were resolved in the New Testament period in favor of the *paterfamilias,* through adoption of the popular morality manifested in the *Haustafeln.*   Cf. the discussion of Sanders, pp. 73-76. Sanders ultimately defines these materials as "completely

worthless for Christian ethics." However this may be from the point
of view of ethics, historically they formed an important element in
the moral teaching of the early church. Schilling, pp.
39-40, was right to hold that the tension between
rich and poor was not an important factor within the early church; for
the tension was resolved early on in favor of the status quo.

⁷For a recent summary of the discussion of Paul's opposition at
Corinth, see Hans Conzelmann, *First Corinthians,* trans. James W.
Leitch, with bibliography and references by James W. Dunkley, ed.
George W. MacRae (Philadelphia: Fortress Press, 1975), pp. 14-16.
Some literati of the Empire came from "poor" families, e.g.,
Lucian of Samosata, who was first apprenticed to his uncle, a statu-
ary (*Somnium* 1-4). Nonetheless, the educated constituted an elite
closely allied to the elite of wealth and power; and Paul had to de-
fend himself against their efforts to take charge of the church.
With I Cor. 3:18-20, cf. I Cor. 1:20 (ποῦ σοφός;), Rom. 1:14 (...
σοφοῖς τε καὶ ἀνοήτοις ὀφειλέτης εἰμί), Phil. 3:12-16 (those who
think they are τέλειοι are not yet so), Col. 2:8 (dangers of "philosophy"). The problem did not end with Paul's time, for Irenaeus made
a similar protest against the pretensions of the educated, *Adv. haer.*
1.10.3-4 (1.10.2-3): οὐδεὶς γὰρ ὑπὲρ τὸν διδάσκαλον. J. Lebreton,
"Le désaccord de la foi populaire et de la théologie savante dans
l'Eglise chrétienne de IIIe siècle," *Revue d'histoire ecclésiastique*
19 (1923):481-506 and 20 (1924):5-37, explained the classical
heresies as a kind of rebellion of intellectuals against ordinary
church life; see especially 19:481 and 20:34-37.

⁸For local officers in Corinth, see I Cor. 16:15-16, where Paul
urges the congregation to obey Stephanas, the first convert of Achaia,
and "every fellow worker and laborer." Except for Paul's distant
oversight, the Corinthian congregation presents an appearance of "organized chaos"; Hans von Campenhausen, *Ecclesiastical Authority and
Spiritual Power in the Church of the First Three Centuries,* trans.
J. A. Baker (London: Adam & Charles Black, 1969), p. 64 (cf. the discussion of Paul's concept of apostolic authority, pp. 39-54).
Civic patriotism ultimately triumphed; see above p. 167.

⁹For the church order of the Pastorals, see Campenhausen, pp.
106-19, 155-57. Campenhausen necessarily regards the theme of the
"apostolic delegate" as a fiction, since he rejects Pauline authorship
of the letters; but he recognizes that the author was attempting to
provide some objective, external authorization for ministry; see
especially pp. 108-10. The question of authorship is not crucial to
our argument, for the conclusions of J. N. D. Kelly, pp. 13-16, are
strikingly similar, with the exception that he regards the letters
themselves and therefore the position of "apostolic delegate" as
authentic.

¹⁰Kelly, pp. 65-68. Dibelius and Conzelmann, pp. 44-47, suggest

that the verses on women were originally paraenetic material pertain-
ing to general behavior, not to the specific question of behavior
during services. They agree, however, that in the present context,
it is the latter that is in view.

[11]Kelly, pp. 147-49, holds that this message to the rich is
merely meant to counteract the negative effect of verses 9-10 preceding ("Those who want to be rich fall into temptation..."). This is
possible, but Kelly has overlooked the distinction in subject-matter:
vss. 17-19 refer to rich laymen; vss. 9-10 are concerned with Christian teachers who invent new teachings in order to make money.
Dibelius and Conzelmann, p. 84, hold that the warning against
greed in vss. 9-10 is "only superficially connected with the polemic
against heresy in 6:3-5." Nonetheless, it is so connected. As for
6:17-19, they simply give up asking why they were included (p. 91).
Surely, even a pseudepigraphical author would say something of significance to himself as his last word.

[12]Campenhausen, pp. 86-91.

[13]William Wrede, *Untersuchungen zum Ersten Klemensbriefe* (Göttingen: Vandenhoeck & Ruprecht, 1891), p. 33, rejected the suggestion
that the rebels at Corinth could have been rich or powerful, but on
the basis of a priori assumption that there were no such people in
the church by the end of the first century.

[14]There are other passages as well which indicate a special concern about the rich: 13.1-2 (almsgiving and detachment from wealth are
aids to humility); 37.1-4 (great and small need eath other, on the
analogy of leaders and followers in an army); 38.1-2 (rich and poor
need each other). R. M. Grant, *Apostolic Fathers*, 2:21, observed that
Clement may have had in mind "the kind of proverbial wisdom expressed
in a phrase like 'prosperity brings forth *hybris*.'" This was indeed
an appropriate sentiment for the occasion.
Donfried, pp. 1-15, has argued that *II Clement* was written by the
Corinthian presbyters who had been expelled from office as "a call to
the congregation to repent of their past errors." If this is correct,
the emphasis on almsgiving as an atonement in *II Clem.* (see above, p.
111) would gain added significance from our argument that the Corinthian insurgents were rich. Donfried's hypothesis is not, however,
universally accepted; see reviews by Robert M. Grant, *JBL* 94 (1975):
472-73, and Elaine H. Pagels, *Church History* 45 (1976):98-99.

[15]Joseph Barber Lightfoot, ed., *The Apostolic Fathers*, 5 vols.
(London: Macmillan & Co., 1885-90; reprint edition, Hildesheim: Georg
Olms Verlag, 1973), 1:378, failed "to discover any traces of heretical
doctrine at Corinth refuted in Clement's Epistle," apart from a certain scepticism about the resurrection, comparable to that which Paul
dealt with in I Cor. 15. Cyril C. Richardson, on the other hand, in
Early Christian Fathers (New York: Macmillan Publishing Co., paperback

1970), p. 34, argued that the rebels did have distinctive religious
characteristics: asceticism (38.2), gnosis (48.5), charismata (21.5;
57.2). But he admitted that the last two passages are equally open
to the interpretation that the men were capable rhetoricians. The
reference to gnosis is included in a broad list of spiritual gifts
based on I Cor. 12 (R. M. Grant, *Apostolic Fathers*, 2:79). The reference to asceticism is paralleled, in the same context, by one to
wealth.

Donfried, pp. 8-9, tried to bolster the argument for charismatic
rebels by adducing the polemic against arrogance in *I Clem*. 13, 15-19
and the emphasis on orderly worship in 40-41. But charismatics had
no monopoly of arrogance; and the point of Chaps. 40-41 is rather
that the layman must keep his place.

[16]For Theodotus the banker, see Eusebius, *H.E.* 5.28.9; the foun-
der of the movement, however, was a cobbler.

[17]Tertullian, *De praescr. haer.* 30.1-2 (Marcion and Valentinus);
41.4-8 (heretical orders). The list of those whom the heretics or-
dain echoes contemporary concern over the rich as tending to lapse.
On Marcion, cf. Robert M. Grant, *From Augustus to Constantine: The
Thrust of the Christian Movement into the Roman World* (New York:
Harper & Row, Publishers, 1970), p. 124.

There was an important social element in the schism of Hippolytus at Rome, too; but Hippolytus, though well-connected socially and
probably rich, was not a layman. See Henneke Gülzow, "Kallist von
Rom."

[18]In addition, we should note the claim by Ignatius of Antioch
(*Smyrn.* 6) that heretics have no concern for the poor and the implica-
tion of Irenaeus, *Adv. haer.* 1.7.2 (1.13.3-4), that the Marcosian
Gnostics addressed themselves primarily to an audience of rich women.

One recent scholar has concluded, on sociological grounds, that
the Gnostics of the second and third centuries were recruited from
disaffected and politically impotent intellectuals: Hans G. Kippenberg, "Versuch einer soziologischen Verortung des antiken Gnostizismus," *Numen* 17 (1970):211-31. The sociological criticism of Kippenberg's article by Peter Munz, "The problem of 'Die soziologische
Verortung des antiken Gnostizismus,'" *Numen* 19 (1972):41-51, is beyond my competence to judge; but Munz ends by giving the Gnostics no
recognizable social locus at all in the ancient world. Neither writer
attempted to test his hypothesis historically. John Gager, pp. 82-83,
has also affirmed the intellectual's role in early Christian heresy.
Insofar as the interests of the rich and of intellectuals were aligned
in antiquity, the argument of this paragraph may lend historical
strength to the hypotheses of Kippenberg and Gager. For an analysis
of needed research, see Henry Alan Green, "Suggested Sociological
Themes in the Study of Gnosticism," *VC* 31 (1977):169-80.

[19]The primitive church at Jerusalem may have used more than one

house, for Peter found only a part of the congregation at the house
of Mary after his escape from prison.

[20]The house church has a further significance, for the spread of
Christianity must have been dependent on conversion of people rich
enough to supply such facilities. Cf. Floyd V. Filson, "The Significance of the Early House Churches," *JBL* 58 (1939):105-12, and Judge,
pp. 35-37. See, too, the excellent discussion in Malherbe, *Social Aspects,* pp. 60-91. G. Heinrici, "Zur Geschichte der Anfänge paulinischer Gemeiden," *ZWT* 20 (1877):89-130, especially p. 103, proposed
that the earliest Christian societies were analogous to the household
collegia, clubs limited entirely to the members of a certain *familia.*

[21]The house was built in A.D. 232-33. One room may have been
used for Christian worship from the start, and the building had been
appropriated in its entirety to Christian use before its destruction
soon after 256. See Jack Finegan, *Light from the Ancient Past: The
Archeological Background of Judaism and Christianity,* 2d ed., 2 vols.
(Princeton: Princeton University Press, paperback ed., 1969), 2:495-
501. The size of the house indicates an owner of some means; Filson,
pp. 107-8. The wall paintings indicate some pretensions to elegance,
though they are inferior in quality and scope to those of the synagogue at Dura.
The ideal house for church use was one of the great private
dwellings that contained a basilica, a hall in imitation of the large
public buildings by that name. We hear of such a house being given
to the church in pseudo-Clement, *Rec.* 10.71. While there is no reason to believe that any accurate, first-century historical tradition
lay behind the account, the narrative probably seemed reasonable to
the author in his own day.

[22]Minucius, *Oct.* 9.1, cf. 32.1; Eusebius, *H.E.* 7.13.

[23]Fernand de Visscher,"Le régime juridique des plus anciens
cimetières chrétiens à Rome," *Analecta Bollandiana* 69 (1951):39-54,
especially pp. 42, 48-49, 52-54. On the role of Callistus, see
Gülzow, pp. 116-18. George LaPiana argued that Victor acquired the
"Cemetery of Callistus" late in the reign of Commodus (180-92) in
order to free the church from dependence on its rich members for use
of their private *areae;* "The Roman Church at the End of the Second
Century: The Episcopate of Victor, the Latinization of the Roman
Church, the Easter Controversy, Consolidation of Power and Doctrinal
Development, the Catacomb of Callistus," *HTR* 18 (1925):201-77,
especially pp. 254-71.

[24]"There is no stylistic difference between Christian paintings
of the third and fourth centuries and the contemporary pagan work";
Ernst Kitzinger, *Early Medieval Art* (Bloomington, Ind.: Indiana University Press, 1964), p. 5. For an appreciation of the paintings as
a chapter in art history, see Wladimiro Dorigo, *Late Roman Painting,*

with a foreword by Sergio Bettini, trans. James Cleugh and John War-
rington (New York: Praeger Publishers, 1970), pp. 117-26.

[25]See above, pp. 72-73, on peculation. On the role of the clergy,
see Chastel (Eng.), p. 95; Uhlhorn (Eng.), pp. 123-24, 160-62; Edwin Hatch,
The Organization of the Early Christian Churches, 4th ed. (London:
Longmans, Green & Co., 1892), pp. 40-48; Haller, pp. 558-61; Harnack,
Constitution and Law, pp. 138-39. The later *Apostolic Constitutions*
even forbade private almsgiving; but this was a unique and extreme
position. See Seipel, pp. 241-43.

[26]Hospitality already played an important role in Paul's time;
Enslin, pp. 292-93.

[27]In III Jn. 9, I take the participle φιλοπρωτεύων to imply that
Diotrephes was not yet a church officer, but aspired to be. But cf.
R. M. Grant, *Augustus to Constantine,* pp. 67-68. See Abraham Mal-
herbe, "The Inhospitality of Diotrephes," in *God's Christ and His
People: Studies in Honor of Nils Alstrup Dahl,* ed. Jacob Jervell and
Wayne A. Meeks (Oslo: Universitetsforlaget, 1977), pp. 222-32.

[28]Henry Chadwick, "Justification by Faith and Hospitality,"
Studia Patristica 4, pt. 2 (*TU* 79):281-85.

[29]On compensation of clergy, see R. M. Grant, *Augustus to Constantine,* pp. 161-62; cf. Adolf Harnack, *The Mission and Expansion of
Christianity in the First Three Centuries,* trans. James Moffatt,
intro. Jaroslav Pelikan (New York: Harper & Row, Torchbook edition,
1962; reprint ed., Gloucester, Mass.: Peter Smith, 1972), pp. 158-59.
     On Origen, see Eusebius, *H.E.* 6.3.9. Origen did not object to
dependence on rich lay persons. He himself had depended on the generosity of a rich Alexandrian woman after his father's martyrdom and
the confiscation of the family's goods (*H.E.* 6.2.13); and he defended
the maintenance of Jesus by rich women (Lk. 8:2-3) in *Cels.* 1.65.

[30]On the legal analogy, see, most recently, David Daube, review
of *Personality in Roman Private Law,* by P. W. Duff, in *JRS* 33 (1943):
86-93 and 34 (1944):125-35. See also Ernest George Hardy, *Studies in
Roman History* (London: S. Sonnenschein & Co., 1906), pp. 140-49.
     On the social analogy, see Robert L. Wilken, "Collegia, Philo-
sophical Schools, and Theology," in *The Catacombs and the Colosseum:
The Roman Empire as the Setting of Primitive Christianity,* ed. Stephen
Benko and John J. O'Rourke (Valley Forge, Pa.: Judson Press, 1971),
pp. 268-91. See also Franz Poland, *Geschichte des griechischen
Vereinswesens* (Leipzig: B. G. Teubner, 1909; reprint ed., Leipzig:
Zentral-Antiquariat der Deutschen Demokratischen Republik, 1967), p.
534. For an interesting new approach to this question, see J. Paul
Sampley, "Societas Christi: Roman Law and Paul's Conception of the
Christian Community," in *God's Christ and His People: Studies in Honor
of Nils Alstrup Dahl,* ed. Jacob Jervell and Wayne A. Meeks (Oslo:
Universitetsforlaget, 1977), pp. 158-74.

[31]On real estate, see Theodor Mommsen, *De collegiis et sodaliciis romanorum* (Kiel: Libraria Schwersiana, 1843), pp. 96-97; Poland, pp. 453-66. On terminology, see Poland, pp. 417, 488-89; Hatch, p. 37. On communism, see Kalthoff, *Entstehung des Christentums,* pp. 91-108; cf. Poland, pp. 463-64.

[32]Poland, pp. 328-29; Tod, pp. 84-85.

[33]Mommsen, pp. 98-99, 107-12, showed that the banquets were paid for by patrons, with the club itself supplying only table service, bread and wine. On foundations and temples, see Poland, pp. 271-73, 468, 478-83. In general, see *PW,* sv. "Collegium," by E. Kornemann, 7:424-26. On the role of patrons in Latin-speaking clubs, see J. P. Waltzing, *Étude historique sur les corporations professionnelles chez les Romains depuis les origines jusqu'à la chute de l'Empire de l'Occident,* Tome 1 (Louvain: Charles Peeters, 1895), pp. 426-46.

[34]For two exemplary inscriptions in English translation, see Naphtali Lewis and Meyer Reinhold, *Roman Civilization,* 2 vols. (New York: Harper & Row, Torchbook ed., 1966), 2:272-76. For further examples, see *ILS,* nos. 7212-18, and *SIG,* nos. 426-27.

[35]*Epistle of the Apostles* even promises this title to poor Christians who give alms (46, Coptic version).

[36]On titles, see Poland, pp. 437-39; on birthdays, pp. 250-51; on inscriptions, pp. 280-81, 423-31, 440-41. Poland observed, pp. 501-2, that the rich club member certainly got as much from the club as he put into it.

[37]On Roman clubs, see Mommsen, pp. 106-7, Waltzing, pp. 357-68, 383-425, and Kornemann, cols. 418-24. On Greek clubs, see Poland, pp. 339-51, 375-87, 413-16, 419-21. Compensation for officers was usually limited to honors, sacrificial portions, and exemption from dues; Poland, pp. 421-22.

[38]Poland, pp. 418, 494-98; Tertullian, *Apol.* 39.5.

[39]Insofar as the church originated as a millenarian community, status distinctions were probably ruled out in theory; Gager, pp. 33-34.

[40]On guilds of actors, see *OCD,* s.v. "Clubs, Greek," by Marcus Niebuhr Tod. On the change in Christian organization, see Harnack, *Mission and Expansion,* pp. 445-82. For imported bishops, see Eusebius, *H.E.* 7.32.5-6, on Eusebius and Anatolius, two successive bishops of Laodicea who were both Alexandrians. Cf. Lebreton, 20:12.

[41]Stephanas was not a "clergyman," since Paul's conception of ministry was informal; but he was a forerunner of the officials of the

time of *I Clement.* See Conzelmann, p. 298. Since the household of
Stephanas took upon themselves "the service of the saints," they must
have had resources that made it possible for them to neglect their
own business. Cf. Case, *Social Origins,* p. 153.

[42]Similar requirements for deacons are given in I Tim. 3:12:
διάκονοι 'έστωσαν μιᾶς γυναικὸς ἄνδρες, τέκνων καλῶς προϊστάμενοι καὶ
τῶν ἰδίων οἴκων. The exact orders of ministry envisaged in the Pastorals (cf. Dibelius and Conzelmann, pp. 54-57) do not concern us
here. The important thing is that all ranks of ministers are expected
to display the virtues appropriate to prosperous householders; they
are to be drawn from among the elite of the church.

[43]On Polycarp, see above, p. 141. On Polycrates, see Eusebius, *H.E.* 5.24.6; but perhaps we should think of a family of professional clerics, such as Origen knew of (Campenhausen, p. 253). On
Hippolytus, see R. M. Grant, *Augustus to Constantine,* p. 181, and
Gülzow, p. 118. On Gregory, see Quasten, 2:123. On Cyprian, see below, pp. 184-85. On Dionysius of Alexandria, see R. M. Grant, *Augustus to Constantine,* pp. 209-12; the special treatment (banishment)
accorded him during the Valerian persecution marks him as a person
of distinction. We should perhaps add Geminius, Bishop of Furni
Africa in the mid-third century; Michael Sage, *Cyprian,* Patristic
Monograph series, no. 1 (Cambridge, Mass.: Philadelphia Patristic
Foundation, 1975), 148.

[44]On new members seeking a role in government, see I Tim. 3:6,
which forbids their ordination. The tradition of life tenure was
based on the apostolic origins of the church. Since the first Christian authorities received their commissions directly from Jesus, they
were not subject to removal by the congregation.

[45]On the size of Greco-Roman clubs, see Poland, pp. 282-87; Duncan-Jones, pp. 277-82. On the number of Christians at Rome in the
mid-third century, see R. M. Grant, *Augustus to Constantine,* p. 184,
who places it at 30,000 to 50,000. Eusebius claimed that the church
had grown rapidly in the reign of Commodus (*H.E.* 5.21.1); but his un-
supported statement is not compelling, since it appears to be a device
for introducing the martyrdom of Apollonius, which Eusebius mistakenly
set in the Roman Senate. Otherwise, there is no reason to think that
the comparatively large number of Christians at Rome was a wholly new
feature of the third century.

[46]Jean Beaujeu, "La religion de la classe sénatoriale à l'époque
des Antonins," in *Hommages à Jean Bayet,* ed. Marcel Renard and Robert
Schilling (Brussels: Latomus, 1964), pp. 54-75, especially pp. 64-75,
traced in the religious groups of the second century "une tendance
à la fraternisation entre les classes sociales," and he remarks that
"ce charactère n'était donc pas un privilège du Christianisme...."
Pliny (as Judge, p. 61, noted), was not surprised that Christians

were to be found at all levels of society; he was disturbed rather
that they were spreading into the countryside.

[47]On salaries for heretical ministers, see Eusebius, *H.E.* 5.18.2
(Montanists), 5.28.9 (Adoptionists). For Tertullian as a man of
wealth, see Barnes, p. 138. For a different interpretation of the
significance of salaries, see R. M. Grant, *Early Christianity,* pp.
140-41; Grant sees the Catholic objections as based on Catholic use
of a "dividend principle" in paying clergy.
        John Morris, "Early Christian Orthodoxy," *Past and Present,* no.
4 (February 1953): pp. 1-14, suggests that heretics in general tended
to be rich; but his argument is not entirely clear.

[48]Tertullian, *Adv. Marc.* 4.15.

CHAPTER SIX

CYPRIAN OF CARTHAGE: A CASE STUDY IN THE
THEORY AND PRACTICE OF CHRISTIAN RICHES

CYPRIAN OF CARTHAGE AND
HIS ABANDONMENT OF WEALTH

The argument thus far has shown that attitudes toward wealth in Early Christian writings were closely tied to the role of the rich within the church. But we have had to assemble our picture of both attitudes and roles largely from a patchwork of isolated statements, even though we have followed an outline based on the writings of Clement of Alexandria. In no one author could we clearly demonstrate the full range of attitudes, the social realities of early church life, and their interconnection. We are fortunate, then, that one Early Christian writer, Cyprian of Carthage, has left us enough material of the right sort that we can hope to analyze the relation between attitudes and social roles in his own thought on wealth and in the church with which he was associated.[1]

Cyprian presided over the church at Carthage (one of the principal metropolitan centers of the Roman world) during a period of extraordinary crisis, when every aspect of Christian doctrine and organization was undergoing a severe test. He had been bishop only a few years when the Emperor Gecius launched his persecution of the church (250-51)—the first empire-wide persecution of Christianity and one which was particularly devastating by reason of the Emperor's requirement that every person in the empire should offer sacrifice to the pagan gods.

This persecution caused the lapse of a great many

Christians in Carthage and elsewhere; and the efforts of
the lapsed to gain readmission to the church subsequently
gave rise to schisms at Carthage and Rome. Cyprian and
the Roman bishop at first supported each other in the matter; but they fell out over the question of the validity
of schismatic baptism and so became involved in a battle
that threatened to split the whole empire-wide church.
Meanwhile, Carthage was visited by the great plague of 252,
which brought with it the threat, if not the reality, of
renewed persecution. Finally, the emperor Valerian renewed the persecution in 257-58, at which time Cyprian himself suffered martyrdom.

We do not know a great deal about Cyprian himself.
We are fortunate to possess a *Vita* written shortly after
his death by his deacon Pontius. The work, however, is
more a memorial of his martyrdom and defence of his episcopate than a biography. Pontius often alluded briefly to
matters we should like to have known a great deal about;
and what we learn of Cyprian from this source is sometimes
more tantalizing than useful.[2]

We can, however, be sure that Cyprian was a man of
wealth and standing before he became a Christian. He was
a well-educated man, as his writings show (despite the
fact that he deliberately simplified his style and excluded all pagan imagery from his writing after he became a
Christian).[3] It is also said that he had practiced law
and taught rhetoric in Carthage before his conversion. At
the end of his life, his treatment at the hands of the law
demonstrated his high status. After his arrest, he was
first deported and allowed to live in retirement for a
time. At no time was he tortured; and at the end, he was
beheaded, not burned at the stake. In the middle of the
third century, such respectful treatment was accorded only
to the foremost ranks of society.[4]

It is particularly interesting, then, to read in
Pontius's *Vita* that Cyprian gave away his fortune at the
very beginning of his life as a Christian:

> By distributing his means for the relief
> of the indigence of the poor, by dis-
> pensing the purchase-money of [almost]
> entire estates, he at once realized two
> benefits—the contempt of this world's
> ambition,...and the observance of that
> mercy which God has preferred even to
> His sacrifices,...whereby with premature
> swiftness of piety he almost began to be
> perfect before he had learnt to be per-
> fect (2).

Pontius stressed the unheard of nature of this sacrifice,
without telling us how Cyprian went about the distribution
of his goods—whether he handed them over personally to
the poor, or whether he gave them to the clergy for redis-
tribution. He also left it unclear how completely Cyprian
had divested himself of property.[5]

There are several signs, both in Pontius and in
Cyprian's own writings, that the surrender was less than
complete. In the *Ad Donatum,* an early treatise, Cyprian
still wrote in the character of a gentleman farmer or
rural landowner.[6] Later, during the Decian persecution,
Cyprian wrote in a letter of having left a sum of his own
money (*quantitate mea propria*) with the clergy in Carthage
for relief of the distressed; and he promised to send yet
more (*Ep.* 7).[7] Finally, at the time of his martyrdom in
258, Cyprian was again in possession of gardens near
Carthage that he had sold years before. Pontius did not
explain how these came back into Cyprian's hands, though
he did claim that it was only the disturbed character of
the times that had prevented him from selling them again.[8]

We have already seen that there was no living tradition within the early church that new converts should
abandon their wealth.[9] It is puzzling, then, that Cyprian

should have insisted on doing so; and it seems likely that
his motives owed as much to a familiar philosophical tradition as to the example of Jesus or the apostles. Cyprian
may simply have been making a philosophical retreat from
the cares of active life—a retreat into Christianity as
if it were one of the Greek schools. In the same way, the
Cynic philosopher Crates, many centuries before, had put
his wealth in trust for his children to free himself for
philosophy. Seneca, in the first century A.D., had recommended the limitation of wealth for the same purpose. And
long after Cyprian's time the ideal of philosophical retirement remained alive—for example, when it influenced
Augustine and his friends to take up their communal life
at Cassiciacum.[10]

The original objective, however, in the pursuit of
philosophical retirement was not that of benefiting the
poor—a matter of little interest to the Greeks in any
case. The objective was to free oneself from unnecessary
involvement in secular business. Therefore, one might put
one's wealth in trust, like Crates, or commit it to relatives, like the Jewish Therapeutae who followed this Greek
pattern. The donor retained enough income for an untrou-
bled life, free from luxury and the cares of business; and
in this way he could be free from both kinds of financial
worries—those of too much money and those of too little.[11]

What did Cyprian do? If he really gave all his
money to the poor, as Pontius claimed, it is difficult to
understand how he came still to possess both money and
property later in life. On the other hand, if he merely
put his wealth in trust, so that he could retire from active involvement with it, why did Pontius claim that he
had given it to the poor? The event must still have been
fresh in the minds of many when Pontius wrote, and it
would have been difficult to misrepresent it completely.

While any explanation must be hypothetical, we can most easily explain all our information by supposing that Cyprian, on his conversion, turned his wealth over to the church itself as a trust. He would have retained a comfortable income for himself and assigned the remainder to the benefit of the poor. When he subsequently became bishop, however, he would have found himself in the odd position of being his own trustee; and this explains how his "private funds" and the garden in Carthage came back into his personal control.

If this hypothesis is correct, it means that Cyprian never intended to and never did impoverish himself. His main objective was to separate himself, not from his wealth as such, but from the distractions which that wealth entailed. This agrees with the attitude toward wealth expressed in Cyprian's earliest works, particularly the *Ad Donatum*. If Cyprian had been inspired by ascetic or rigorist notions, we should expect to find traces of them here; but we do not. Instead, Cyprian inveighs equally against all the far-ranging evils of the world—the crimes of arena and theater, sexual immorality, injustice and torture in the courts, and the instability of the so-called goods of this world, including riches and power.

Wealth, therefore, was but one object of attack among many for Cyprian; and his attack upon it was aimed less at wealth itself than at the attachment of the rich to it. They think of nothing but acquisition; and they are forever tormented by fear of theft and jealousy of those who have more. They will not spare a little something even for their own clients, much less for the poor; and, miserable though they are, they "obstinately cling to their tormenting hoards" (*poenalibus cumulis pertinaciter adhaerere*). In brief, Cyprian vindicated that doctrine which was common to both the philosophers and his Christian

teachers: that the vice resides not in wealth itself, but
in the way it is used. He mocked the unenlightened because "they call those things 'goods,' which they absolute-
ly put to none but *bad* use" (12).[12]

THE DECIAN CRISIS: BEFORE AND AFTER

     It is already evident, from the preceding discussion,
that the early Cyprian belonged to the same broad stream
of thinking about wealth as Clement of Alexandria and other Early Christian authors we have considered. This is
true in other respects as well. Not long after he was
elected bishop of Carthage, he wrote a treatise *De habitu
virginum (On the Dress of Virgins)*, in which he argued for
simplicity of life as the proper Christian standard, especially for those women who were regarded as an example of
holiness within the church.

     These virgins whom Cyprian addressed were wealthy
women who had made vows of chastity. They received public
recognition by the church; but they figured in the congregation as a class of individuals, not as an organized body.
They thus differed from later nuns in that each lived in
her own home, retained her own property, and was free to
come and go as she wished—within the limits of propriety
for a woman of her social order.[13]

     Cyprian found these women living in great luxury and
elegance; and he wrote the present treatise in order to
put a stop to this. It was not merely a matter of money.
In a manner reminiscent of Clement of Alexandria's *Paedagogus*, he attacked all kinds of familiar Roman pleasures,
from mixed bathing to the use of cosmetics.[14] But wealth
was at the heart of the problem. Cyprian, at one point,
imagined his readers objecting that they had a right to
use what they owned. He conceded the point, but reminded

them that the New Testament still required moderation in
dress and ornament and that "it does not befit a virgin to
flaunt her riches."[15]

It is sinful to suppose that God gave men riches to
use in a way that does not tend to salvation. One ought
rather to use them "for good purposes...for those things
which God has commanded," that is to say, for almsgiving:

> Let the poor feel that you are wealthy;
> let the needy feel that you are rich.
> Lend your estate to God on interest;
> give food to Christ. Move God by the
> prayers of many to grant you to carry
> out the glory of virginity and to suc-
> ceed in coming to the Lord's rewards....

For Cyprian, as for our other Early Christian authors, alms
are a sure road to divine favor, and the rich can lay
their claim on God through the prayers of the poor. "Every
one who is rather well-off ought by his patrimony to redeem his transgressions rather than to increase them."[16]

The *Ad Donatum* and the *De habitu virginum* thus represent an attitude toward wealth that is already familiar to
us from our study of other Early Christian writings. The
early Cyprian was suspicious of wealth insofar as it contributed to avarice and tempted the Christian to luxury and
ostentation. He endeavored to dissociate himself from it
by surrendering control over his own fortune. Yet, he also believed with his fellow Christians that riches offered
the remedy for the very harm they caused, for almsgiving
was a sure road to salvation.

If we possessed only the early works of Cyprian, we
should have to rank him side by side with Clement of Alexandria as an author relatively friendly toward the rich.
In these early works, he criticized the rich only for luxury and acquisitiveness. Cyprian's rich virgins are so
far from being inferior members of the church, that they
are actually models of piety in most respects. The Decian

persecution, however, brought other themes to the fore in
Cyprian's thinking. Unlike earlier persecutions, it was
empire-wide; and it was based not on casual accusations,
but on a universal command to offer sacrifice, so that no
Christian could expect to escape merely by lying low. The
effect on the church at Carthage was to produce great numbers of lapses, particularly among the rich.[17]

When Cyprian afterwards wrote of this disaster in
the treatise *De lapsis (On the Lapsed)*, he laid the whole
blame on wealth, and this in two ways. He regarded the
persecution itself as divine punishment for the avarice
that had become characteristic of Christians; and he also
claimed that attachment to riches was the principal reason
why so many had lapsed. Thus, the persecution was necessary because wealth (or, more precisely, the acquisitive
temper) had undermined the church's faith. People had been
neglecting their religious duties, including almsgiving, in
order to devote themselves to expanding their possessions.
The clergy themselves had neglected their charges in order
to tour the markets of the empire on business; some, he
claimed, had even resorted to fraud and the worst sort of
usury in the process of building estates. It was a mercy
on God's part to send a persecution and so strengthen the
church's waning faith.[18]

But the power of avarice proved too much for most of
the rich; they gave way to it and denied their faith rather
than suffer confiscation. Some rushed to perform sacrifice
before there was even a suggestion of coercion; and having
sacrificed, they encouraged others to do the same.[19]
Cyprian himself fled from Carthage to avoid arrest, and he
recommended this course of action to others. But the rich
had been unable to do even this, since it would have meant
sacrificing their wealth, if not their lives. "Their property held them in chains," Cyprian declared. None of this

would have happened if, like Cyprian himself (though he
does not say this), they had put their wealth at the service of the poor; for "no man could be overcome by the
world if he had nothing in the world to overcome him."[20]
God had thus imposed the persecution on the church as a
test of avarice; and a great many had failed the test and
lapsed.

The problem of the rich did not end with the persecution. During the troubles they had proved themselves
marginal Christians; after the persecution was past, they
turned rebellious as well. Cyprian complained that people
who ought to be living the life of penitents, with fasting,
weeping, and mourning, were living sumptuously instead.
From the very day of their lapse, they were still to be
found enjoying the baths and belching from last night's
overindulgence; lapsed women were still appearing publicly
in their finest clothes and their jewels.[21]

Such behavior suggests that the rich lapsed were refusing to accept Cyprian's verdict on them as sinners and
the penitential discipline that he wished to impose. Other
evidence confirms this. Many felt that they had done
nothing wrong by performing an act of external confirmity.
Some had, in fact, done nothing more than acquire (by influence or purchase) certificates which *said* they had sacrificed when they had not.[22] A good many of the lapsed had
subsequently got hold of papers which they regarded as the
equivalent of a full pardon from God—something the church
could scarcely, in their opinion, fail to recognize.

These papers were the so-called *libelli pacis* (certificates of peace), issued by confessors who had suffered for
their faith during persecution. The church had long es-
teemed these people as heroes, very close in rank to the
martyrs themselves; and their merits entitled them to a
certain influence with God. If anyone could forgive sins,

it was certainly they; and some of them began issuing
libelli pretty freely to the lapsed. Cyprian, however refused to acknowledge these, since he was intent on reim-
posing normal ecclesiastical discipline. The consequence
of his refusal was a rebellion on the part of the lapsed
themselves.[23]

This situation was made more difficult for Cyprian
by the fact that a schism had opened up within the church
while he himself was in hiding during the persecution.
The original leader, a presbyter named Novatus, is a shad-
owy figure for us. But it is probable that he had been a
rival of Cyprian's for election as bishop of Carthage and
that he was in charge of a district of the city (the Byrsa)
that included the main public buildings along with much
wealth and influence. Novatus and some other presbyters
declared their independence of Cyprian by readmitting the
lapsed to communion without any prolonged period of penance
or any verdict of the bishop. Thus, the schism threatened
to attract to itself many of the rich members of the church
who were in revolt against Cyprian's rigid penitential
discipline.[24]

Between lapse and schism, Cyprian's church lost the
majority of its rich members. We can appreciate the gravi-
ty of this only when we see the extraordinary financial
drain that affected the church during this same period. To
begin with, there were the normal demands on the church to
support widows, orphans, and other destitute people. We do
not know how many of these the church in Carthage was maintaining, but the older and larger church of Rome had about
1,500 on its rolls at this time.[25] This group included
people who had been required to give up "immoral" professions on becoming Christians; and since the preceding decades had been a period of expansion, there may have been a
number of these, too.[26]

The clergy also received a monthly stipend. At Rome there were 155 of these, at Carthage probably fewer. (We know specifically of twenty-five priests, deacons, and sub-deacons; but there is no reason to suppose that we have a complete list.) Even if these men were not paid magnificently, they probably received more than the indigent people on the relief rolls; and the total outlay may have been large. Since it was particularly important in a time of schism to secure the continuing loyalty of the clergy, the regular payment of stipends was important as a bond between the bishop and the lower orders.[27]

Expenses for welfare and clergy, then, constituted a heavy, if normal, burden for any church. In addition, persecution created extraordinary demands on the church's resources. The confessors in prison had to be cared for: even to maintain contact with them must have cost a certain amount in bribes to jailers, and the church also made it a standing practice to improve their lot by bringing them better food. In addition, the church must have taken some responsibility for the families of confessors; and it had to do something for those left destitute by confiscations. In short, the relief rolls will have mushroomed during the years 251-52.[28]

No sooner had the persecution itself ceased when another emergency arose. Barbarian raiders in Numidia carried off large numbers of Christians among their hostages, and the Numidian bishops called for help in ransoming them. Since Carthage enjoyed a position of leadership among Christians in Numidia as well as in the province of Africa, Cyprian could not fail to respond. Accordingly, he raised 100,000 sesterces in Carthage, plus sums from other African churches, which he forwarded to the Numidian bishops. Along with the donation, he sent a list of contributors, which shows that the money did not come from regular church funds, but had to be raised by special appeal from a limited number of rich donors.[29]

The church treasury was depleted at this point partly because of the defection of one of Cyprian's deacons,
Felicissimus, to the party of Novatus, where he assumed a
position of leadership. Since deacons were the usual financial officers of a church such as that of Carthage, we
can assume that he took with him, when he defected, a substantial portion of the church's treasury. (Cyprian had,
in fact, distributed large funds among his clergy during
the persecution to simplify problems of distribution to the
needy.) Since Felicissimus now recognized the party of
Novatus as the true church of Carthage, he would naturally
turn over to them any funds at his disposal.[30]

Finally, in the year 252, a plague struck the empire,
working devastation in Carthage as elsewhere. The situation demanded heroic efforts in the care of the sick and
the burial of the dead. The disruption of normal agriculture and trade must have called for outlays of cash as well,
in order to ensure distribution of necessary food supplies.
Cyprian, moreover, called on his congregation to devote
themselves to caring not only for their own sick, but for
pagans as well.[31]

The years 250-52 were thus a time of inordinate financial strain for the church at Carthage, compounded by
the fact that so many of the congregation's wealthy members
had lapsed in the persecution at the very beginning of this
period. One suspects that offerings to the church fell off
at least as markedly as expenses increased. It is not surprising, then, to find Cyprian at exactly this time lament-
ing the lost days of the apostles and the fabled generosity
of the primitive Christians:

> In those days, they would sell their
> houses and their estates...giving the
> money to the apostles for distribution
> to those in need. But now, we do not

> even give tithes on our patrimony, and
> whereas the Lord tells us to sell, we
> buy instead and accumulate.

This is the lament of a man who cannot make ends meet. As
Cyprian's need for the alms of the rich mounted, he became
more conscious both of the frequently marginal character of
their attachment to the church and of the danger of their
seeking to wrest control from the church's constituted officers.[32]

ALMSGIVING: THE ONLY SOLUTION

Thus it happened that in 251-52, the distinct problems of the lapsed and of the church's financial predica-
ment became, for Cyprian, a single problem. The fallen
stood in need of penance and good works by which they might
purge their sin and prove the genuineness of their repentance. The community as a whole stood in need of larger resources to maintain its own unity and to serve the brethren
in need. Why should not the lapsed win their own salvation
at the same time that they came to the rescue of the church
—by giving alms?[33]

The value of almsgiving in this connection had already occurred to Cyprian early in this disastrous period.
In *De lapsis,* he urged everyone who had any crime to atone
for that he should give alms quickly and lavishly. A little later, in his treatise *De dominica oratione (On the
Lord's Prayer)*, he declared that prayer itself "is ineffect-
ual when it is a barren entreaty that beseeches God...."
Only almsgiving can give one the right to have one's prayers
heard. This extreme doctrine is novel, it seems, with
Cyprian; the closest approach to it in an earlier author is
the statement in *II Clement* that almsgiving is better than
prayer.[34]

Finally, Cyprian summed up his reasoning in the

treatise *De opere et eleemosynis,* a title which we can
translate as *On Good Works and Alms*—or better (as a hen-
diadys) *On Almsgiving as a Good Work*. This essay must be
dated near the end of the period of persecution, schism
and plague, and it contains Cyprian's most developed treatment of the question of almsgiving. In it Cyprian addressed
the laity of Carthage (*fratres carissimi*), urging them to
give alms for their souls' salvation. It was primarily the
rich laity that he had in mind, even if he did allude to
the widow's mite to show the poor that they, too, should
give alms (15). Like Tertullian, Cyprian thought of the
poor as recipients of alms, not givers—and this is true
not only for the *egentes* (indigent), but also for the
pauperes (people of limited means) (23).[35]

The treatise is a barrage of threats and promises,
all of them affirming that one's salvation is intimately
dependent on almsgiving. Cyprian began by arguing that
everyone in the church has sins to atone for and that almsgiving is the one certain method of accomplishing this—
superior to prayer, lamentation and fasting. He even compared it to baptism—to the disadvantage of the latter, in
which sins are remitted only once (2). By the same token,
refusal to give alms is dangerous, for it lowers a person's
standing "in the sight of God" (13).[36]

At one point, Cyprian painted complete abandonment
of goods as the only alternative to eternal damnation. In
the usual Early Christian manner, however, he was simply
shaping an *a fortiori* argument: if Jesus really demands
complete abandonment, then one must all the more give alms
(7). The same device reappears at the end of the work,
where Cyprian invoked the communism of the primitive church
and God's universal gift of sun, air, and water as arguments not for communism but for almsgiving:

He who has possessions and, according to

this example of equality (*or* equity),
shares on earth his returns and income with his brethren, in being universal and equitable in his gratuitous
generosities, is an imitator of God
the Father (25).

It is a question not of total surrender, but of "gratuitous
generosities." Cyprian himself may have surrendered control of his wealth, but he did not treat this as a norm for
his flock. [37]

Finally, in a splendid peroration, Cyprian described
the glory that awaits those who give alms, insisting that
the hope of this glory is the best possible motive for good
works. He stressed the simplicity of this path to salvation, which is within the reach of both weak and strong.
He compared almsgiving with martyrdom, promising a white
crown to those who triumph "in time of peace," comparable
to the purple crown of those "victorious in time of persecution" (26). There is even the suggestion that the white
crown prepares the way for the second, purple crown of
martyrdom. [38]

Nothing in this treatise is unusual in Early Christian terms, unless it is the thorough-going way in which
the calculus of merit has been worked out, with almsgiving
evaluated as the peacetime equivalent of martyrdom. The
simple conviction that almsgiving wins God's favor and provides a reliable path to salvation was not new with Cyprian.
Yet the treatise *De opere et eleemosynis* provokes a certain
antipathy from modern students of the early church. Arch-
bishop Benson, for example, referred to Cyprian's words on
the topic as "a commencement of much medieval trouble."
It is true that Cyprian's work supplied later ages with a
crude and potent statement of the doctrine of salvation by
works, if only because it was the most comprehensive and
explicit Early Christian work on the subject. [39]

Still, we must understand the treatise, like most of
Cyprian's works, as an occasional piece, prompted by a specific situation. I have already sketched the financial
situation at Carthage which made almsgiving so important at
this juncture. In addition, Cyprian was also concerned for
lapsed Christians who had been allowed back into the communion of the church, without, in his opinion, a sufficient
period of penance. During the plague, those of the lapsed
who seemed in danger of death had been reconciled to the
church; and when some of them subsequently recovered, their
reconciliation could not be revoked. This meant that some
of the lapsed had been reconciled and some not; and the injustice of this, coupled with the threat of renewed persecution as a result of the plague, moved the African bishops
in 252 to declare a general reconciliation of all the
lapsed from the Decian persecution who had been living
penitently for the intervening time.[40]

Cyprian, however, felt a continuing concern for
these people and a fear that their incomplete reformation
would contribute to another lapse in the future. Hence,
the note of warning in *De opere* 2: there is *no one* in the
church without need of atonement. Hence, too, the association of almsgiving with martyrdom in the last lines of the
treatise. The ideal for the lapsed would be that they repair their former failure with a bold confession under persecution. That opportunity may yet be theirs, but in the
meantime, they must concentrate on winning the white crown
of almsgiving, in the course of which they will prepare
themselves for a "second crown, purple for their suffering."
Cyprian's intensity, then, in this matter of almsgiving was
a measure of his concern for the newly (and prematurely)
reconciled lapsed as well as an indication of the financial
straits of his congregation.

The doctrine he propounded was by no means new; but

he propounded it with an energy and a simplicity which—it
cannot be denied—encouraged later, more mechanical notions about the relationship of almsgiving and divine favor. For Cyprian, almsgiving was a means of separating
oneself from the things of this world, which had overcome
so many in the Decian persecution, as well as a claim on
God's favor. For later Christians, reading his works
without full consciousness of the circumstances which
prompted them, it must appear that he thought of almsgiving as the means by which the rich could purchase the
Kingdom.[41]

CONCLUSIONS

        In the writings of Cyprian we have an unusually full
picture of the interaction between clergy and rich laity,
between traditional attitudes toward the rich and their actual role in the church. Cyprian stood in the same tradition as Clement of Alexandria and the other authors we
have studied: he advocated detachment from wealth and simplicity of life; he made use of the ideals of abandonment
and communism as the foundation for an *a fortiori* argument for
almsgiving; he saw in almsgiving itself an assured path to
God's favor. Cyprian also found himself confronted, in a
critical manner, by the same realities of church life as
his predecessors were: the marginality of the rich, their
tendency to be insubordinate toward the clergy, and the essential nature of their contribution to church life.
        Cyprian's work bear out what we have already
learned about the attitudes toward wealth and the role of
the Early Christian rich. At the same time, what we have
learned from other Early Christian writers illuminates
Cyprian's life and thought, helping to explain the difference in emphasis between Cyprian's early and late writings,
particularly his increasing hostility toward the rich and

his ever higher doctrine of almsgiving. The moral attitudes of the early Christians, in this matter, were directly linked to the practical experience of their communities.[42]

FOOTNOTES

[1]We are fortunate that Cyprian has left us not only treatises that bear on our topic but also letters that enable us to reconstruct some of the events of his episcopate. The translations of Cyprian and Pontius are my own, except that I have made use, for two treatises, of Maurice Bévenot, ed. and trans., *Cyprian: De Lapsis and De Ecclesiae Catholicae Unitate, OECT* (Oxford: Clarendon Press, 1971).

[2]Pontius completely neglected Cyprian's life before his conversion: "Unde igitur incipiam? unde exordium bonorum eius adgrediar, nisi a principio fidei et nativitate caelesti? siquidem hominis Dei facta non debent aliunde numerari, nisi ex quo Deo natus est" (*Vita* 2).

[3]Paul Monceax noted that Cyprian was unusual among educated Christians in his complete renunciation of pagan imagery: *Histoire littéraire de l'Afrique chrétienne depuis les origines jusqu'à l'invasion arabe*, vol. 2: *Saint Cyprien et son temps* (Paris: E. Leroux, 1902), pp. 207-8.

[4]Peter Hinchliff, *Cyprian of Carthage and the Unity of the Christian Church* (London: Goeffrey Chapman, 1974), pp. 20-22. Edward White Benson, *Cyprian: His Life. His Times. His Work* (New York: D. Appleton & Co., 1897), pp. 471-72, rightly contrasted the fate of the nine Numidian bishops who were sent to the mines. Condemnation to *metallum* was normally a lower-class penalty, from which those who ranked as decurions or above were exempted: Garnsey, pp. 134-35.

[5]In the quotation from Pontius, the word "almost" (*prope*) is a conjecture by W. Hartel in his edition (*CSEL*) of Cyprian, based on the unintelligible *pro* of one manuscript. Joseph H. Fichter, *Saint Cecil Cyprian, Early Defender of the Faith* (St. Louis: Herder Book Co., 1942), p. 124, was perplexed that "during all the subsequent years, Cyprian seemed always able to dip into some other reserves." Joseph Boutet, *Saint Cyprien, Evêque de Carthage et martyr* (Avignon: Aubanel Freres, 1923), p. 11, excuses these as "Sages réserves qui, faut-il le dire, n'enlèvent rien à la grandeur du sacrifice spontanément consenti." For the most recent discussion, see Sage, pp. 132-34.

[6]It is possible, however, that we should ascribe the elegantly rustic tone of the work to the classical manner that suffuses it. Cf. Joseph Ludwig, *Der heilige Märtyrerbischof Cyprian von Karthago: Ein kulturgeschichtliches und theologisches Zeitbild aus der afrikanischen Kirche des 3. Jahrhunderts* (Munich: Karl Zink Verlag, 1951), pp. 20-21.

[7]There is a variety of systems for numbering the *Epistles* of Cyprian. All references here are to the edition of Hartel. Cf. *Ep.* 66.4, where Cyprian complains that he had suffered at this time from an order of confiscation: "si quis tenet possidet de bonis Caecili

Cypriani episcopi christianorum...."

[8]*Vita* 15.1. Benson, p. 18, suggested that "friends bought them in, and insisted on his residing there"; but Pontius seems to mean that he actually owned them at the time of his death. Cf. Monceaux, *Histoire littéraire,* 2:206-7, who thinks that friends bought the property and restored it to Cyprian.

[9]See above, pp.114-18. Cyprian once referred to Christians as those "who have renounced the world, and have cast away its riches and pomps..." (*De dom. or.* 18). This is simply a reference to the baptismal renunciations. In another place, he advocated that Christians abandon their property "ut apostoli et sub apostolis multi et nonnulli saepe fecerunt" (*De laps.* 11). But the vague terms "multi" and "nonnulli" scarcely suggest an exact historical tradition.

[10]On Crates, see Donald R. Dudley, *A History of Cynicism from Diogenes to the Sixth Century A.D.* (London: Methuen & Co., 1937), p. 48. The later Cynic tradition was that Crates threw his money into the sea at the urging of Diogenes (p. 42). For the ideas of Seneca, see his *Ep.* 17. For discussion of Seneca's extensive influence on Cyprian, see Hugh Koch, *Cyprianische Untersuchungen,* Arbeiten zur Kirchengeschichte, no. 4 (Bonn: A. Marcus & E. Weber, 1926), pp. 286-313. On Augustine, see Peter Brown, *Augustine of Hippo: A Biography* (Berkeley: University of California Press, paperback edition, 1969), pp. 90-91, 115-16, 132-33.

[11]On the Therapeutae, see Philo, *Vit. cont.* 13-17. Seneca urged his protégé Lucilius to abandon the pursuit of wealth and devote himself to philosophy instead; but he tipped his hand when he explained that Lucilius was already "next-door to being rich" (*Ep.* 17.10). It was not so much poverty that Seneca preached as contentment with moderate wealth—preferably inherited, since that is less distracting (20.10). "The best measure of money is one that neither falls into poverty nor departs far from it..." (*Tranq.* 8.8).

[12]For the stereotyped character of Cyprian's attack on the avarice of the rich, see Daniel David Sullivan, *The Life of the North Africans as Revealed in the Works of St. Cyprian,* Catholic University of America Patristic Studies, vol. 37 (Washington: Catholic University of America, 1933), pp. 54-56.

[13]The virgins had to be well-off, since they lived off their own income, not a church stipend; cf. the letter of Cornelius of Rome (Eusebius, *H.E.* 6.43.11), where they are omitted from the list of those supported by the church. See Benson, pp. 55-56, and Angela Elizabeth Keenan, *Thasci Caecili Cypriani De Habitu Virginum: A Commentary, with an Introduction and Translation,* Catholic University of America Patristic Studies, vol. 34 (Washington: Catholic University of America, 1932), p. 7.

[14]*De hab. virg.* 18-19. It has been suggested that Cyprian may have known Clement's work, but since most of what the two authors have in common is of the nature of Stoic commonplace, it is difficult to be sure. Cf. Keenan, pp. 28-32.

[15]*De hab. virg.* 7-10.

[16]Ibid., 11.

[17]R. M. Grant, *Augustus to Constantine*, pp. 168-69. As for those who held firm in the persecution, "The majority of the confessors of whom any record has survived seem to have been far from eminent"; Frend, *Martyrdom and Persecution*, p. 306.

[18]*De laps.* 5-6.

[19]Ibid., 8-9. Roman officials probably aimed at just this result. The prefect Culcianus, in the persecution of Diocletian, took special pains to secure the apostasy of Phileas because his wealth and influence would have induced others to apostatize; *Apology of Phileas, Bishop of Thmuis,* ed. Victor Martin, *Papyrus Bodmer,* 20:15-16.

[20]*De laps.* 11. In Chap. 3, Cyprian placed those who fled second only to those confessors who actually underwent torture. In this way, he excused his own flight from the city, as Pontius was still doing when he wrote the *Vita*. It is difficult to say how thorough the government was about confiscating property, for Cyprian still possessed property after the Decian persecution and even after his own *deportatio* to Curubis, which should have involved confiscation (Benson, pp. 466-67).

[21]*De laps.* 30.

[22]We may guess that this expedient was available only to people with influence or the means to pay the necessary bribes. Cyprian does not tell us this, but Tertullian had spoken of the prevalence of bribery in *De fuga*. Cyprian viewed the case of the *libellatici* with as much seriousness as that of the *sacrificati* who had actually participated in the pagan rites (*De laps.* 27); but the African bishops in council treated them more leniently (*Ep.* 55.13-14). Goeffrey E. M. de Ste. Croix, "Aspects of the 'Great' Persecution," *HTR* 47 (1954):75-113, especially pp. 87-88, argues that the church in the East tolerated purchase of *libelli* even in the Decian persecution; but the argument is one *ex silentio*.

[23]Hinchliff, pp. 52-60; Sage, pp. 211-12.

[24]On Novatus, see Benson, p. 112; Hinchliff, pp. 38-39; Sage, pp. 138-43. On readmission of the impenitent, see Cyprian, *Ep.* 17.2;

34.1. Cyprian held that only the sacrifice offered by the bishop himself could purge the sins of the lapsed (De laps. 16).

Cyprian viewed the schism as a worse and more ominous disaster
than the persecution; see Géza Alföldy, "Der heilige Cyprian und die
Krise des römischen Reiches," Historia 22 (1973):479-501, especially
pp. 484-86.

[25]Letter of Cornelius of Rome in Eusebius, H.E. 6.43.11. Benson,
p. 68, estimated the Roman church at under 50,000; Uhlhorn, pp.
158-59, put the Carthaginian church at no more than 3,000 to 4,000.
All such estimates are dubious.

[26]We know of one such case outside Carthage, where Cyprian wrote
to prohibit a converted actor from teaching his profession and offered to support him at Carthage if he had no other means of livelihood (Ep. 2.2). The early church prohibited the practice of a number of professions; abandonment of them was a condition of being admitted to the catechumenate, according to Hippolytus, Apost. Trad. 16.

Cyprian himself, Ep. 41, stressed the importance of alms as tying
the people to their bishop.

[27]Cornelius (Eusebius, H.E. 6.43.11) on the Roman clergy. On
Carthage, see Hinchliff, p. 140, n. 5, citing S. Thani Nayagam, The
Carthaginian Clergy during the Episcopate of Cyprian (N.p.: Tamil
Literature Society, 1950), pp. 49-50.

[28]On care of imprisoned confessors, see Tertullian (De ieiun.
12.3), who poured contempt on the orthodox for maintaining their confessors in what he considered luxury. Cf. the picture of these
charities in Lucian, Peregr. 11-13.

[29]Ep. 62. Cf. the rabbinic practice of keeping lists of donors;
Montefiore and Loewe, p. 423. There is uncertainty as to the year of
this event, since the letter itself has no indication of date; see
Sage, pp. 36, 287-88, 365.

[30]For Cyprian's distribution of funds, see Ep. 5.1. A deacon
"had the opportunity of enriching with both adherents and property
any section which he pronounced to be the true church. And it is
from such transferences probably that the accusations of 'fraud and
rapine' arise which are so frequently showered upon unorthodox deacons..." (Benson, p. 115).

[31]Pontius, Vita 9. The epidemic was not bubonic plague, but "a
synchronous prevalence of many diseases, among which forms of menin-
gitis and probably acute bacillary dysenteries were frequent...";
Hans Zinsser, Rats, Lice and History (New York: Bantam Books, 1971),
pp. 102-4.

[32]De unit. 26.

[33]The lapsed were not at first allowed to make offerings at the Eucharist (*Ep.* 15.1). But those formally admitted as penitents could apparently give alms (*De laps.* 35).

[34]*De laps.* 35; *De dom. or.* 32. Contrast Mt. 21:20-22, where it is *faith* that makes prayer effective. Tertullian regarded good works as the normal accompaniment of prayer (*De orat.* 28).
The date of *De dominica oratione* has been disputed. The ancient list of Cyprian's works that stood behind the seventh chapter of Pontius' *Vita* suggests a date early in 252, after *De laps.* and the first edition of *De unit.* But it is not completely certain that Pontius' list was meant to be chronological. Recently, Michel Réveillaud, *Saint Cyprien, L'oraison dominicale: Texte, traduction, introduction et notes* (Paris: Presses Universitaires de France, 1964), pp. 36-39, has argued that the work can be dated precisely to late April 250. Réveillaud advances two principal arguments: (1) that the absence of any reference to the collegial unity of bishops requires a date before the schism of Novatian and the composition of *De unit.;* (2) that the reference to *tormenta* and the fact that some Christians have suffered martyrdom brings us to the second part of April 250— but no later, since there is no reference to apostasies. Neither argument is valid. Réveillaud himself notes that the work is essentially catechetical; a discussion of the collegial unity of bishops would be unnecessary in instructing new converts. And in *De laps.* 8, Cyprian declares that the apostasies were caused by the threat of confiscation and did not wait on actual martyrdoms. The best dating for the treatise remains late 251 or early 252; Koch, pp. 136-39; Paul Monceaux, *Saint Cyprien, évêque de Carthage (201-258),* 2d ed. (Paris: J. Gabalda, 1914), p. 122; Sage, p. 381.

[35]The date of *De op. et eleem.* has also been questioned. The early lists of Cyprian's works suggest a date after the plague of 252 and before *De bono patientiae* (c. 256). See Cuthbert Hamilton Turner, *Studies in Early Church History* (Oxford: Clarendon Press, 1912), pp. 258-65. This dating is still the most probable; cf. Koch, pp. 145-48, Monceaux, *Histoire littéraire,* 2:243-44, 252, and Sage, pp. 381-82. Other proposals, however, have been advanced. E. W. Watson, "The *De Opere et Eleemosynis* of St. Cyprian," *JTS* 2 (1901):433-38, dates the work to the high point of the schism and interprets it as Cyprian's defense of his use of personal funds to reinforce his party during the struggle. But Watson based his argument on a misunderstanding. In *De op. et eleem.* 12, Cyprian characterized the opponents of almsgiving as "Pharisees," a term which Watson took to mean "rigorists" (representatives of a Novantianist attitude which was in fact different from that of the Carthaginian schismatics). But Cyprian was alluding to Lk. 16:14, where the Pharisees are styled "lovers of money"; in context, that is the whole meaning of the term.
Another effort to redate *De op. et eleem.* is that of Edward V. Rebenack, *Thasci Caecili Cypriani De Opere et Eleemosynis: A Translation with an Introduction and a Commentary,* Catholic University of

America Patristic Studies, vol. 94 (Washington: Catholic University
of America Press, 1962), pp. 5-8; his principal argument is that,
since "the Decian persecution could not have failed to produce a puri-
fying effect on the Christians" and since *De op. et eleem.* is addressed to "Christians who were worldly-minded, avaricious, and loath
to help the poor and needy," the treatise must have been written before the persecution, about the time of *De hab. virg.* Rebenack, pp.
12-14, cites certain "similarities of thought" between the two works
in support of this dating; but these are not verbally close. He fails
to note the radical difference between them as regards the power assigned to almsgiving: in *De hab. virg.* 11, alms are valuable as
winning the prayers of the poor; in *De op. et eleem.* 5, prayers themselves are valueless without almsgiving. Since Rebenack's picture of
a church perfected by the Decian persecution contradicts the evidence
of Cyprian's letters and of *De laps.* (especially Chap. 30), there remains no foundation for his dating of the work.

Rebenack is right, however, to point out that the work was written at a moment when persecution was not a current reality (pp. 5-8),
for Cyprian says little in *De op. et eleem.* about martyrdom. Still,
he gives martyrdom pride of place in his peroration. This suggests
that we should place the work in a period of uncertainty. Just after
the accession of Valerian in 253, when the threat of persecution by
Gallus was postponed, would be a suitable locus.

[36]On the role of *satisfactio* in Cyprian's conception of penitential discipline, see Adhémar d'Alès, *La théologie de saint Cyprien*
(Paris: Gabriel Beauchesne, 1922), pp. 272-81.

[37]Cf. Schilling, pp. 59-62, for use of these passages to prove
that early Christianity was socialist.

[38]Cyprian still regarded martyrdom as the best method of purging
oneself of apostasy (*De laps.* 36). For him, as for Tertullian, martyrdom "indefeasibly guarantees salvation"; Barnes, p. 174, citing
Scorp. 6.9.

[39]Benson, p. 249. The sense of embarrassment has often been
acute. Thus Uhlhorn, pp. 214-15, pretended that Cyprian's ideas were
isolated and unique in the pre-Constantinian church. Seipel, pp.
227-29, argued that Cyprian only meant that almsgiving would help the
penitent detach himself from love of money. Monceaux, *Saint Cyprien*,
pp. 123-24, ignored the whole idea of redemptive alms in his summary
of *De opere.* Phillips, pp. 88-91, detected "a certain lowering of
the moral atmosphere," but excused Cyprian by saying that "not the
writer but his hearers are primarily responsible." But John Burnaby,
Amor Dei, A Study of the Religion of St. Augustine (London: Hodder &
Stoughton, 1938), pp. 132-33, 235, blamed Augustine's shortcomings in
this regard squarely on Cyprian. Schellhase, pp. 443-44, is excep-
tional in at least expressing sympathy for the enormous burden Cyprian
carried in the matter.

⁴⁰Hinchliff, pp. 80-81; Sage, pp. 280-82. (Sage, however, dates *De op. et eleem.* before the extension of a general peace, p. 273.) On Gallus and the threat of renewed persecution, see Monceaux, *Histoire littéraire,* 2:23.

⁴¹Cf. LaPiana, p. 276: "...African Christianity, in striking contrast with the hellenistic churches, shows from the beginning little or no interest in merely speculative problems; emphasis was primarily, if not entirely, concentrated on moral issues and on disciplinary and sacramental implications."

⁴²Cf. Eric Osborn, p. 2; "The determining ideas in ethics are never simply ethical and this is clearly the case in early Christian writings." See also Sage, p. 335, on the practical foundations of Cyprian's thinking.

CONCLUSIONS

SUMMARY

Early Christian attitudes toward wealth were a peculiar mixture of positive and negative themes. On the
negative side, the writers we have studied treated wealth
as something from which to separate oneself by spiritual
detachment and physical simplicity of life. They considered acquisition of further riches sinful, since it implied an unhealthy attachment to the things of this world.
They spoke of the poor as more pious and more acceptable
to God than the rich. They toyed with the ideal of complete abandonment of wealth and with the principles of
ancient communism.

On the other hand, there were limits to the radicalism of these early Christians. Abandonment of property
never became a norm for Christians as it was for Cynic
philosophers. Communism was never formally imposed on any
Christian congregation, although there was great social
pressure toward it in the primitive church of Jerusalem.
What is more striking—our authors actually ascribe one
major, positive religious value to the possession of
wealth: by distributing it in alms, the rich could earn
their own salvation. Thus, they left control of wealth in
the hands of those who held it, even though they tried to
prescribe the way in which they should expend it.

The incongruities of the Early Christian attitude toward riches are perplexing at first sight, but they arose
from tensions and ambiguities within the life of the

Christian congregation itself. For there were two basic
problems in the roles assigned to the Christian rich.
First, the church assigned a central role in the support
of its institutions to rich Christians who were apt to be
marginal members of the congregation because of their
larger horizons. Second, the church expected the rich to
provide for it financially at the same time that it denied
them the honors, powers, and rewards which Greco-Roman
culture led them to expect in return for their beneficence.
The first of these tensions led to uncertainty about the
reliability and perseverance of the rich. The second encouraged rivalry between the rich and the clergy for leadership of the church.

     Most of our Early Christian literature comes to us
from the hands of clergymen (or of exceptionally pious laymen), who were concerned to maintain their own prerogatives and yet were also intent on seeing that the church's
treasury was kept full. It was natural that most of them
should condemn the rich for the marginal character of their
faith and for their tendency to rebel, while yet stressing
the great spiritual opportunity that their wealth gave them
to buy salvation with alms. Thus, Early Christian attitudes toward wealth, however confused they may seem on the
purely rational plane, become intelligible, even in their
apparent inconsistencies, once we have placed them against
the background of social realities within the early
church.[1]

IMPLICATIONS FOR FURTHER WORK

     Throughout the present work, I have endeavored to
understand the teaching of early Christian thinkers and
writers as an aspect of the social life of the early
churches, rather than treating intellectual history as

autonomous. This approach vindicates itself, I think, insofar as it accounts for the apparent inconsistencies in the attitude of early Christian writers toward the rich. Whether all intellectual history should be treated in this way, I am in doubt; but all issues of morality or ethics have a strong claim to be examined in the light of social history, for it is on the social plane that morality and ethics live and breathe. Only when we see them in their full social ramifications, will the ideas of ancient writers be quite intelligible.

Unfortunately, it is not at all easy to acquire an understanding of the social life of early Christianity. It is not enough merely to comb the Christian texts or consult our meager archeological remains; we must also reconstruct an image of the whole of first-century life as it is relevant to our subject. Apart from the fact that no one person is likely to be fully competent and up-to-date in all the relevant disciplines, one must cope with the inevitable human tendency to interpret the unknown in terms of the familiar—the first century, in this case, in terms of the nineteenth or twentieth. There are, to be sure, human continuities—greed, self-interest, fear and, equally, generosity, nobility and love. Yet, the socially channeled expressions of these constants may vary widely.

For these reasons, I think it important to stress what we might call the "strangeness" of the Greco-Roman and Jewish-Palestinian worlds in which Christianity originated. Until we recognize the gulf between them and us, we cannot cross it in any meaningful way nor begin to make sense, in our own terms, of their alien experience. Good historians, of course, have always grasped this truth, consciously or unconsciously. I merely reaffirm that one of the cardinal purposes of the student of early Christianity must be to pursue this distinction, for without doing

so, he may find himself with nothing more than the odd
pieces of a puzzle which cannot be fitted together, half of
them being modern and half ancient.

The influence of modern sociology and social anthro-
pology creates particular opportunities in this regard,
even while it raises new problems. Modern social theory
may stimulate the social historian to ask new questions
and to see his material in new lights. This is a great
advantage, if it helps to integrate our fragmentary data.
On the other hand, the modern sociologist is used to
working with abundant data, immeasurably more so than the
historian of early Christianity. With the help of such
data, he can construct compelling models of social behavior, which command assent by their appearance of complete-
ness and by the documentation provided for them. There
is a temptation, then, to apply such models cross-cultural-
ly with no further ado, a method which is little better
than that of the Marxist-Roman Catholic polemics which we
surveyed in the Introduction to this work.

I do not wish to deny that modern sociological and
social anthropological theory may be useful to the historian; but he must use it with care. If the theory is of a
high enough order of abstraction, one may be able to argue
that it is applicable to all cultures alike. If the theory
can be grounded in incontestably universal human characteristics—a difficult feat in itself—one might argue the
same. Otherwise, the social historian who wishes to make
use of modern models of social behavior must demonstrate
clearly that there is a legitimate analogy between the
relevant ancient and modern social institutions. No
amount of sociological insight can ever take the place of
the historian's work, even though it may illuminate it.

If I have succeeded in clarifying the social role of
one group within the early Christian communities, this

still falls far short of providing a complete conception of the social nature of early Christianity. It seems to me that the logical next step in investigation will be to examine the social roles of the Christian ministry under the Early Empire.[2] The role of the poor is also of great importance, but I believe that it will prove virtually inaccessible to us, since the poor of antiquity did not have much access to literary immortality. In any case, the implications of this study for our understanding of early Christianity are sufficiently broad that they will need to be confirmed or refuted by much further research, which must include both broad studies, like this one, of various aspects of the Christianity of the Early Empire and also detailed studies of specific documents, places and people.

Finally, it is important to say something about the relationship between this historical study of the rich in the early church and the modern social and economic concerns which have stimulated modern interest in our topic. The importance of creating an ethical evaluation of wealth and some moral direction for its use is certainly no less in 1980 than it was just after 1848, when Étienne Chastel wrote, even if the simple opposition between socialist and Christian is now partly obsolete. At the same time, the emphasis I have laid on the strangeness of first-century life implies that it will be more difficult than before to make of early Christianity a patron of one's own point of view or a whipping boy for that of the opposition. Much less can anyone look to early Christianity for any detailed guidance in the quandaries of modernity. This not to say, however, that the Gospel of those Christians has nothing to say to our century—only that we must use the utmost care in making any translation from their world to ours.

According to one recent author on early Christian

ethics, "Christianity, as a religion of divine incarnation,
is committed to both a sense of perfection and a respect
for the contingent."[3]   Perhaps the opportunism of early
Christianity in accepting the social structures of its
place and time and seeking to transform them to the service of transcendence and the benefit of the poor is the
primary ethical message which it has to impart. Social
institutions and social movements alike have a certain
autonomy which does not require the church either to
initiate or to approve them. The ancient Christians did
not shrink, however, from active involvement with these
autonomous phenomena in an effort, at least partially
successful, to subordinate them to higher ends.

FOOTNOTES

[1]For a related summary, see above, pp. 171-73.

[2]For a first step, see my article "The Intellectual Role of the Early Catholic Episcopate," *Church History,* 48 (1979):261-68.

[3]Osborn, p. 5.

LIST OF ABBREVIATIONS

ANF	The Ante-Nicene Fathers
CSEL	Corpus scriptorum ecclesiasticorum latinorum
Eng.	English translation
GCS	Die griechischen christlichen Schriftsteller der ersten drei Jahrhunderte
HTR	Harvard Theological Review
ICC	International Critical Commentary
ILS	Hermann Dessau, Inscriptiones latinae selectae
JRS	Journal of Roman Studies
JTS	Journal of Theological Studies
LCL	Leob Classical Library
NTS	New Testament Studies
OCD	The Oxford Classical Dictionary, 2d ed.
OECT	Oxford Early Christian Texts
PW	Real-Encyclopädie der klassischen Altertumswissenschaft (Pauly-Wissowa)
RAC	Reallexikon für Antike und Christentum
RSR	Recherches de science religieuse
SIG	Wilhelm Dittenberger, Sylloge Inscriptionum Graecarum, 1883
TDNT	Theological Dictionary of the New Testament
TS	Texts and Studies
TU	Texte und Untersuchungen zur Geschichte der altchristlichen Literatur
TZ	Theologische Zeitschrift
VC	Vigiliae Christianae
ZTK	Zeitschrift für Theologie und Kirche
ZNW	Zeitschrift für die neutestamentliche Wissenschaft
ZWT	Zeitschrift für wissenschaftliche Theologie

BIBLIOGRAPHY

I. Texts and Translations of Ancient
   Jewish and Christian Works

Ante-Nicene Fathers, The. Edited by Alexander Roberts and James Donald-
    son. American edition edited by A. Cleveland Coxe. 8 vols.
    Buffalo: Christian Literature Publishing Co., 1885-86.

Apology of Phileas, Bishop of Thmuis. Edited by Victor Martin.
    Papyrus Bodmer XX. Cologny-Geneve: Bibliotheca Bodmeriana,
    1964.

Apostolic Fathers. Translated by Kirsopp Lake. Loeb Classical Libra-
    ry. 2 vols. London: William Heinemann, 1912-13.

Athenagoras. Legatio and De resurrectione. Edited and translated by
    William R. Schoedel. Oxford Early Christian Texts. Oxford:
    Clarendon Press, 1972.

Chadwick, Henry, ed. The Sentences of Sextus, A Contribution to the
    History of Early Christian Ethics. Texts and Studies, n.s.,
    vol. 5. Cambridge, England: University Press, 1959.

Charles, R. H., ed. The Apocrypha and Pseudepigrapha of the Old Testa-
    ment. 2 vols. Oxford: Clarendon Press, 1913.

Clement of Alexandria. Werke. Edited by Otto Stählin. Die griechis-
    chen christlichen Schriftsteller der ersten drei Jehrhunderte.
    3 vols. Leipzig: J. C. Heinrichs, 1905-6.

_____. The Exhortation to the Greeks, The Rich Man's Salvation,
    and the Fragment of an Address Entitled To the Newly Baptized.
    Translated by G. W. Butterworth. Loeb Classical Library. Lon-
    don: William Heinemann, 1919.

Cyprian. Opera Omnia. Edited by Guilelmus Hartel. Corpus scriptorum
    ecclesiasticorum latinorum, vol. 3. 2 vols. Vienna: C. Geroldi
    Filius, 1868-71.

_____. De habitu virginum. Translated, with a commentary, by
    Angela Elizabeth Keenan. Catholic University of America

Patristic Studies, vol. 34. Washington: Catholic University of
America, 1932.

_____. De lapsis and De ecclesiae catholicae unitate. Edited and
translated by Maurice Bévenot. Oxford Early Christian Texts.
Oxford: Clarendon Press, 1971.

_____. L'oraison dominicale. Edited and translated by Michel
Réveillaud. Paris: Presses Universitaires de France, 1964.

_____. De opere et eleemosynis. Translated, with a commentary, by
Edward V. Rebenack. Catholic University of America Patristic
Studies, vol. 94. Washington: Catholic University of America
Press, 1962.

Eusebius. The Ecclesiastical History. Translated by Kirsopp Lake and
J. E. L. Oulton. Loeb Classical Library. 2 vols. London:
William Heinemann, 1926-32.

Hennecke, Edgar, ed. New Testament Apocrypha. New edition edited by
Wilhelm Schneemelcher. English translation edited by R. McL.
Wilson. 2 vols. Philadelphia: Westminster Press, 1963.

Hippolytus. The Apostolic Tradition. Edited and translated by Burton
Scott Easton. Cambridge: University Press, 1934; reprint ed.,
[Hamden, Conn.]: Archon Books, 1962.

Irenaeus. Libri quinque adversus haereses. Edited by W. Wigan Harvey.
2 vols. Cambridge: Typis Academicis, 1857.

Justin Martyr. Apologies. Edited by Louis Pautigny. Paris: Alphonse
Picard & Fils, 1904.

_____. Dialogue avec Tryphon. Edited by Georges Archambault.
Paris: Alphonse Picard & Fils, 1909.

Krüger, Gustav, ed. Ausgewählte Märtyrerakten. Sammlung ausgewählter
kirchen- und dogmen-geschichtlicher Quellenschriften, n.s., no.
3. 4th ed. With appendix by Gerhard Ruhbach. Tübingen: J. C.
B. Mohr (Paul Siebeck), 1963.

Minucius Felix. Octavius. Translated by Gerald H. Rendall. Loeb
Classical Library. (With Tertullian, Apology and De spectaculius.)
Cambridge, Mass.: Harvard University Press, 1931.

Origen. Opera omnia. Edited by C. H. E. Lommatzch. Berlin: Haude &
Spener, 1831-48.

_____. Werke. Edited by Paul Koetschau and others. Die griechis-
chen christlichen Schriftsteller der ersten drei Jahrhunderte.

12 vols. Leipzig: J. C. Heinrichs, 1899-1925.

_____. On First Principles. Translated by G. W. Butterworth.
London: S. P. C. K., 1936.

Tertullian. Opera. Various editors. Corpus christianorum. Series
latina, vols. 1-2. 2 vols. Turnhout, Belgium: Brepols, 1954.

Vermes, Geza. The Dead Sea Scrolls in English. Revised reprint.
Harmondsworth: Penguin Books, 1968.

II. Background and General Works

A. Jewish Background

Abrahams, Israel. Studies in Pharisaism and the Gospels, First
Series. Cambridge: University Press, 1917.

Baeck, Leo. The Pharisees and Other Essays. Introduction by Krister
Stendahl. New York: Schocken Books, paperback edition, 1966.

Birkeland, Harris. The Evildoers in the Book of Psalms. Avhandlinger
utgitt av Det Norske Videnskaps-Akademi i Oslo II, Historisk-
Filosofisk Klasse, 1955, no. 2. Oslo: Jacob Dybwad, 1955.

Encyclopedia Judaica. S. v. "Armut im Talmud," by A. Marmorstein.

Farmer, W. R. "The Economic Basis of the Qumran Community." Theologische Zeitschrift 11 (1955);295-308.

Finegan, Jack. Light from the Ancient Past: The Archaeological Background of Judaism and Christianity. 2d ed. 2 vols. Princeton:
Princeton University Press, paperback edition, 1969.

Finkelstein, Louis. The Pharisees: The Sociological Background of
their Faith. 2 vols. Philadelphia: Jewish Publication Society
of America, 1938.

Flusser, David. "Blessed Are the Poor in Spirit." Israel Exploration
Journal 10 (1960):1-13.

Geiger, F. Philon von Alexandreia als sozialer Denker. Tübinger
Beiträge zur Altertumswissenschaft, no. 14. Stuttgart: W.
Kohlhammer, 1932.

Goodenough, Erwin R. An Introduction to Philo Judaeus. 2d ed. Oxford: Basil Blackwell, 1962.

Jeremias, Joachim. Jerusalem in the Time of Jesus: An Investigation
    into Economic and Social Conditions during the New Testament
    Period. Translated by F. H. and C. H. Cave. London: SCM Press,
    1969.

Johnson, A. R. "The Psalms." In The Old Testament and Modern Study:
    A Generation of Discovery and Research. Edited by H. H. Rowley.
    London: Oxford University Press, Oxford Paperbacks, 1961. Pp.
    162-209.

Montefiore, Claude G., and Loewe, Herbert, eds. A Rabbinic Anthology.
    Prolegomenon by Raphael Loewe. New York: Schocken Books, 1974.

Mowinckel, Sigmund. The Psalms in Israel's Worship. Translated by
    D. R. Ap-Thomas. 2 vols. Oxford: Basil Blackwell, 1962.

Neusner, Jacob. First-Century Judaism in Crisis: Yoḥanan ben Zakkai
    and the Renaissance of Torah. Nashville: Abingdon Press, 1975.

Oppenheimer, Aharon. The ᶜam ha-aretz: A Study in the Social History
    of the Jewish People in the Hellenistic-Roman Period. Translated
    by I. H. Levine. Leiden: E. J. Brill, 1977.

Rabin, Chaim. Qumran Studies. New York: Schocken Books, paperback
    edition, 1975.

Russell, D. S. The Method and Message of Jewish Apocalyptic, 200 BC-AD
    100. Philadelphia: Westminster Press, 1964.

Smith, Morton. "Zealots and Sicarii." Harvard Theological Review 64
    (1971):1-19.

Tcherikover, Victor. Hellenistic Civilization and the Jews. Trans-
    lated by S. Applebaum. New York: Atheneum, Temple Books, 1970.

Thiering, B. E. "Once More the Wicked Priest." Journal of Biblical
    Literature 97 (1978):191-205.

    B. Greco-Roman Background

Beaujeu, Jean. "La religion de la classe sénatoriale à l'époque des
    Antonins." In Hommages à Jean Bayet. Edited by Marcel Renard
    and Robert Schilling. Brussels: Latomus, 1964. Pp. 54-75.

Bolkestein, Hendrik. Wohltätigkeit und Armenpflege im vorchristlichen
    Altertum: Ein Beitrag zum Problem "Moral und Gesellschaft."
    Utrecht: A. Oosthoek, 1939.

Crook, John. Law and Life of Rome. Ithaca, N.Y.: Cornell University

Press, 1967.

Daube, David. Review of Personality in Roman Private Law, by P. W.
    Duff. Journal of Roman Studies 33 (1943):86-93 and 34 (1944):
    125-35.

Davis, William Stearns. The Influence of Wealth in Imperial Rome.
    New York: Macmillan Co., 1910.

Dill, Samuel. Roman Society from Nero to Marcus Aurelius. 2d ed.
    London: Macmillan & Co., 1925.

Dorigo, Wladimiro. Late Roman Painting. Foreword by Sergio Bettini.
    Translated by James Cleugh and John Warrington. New York:
    Praeger Publishers, 1970.

Dudley, Donald R. A History of Cynicism from Diogenes to the 6th
    Century A.D. London: Methuen & Co., 1937.

Duncan-Jones, Richard. The Economy of the Roman Empire: Quantitative
    Studies. New York: Cambridge University Press, 1974.

Finley, Moses I. The Ancient Economy. Sather Classical Lectures,
    vol. 43. Berkeley: University of California Press, 1973.

Garnsey, Peter. Social Status and Legal Privilege in the Roman Empire.
    Oxford: Clarendon Press, 1970.

Georgi, Dieter. "Socioeconomic Reasons for the 'Divine Man' as a
    Propagandistic Pattern." In Aspects of Religious Propaganda in
    Judaism and Early Christianity. Edited by Elizabeth Schüssler
    Fiorenza. Notre Dame, Ind.: Notre Dame University Press, 1976.
    Pp. 27-42.

Hands, A. R. Charities and Social Aid in Greece and Rome. Ithaca,
    N.Y.: Cornell University Press, 1968.

Hardy, Ernest George. Studies in Roman History. London: S. Sonnen-
    schein & Co., 1906.

Jones, A. H. M. The Roman Economy: Studies in Ancient Economic and
    Administrative History. Edited by P. A. Brunt. Totowa, N.J.:
    Rowman & Littlefield, 1974.

Kitzinger, Ernst. Early Medieval Art. Bloomington, Ind.: Indiana
    University Press, Midland Books, 1964.

Lewis, Naphtali, and Reinhold, Meyer. Roman Civilization. 2 vols.
    New York: Harper & Row, Torchbooks, 1966.

MacMullen, Ramsay. Enemies of the Roman Order: Treason, Unrest, and

Alienation in the Empire. Cambridge: Harvard University Press, 1966.

Mommsen, Theodor. De collegiis et sodaliciis Romanorum. Kiel: Libraria Schwersiana, 1843.

Nickel, Rainer. "Das Verhältnis von Bedürfnis und Brauchbarkeit in seiner Bedeutung für das kynostoische Ideal der Bedürfnislosigkeit." Hermes 100 (1972):42-47.

Oxford Classical Dictionary, 2d ed. S.v. "Clubs, Greek," by Marcus Niebuhr Tod, and "Relegatio," by Adolf Berger and Barry Nicholas.

Poland, Franz. Geschichte des griechischen Vereinswesens. Leipzig: B. G. Teubner, 1909; reprint ed., Leipzig: Zentral-Antiquariat der Deutschen Demokratischen Republik, 1967.

Real-Encyclopädie der klassischen Altertumswissenschaft. S.v. "Collegium," by E. Kornemann.

Reallexikon für Antike und Christentum. S.v. "Autarkie," by P. Wilpert.

Tait, Leo Leslie. "Stoic and Christian Preaching." M.A. dissertation, University of Chicago, 1917.

Tod, Marcus Niebuhr. Sidelights on Greek History: Three Lectures on the Light Thrown by Greek Inscriptions on the Life and Thought of the Ancient World. Oxford: Basil Blackwell, 1932.

Vischer, Rüdiger. Das einfache Leben: Wort-und motivgeschichtliche Untersuchungen zu einem Wertbegriff der antiken Literatur. Göttingen: Vandenhoeck & Ruprecht, 1965.

Waltzing, J. P. Ètude historique sur les corporations professionnelles chez les Romains depuis les origines jusqu'à la chute de l'Empire de l'Occident. Tome 1. Louvain: Charles Peeters, 1895.

C. General Works

Barrett, C. K., ed. The New Testament Background: Selected Documents. London: S. P. C. K., 1958.

Bottomore, T. B. Classes in Modern Society. New York: Vintage Books, 1966.

DeMaria, Richard. Communal Love at Oneida: A Perfectionist Vision of Authority, Property, and Sexual Order. Texts and Studies in Religion, Vol. 2. New York: Edwin Mellen Press, 1978.

Martin, Raymond A. Syntactical Evidence of Semitic Sources in Greek
    Documents. Septuagint and Cognate Studies, no. 3. [Missoula,
    Mont.]: Society of Biblical Literature, 1974.

Marx, Karl, and Engels, Frederick. On Religion. Moscow: Progress
    Publishers, 1975.

Quasten, Johannes. Patrology. 3 vols. Utrecht: Spectrum Publishers,
    1962-63.

Vidler, Alec R. A Century of Social Catholicism 1820-1920. London:
    SPCK, paperback edition, 1969.

Zinsser, Hans. Rats, Lice and History. New York: Bantam Books, 1971.

III. Early Christianity and its Society

A. Social Analysis and History of Christianity

Alfaric, Prosper. Origines sociales du Christianisme. Edited by
    Jacqueline Marchand. Preface by Jean Sarrailh. Paris: Union
    Rationaliste, [1959].

Bauer, Walter. Orthodoxy and Heresy in Earliest Christianity. Appen-
    dices by Georg Strecker. Translated by the Philadelphia Seminar
    on Christian Origins. Edited by Robert A. Kraft and Gerhard
    Krodel. Philadelphia: Fortress Press, 1971.

Baynes, Norman H. The Early Church and Social Life (The First Three
    Centuries), A Selected Bibliography. Historical Association
    Leaflet No. 71. London: G. Bell & Sons, 1927.

Bigelmair, Andreas. Die Beteiligung der Christen am öffentlichen Leben
    in vorconstantinischer Zeit. Ein Beitrag zur ältesten Kirchen-
    geschichte. Munich: J. J. Lentner, 1902.

_____. "Zur Frage des Sozialismus und Kommunismus der ersten drei
    Jahrhunderte." In Beiträge zur Geschichte des christlichen
    Altertums und der byzantinischen Literatur: Festgabe Albert
    Ehrhard. Edited by Albert Michael Königer. Bonn: Kurt Schroeder,
    1922. Pp. 73-93.

Brandon, S. G. F. Jesus and the Zealots: A Study of the Political
    Factor in Primitive Christianity. Manchester: Manchester Uni-
    versity Press, 1967.

Campenhausen, Hans von. Ecclesiastical Authority and Spiritual Power
    in the Church of the First Three Centuries. Translated by J. A.
    Baker. London: Adam and Charles Black, 1969.

Case, Shirley Jackson. The Social Origins of Christianity. Chicago:
     University of Chicago Press, 1923.

_____. The Social Triumph of the Ancient Church. New York: Harper
     & Bros., 1933.

Chastel, Etienne Louis. Etudes historiques sur l'influence de la
     charité durant les premiers siècles chrétiens, et considerations
     sur son rôle dans les sociétés modernes. Paris: Capelle, 1853.

_____. The Charity of the Primitive Churches. Historical Studies
     upon the Influence of Christian Charity During the First Centur-
     ies of our Era, with Some Considerations Touching its Bearing
     upon Modern Society. Translated by G. A. Matile. Philadelphia:
     J. B. Lippincott & Co., 1857.

Deissmann, [Gustav] Adolf. Das Urchristentum und die unteren Schich-
     ten. 2d ed. Göttingen: Vandenhoeck & Ruprecht, 1908.

Dix, Gregory. The Shape of the Liturgy. 2d ed. London: Dacre Press,
     1945.

Eck, Werner. "Das Eindringen des Christentums in den Senatorenstand
     bis zu Konstantin d. Gr." Chiron 1 (1971):381-406.

Fiebig, Paul Wilhelm Julius. War Jesus rebell? Eine historische
     Untersuchung zu Karl Kautsky, Der Ursprung des Christentums, mit
     einem Anhang: Jesus und die Arbeit. Gotha: F. A. Perthes, 1920.

Filson, Floyd V. "The Significance of the Early House Churches."
     Journal of Biblical Literature 58 (1939):105-12.

Foakes Jackson, F. J., and Lake, Kirsopp, eds. The Beginnings of
     Christianity. 5 vols. London: Macmillan & Co., 1922-30.

Frend, William Hugh Clifford. "Heresy and Schism as Social and Na-
     tional Movements." In Schism, Heresy and Religious Protest.
     Edited by Derek Baker. Studies in Church History, vol. 9. Cam-
     bridge: Cambridge University Press, 1972. Pp. 37-56.

_____. Martyrdom and Persecution in the Early Church: A Study of a
     Conflict from the Maccabees to Donatus. New York: New York
     University Press, 1967.

Gager, John G. Kingdom and Community: The Social World of Early
     Christianity. Englewood Cliffs, N.J.: Prentice-Hall, 1975.

Grant, Robert M. From Augustus to Constantine: The Thrust of the
     Christian Movement into the Roman World. New York: Harper &
     Row, 1970.

_____. Early Christianity and Society: Seven Studies. San Fran-
cisco: Harper & Row, 1977.

Green, Henry Alan. "Suggested Sociological Themes in the Study of
Gnosticism." Vigiliae Christianae 31 (1977):169-80.

Groh, Dennis. "Upper-Class Christians in Tertullian's Africa: Some
Observations." In Studia Patristica 14, pt. 3:40-46. Texte
und Untersuchungen 117.

Gülzow, Henneke. "Kallist von Rom: Ein Beitrag zur Soziologie der
römischen Gemeinde." Zeitschrift für die neutestamentliche
Wissenschaft 58 (1967):102-21.

Harnack, Adolf. The Constitution and Law of the Church in the First
Two Centuries. Translated by F. L. Pogson and H. D. A. Major.
New York: G. P. Putnam's Sons, 1910.

_____. The Mission and Expansion of Christianity in the First
Three Centuries. Translated by James Moffatt. Introduction by
Jaroslav Pelikan. New York: Harper & Row, Torchbooks, 1962;
reprint edition, Gloucester, Mass.: Peter Smith, 1972.

Hatch, Edwin. The Organization of the Early Christian Churches. 4th
ed. London: Longmans, Green & Co., 1892.

Judge, E. A. The Social Pattern of the Christian Groups in the First
Century: Some Prolegomena to the Study of New Testament Ideas of
Social Obligation. London: Tyndale Press, 1960.

Kalthoff, Albert. Das Christus-problem: Grundlinien zu einer Sozialtheologie. 2d ed. Leipzig: E. Diederichs, 1903.

_____. Die Entstehung des Christentums. Leipzig: E. Diederichs,
1904.

Kautsky, Karl. Der Ursprung des Christentums, eine historische Untersuchung. 9th ed. Stuttgart: J. H. W. Dietz Nachf., 1919.

_____. Foundations of Christianity. Translated by Henry F. Mins.
New York: Russell & Russell, [1953].

Kippenberg, Hans G. "Versuch einer soziologischen Verortung des antiken
Gnostizismus." Numen 17 (1970):211-31.

Knopf, R. "Ueber die soziale Zusammensetzung der ältesten heidenchristlichen Gemeinden." Zeitschrift für Theologie und Kirche 10
(1900):325-47.

Kreissig, Heinz. "Zur sozialen Zusammensetzung der frühchristlichen

Gemeinden in ersten Jahrhunderten u.Z." Eirene 6 (1967):91-100.

LaPiana, George. "The Roman Church at the End of the Second Century: The Episcopate of Victor, the Latinization of the Roman Church, the Easter Controversy, Consolidation of Power and Doctrinal Development, the Catacomb of Callistus." Harvard Theological Review 18 (1925):201-77.

Le Blant, Edmond. "La richesse et la christianisme á l'âge des persécutions." Revue archéologique, ser. 2, 39 (1880):220-30.

Lebreton, J. "Le désaccord de la foi populaire et de la théologie savante dans l'Eglise chrétienne de IIIe siècle." Revue d'histoire ecclésiastique 19 (1923):481-506 and 20 (1924):5-37.

Lohmeyer, Ernst. Soziale Fragen im Urchistentum. Leipzig: Quelle & Meyer, 1921.

Malherbe, Abraham J. Social Aspects of Early Christianity. Baton Rouge, La.: Louisiana State University Press, 1977.

Morris, John. "Early Christian Orthodoxy." Past and Present, no. 3 (February 1953), pp. 1-14.

Mosheim, Johann Lorenz. Dissertationum ad historiam ecclesiasticam pertinentium. 2 vols. Altona and Flensburg: Fratres Korte, 1733-43.

Munz, Peter. "The Problem of 'Die soziologische Verortung des antiken Gnostizismus.'" Numen 19 (1972):41-51.

Riddle, Donald Wayne. The Martyrs: A Study in Social Control. Chicago: University of Chicago Press, 1931.

de Ste. Croix, Geoffrey E. M. "Aspects of the 'Great' Persecution." Harvard Theological Review 47 (1954):75-113.

Schellhase, Reuben Christian. "Social Aspects of Early Christian Charity." Ph.D. dissertation, University of Chicago, 1952.

Schoeps, Hans Joachim. Jewish Christianity: Factional Disputes in the Early Church. Translated by Douglas R. A. Hare. Philadelphia: Fortress Press, 1969.

Schumacher, Rudolf. Die soziale Lage der Christen im apostolischen Zeitalter. Paderborn: Ferdinand Schöningh, 1924.

Stasiewski, Bernhard. "Ursprung und Entfaltung des Christentums in sowjetischer Sicht." Saeculum 11 (1960):157-79.

Thikötter, Julius. Dr. Kalthoff's Schrift "Das Christusproblem" beleuchtet. Bremen: J. Morgenbesser, 1903.

Uhlhorn, G. Die christliche Liebestätigkeit in der alten Kirche. Stuttgart: D. Gundert, 1882.

_____. Christian Charity in the Ancient Church. Translated by Sophia Taylor. Edinburgh: T. & T. Clark, 1883.

de Visscher, Fernand. "Le régime juridique des plus anciens cimetières chrétiens à Rome." Analecta Bollandiana 69 (1951):39-54.

Wallis, Louis. Sociological Study of the Bible. Chicago: University of Chicago Press, 1912.

Wilken, Robert L. "Collegia, Philosophical Schools, and Theology." In The Catacombs and the Colosseum: The Roman Empire as the Setting of Primitive Christianity. Edited by Stephen Benko and John J. O'Rourke. Valley Forge, Pa.: Judson Press, 1971. Pp. 268-91.

B. Social Ethics

Baumgartner, Ephrem. "Der Communismus im Urchristentum." Zeitschrift für katholische Theologie 33 (1909):625-45.

Behm, Johannes. "Kommunismus und Urchristentum." Neue kirchliche Zeitschrift 21 (1920):275-97.

Beyschlag, Karlmann. "Christentum und Veränderung in der alten Kirche." Kerygma und Dogma 18 (1972):26-55.

Brentano, Lujo. "Die wirtschaftlichen Lehren des christlichen Alter-tums." In Sitzungsberichte der philosophisch-philologischen und der historischen Klasse der kgl. Akademie der Wissenschaften. Munich, 1902. Pp. 141-93.

Bruck, Eberhard F. "Ethics vs. Law: St. Paul, the Fathers of the Church, and the 'Cheerful Giver' in Roman Law." Traditio 2 (1944):97-121.

Cadoux, Cecil John. The Early Church and the World: A History of the Christian Attitude to Pagan Society and the State Down to the Time of Constantinus. Edinburgh: T. & T. Clark, 1925.

Chadwick, Henry. Early Christian Thought and the Classical Tradition. New York: Oxford University Press, 1966.

Christophe, Paul. L'usage chrétien du droit de propriété dans l'Écriture et la tradition patristique. Paris: P. Lethielleux, [1964].

Davies, William David. "The Moral Teaching of the Early Church." In
     The Use of the Old Testament in the New and Other Essays: Stud-
     ies in Honor of William Franklin Stinespring. Edited by James
     M. Efird. Durham, N.C.: Duke University Press, 1972. Pp. 310-
     32.

Farner, Konrad. Christentum und Eigentum. Berlin: Verlag A. Francke,
     1947.

_____. Theologie des Kommunismus? Frankfurt/M.: Stimme-Verlag,
     1969.

Funk, F. X. "Über Reichtum und Handel im christlichen Altertum."
     Historisch-politische Blätter 130 (1902):888-99. Reprinted in
     F. X. Funk, Kirchengeschichtlichen Abhandlungen und Unter-
     suchungen, 3 vols. Paderborn: Ferdinand Schöningh, 1897-1907.
     3:150-59.

Giordani, Igino. The Social Message of Jesus. Paterson, N.J.: St.
     Anthony Guild Press, 1943.

_____. The Social Message of the Early Church Fathers. Translated
     by Alba I. Zizzamia. Paterson, N.J.: St. Anthony Guild Press,
     1944.

Haller, W. "Das Eigentum in Glauben und Leben der nachapostolischen
     Kirche." Theologische Studien und Kirtiken 64 (1891):478-563.

Hauck, Friedrich. Die Stellung des Urchristentums zu Arbeit und Geld.
     Gütersloh: C. Bertelsmann, 1921.

Hauschild, Wolf-Dieter. "Christentum und Eigentum: Zum Problem eines
     altkirchlichen 'Sozialismus.'" Zeitschrift für evangelische
     Ethik 16 (1972):34-49.

Healy, Patrick J. "Historic Christianity and the Social Question."
     Catholic University Bulletin 17 (1911):3-19.

_____. "Social and Economic Questions in the Early Church." Catho-
     lic University Bulletin 17 (1911):138-53.

_____. "The Social Value of Asceticism." Catholic University Bul-
     letin 17 (1911):233-56.

_____. "The Economic Aspects of Monasticism." Catholic University
     Bulletin 17 (1911):318-36.

_____. "The Fathers on Wealth and Property." Catholic University
     Bulletin 17 (1911):434-58.

_____. "The Materialistic Interpretation of Early Christian

History." Catholic University Bulletin 17 (1911):656-77.

Hengel, Martin. Property and Riches in the Early Church: Aspects of a
Social History of Early Christianity. Translated by John Bowden.
Philadelphia: Fortress Press, 1974.

Isichei, Elizabeth Allo. Political Thinking and Social Experience:
Some Christian Interpretations of the Roman Empire from Tertullian to Salvian. Christchurch, N.Z.: University of Canterbury,
1964.

Köhler, H. Sozialistische Irrlehren von der Entstehung des Christentums und ihre Widerlegung. Leipzig, 1899.

Kretschmar, Georg. "Ein Beitrag zur Frage nach dem Ursprung der
frühchristlichen Askese." Zeitschrift für Theologie und Kirche
61 (1964):27-67.

Leipoldt, Johannes. Der soziale Gedanke in der altchristlichen Kirche.
Leipzig: Koehler und Amelang, 1952; reprint ed., Leipzig:
Zentral-Antiquariat der Deutschen Demokratischen Republik, 1970.

Maloney, Robert P. "The Teaching of the Fathers on Usury: An Historical Study on the Development of Christian Thinking." Vigiliae
Christianae 27 (1973):241-65.

Meffert, Franz. Der "Kommunismus" Jesu and der Kirchenväter.
M[ünchen]-Gladbach: Volksvereins-Verlag, 1922.

Osborn, Eric. Ethical Patterns in Early Christian Thought. Cambridge:
Cambridge University Press, 1976.

Périn, Charles. De la richesse dans les sociétés chrétiennes. 2d ed.,
revised. Paris: V. Lecoffre, 1868.

Petry, Ray C. Christian Eschatological and Social Thought: A Historical Essay on the Social Implications of Some Selected Aspects
in Christian Eschatology to A.D. 1500. New York: Abingdon, 1956.

Phillips, Charles Stanley. The New Commandment: An Inquiry into the
Social Precept and Practice of the Ancient Church. London:
Society for Promoting Christian Knowledge, 1930.

de Ste. Croix, Geoffrey E. M. "Early Christian Attitudes to Property
and Slavery." In Church, Society and Politics. Edited by Derek
Baker. Studies in Church History, vol. 12. Oxford: Basil
Blackwell, 1975. Pp. 1-38.

Schilling, Otto. Reichtum und Eigentum in der altkirchlichen Literatur: Ein Beitrag zur sozialen Frage. Freiburg im Breisgau:
Herdersche Verlagshandlung, 1908.

_____. "Der Kollektivismus der Kirchenväter." Theologische
    Quartalschrift 114 (1933):481-92.

Seipel, Ignaz. Die wirtschaftsethischen Lehren der Kirchenväter.
    Theologische Studien der Leo-Gesellschaft, no. 18. Vienna:
    Von Mayer & Co., 1907.

Sommerlad, Theo. Das Wirtschaftsprogramm der Kirche des Mittelalters.
    1903.

Troeltsch, Ernst. Gesammelte Schriften. Bd. 1: Die Soziallehren der
    christlichen Kirchen und Gruppen. Tübingen: J. C. B. Mohr
    (Paul Siebeck), 1912.

_____. The Social Teaching of the Christian Churches. Translated
    by Olive Wyon. Introduction by Charles Gore. 2 vols. London:
    George Allen & Unwin, 1931.

Votaw, Clyde Weber. "Primitive Christianity an Idealistic Social
    Movement." American Journal of Theology 22 (1918):54-71.

Walter, Gérard. Les Origines du Communisme, judaïques, chrétiennes,
    grecques, latines. Paris: Bibliothèque historique, 1931.

Wilder, Amos N. "Kerygma, Eschatology, and Social Ethics." In The
    Background of the New Testament and Its Eschatology. Edited
    by W. D. Davies and David Daube. Cambridge University Press,
    1956, pp. 509-36. Reprinted, Philadelphia: Fortress Press,
    Facet Books, 1966.

IV.   Works on the New Testament

A. General Works

Cone, Orello. Rich and Poor in the New Testament: A Study of the
    Primitive-Christian Doctrine of Earthly Possessions. New York:
    Macmillan Co., 1902.

Dibelius, Martin. "Das soziale Motiv im N. T." In Botschaft und
    Geschichte: gesammelte Aufsätze. 2 vols. Tübingen: J. C. B.
    Mohr (Paul Siebeck), 1953-56. 1:178-203.

Dodd, Charles Harold. New Testament Studies. Manchester: University
    Press, 1953.

_____. More New Testament Studies. Grand Rapids, Mich.: William
    B. Eerdmans Publishing Co., 1968.

Grant, Frederick C. "The Economic Background of the New Testament."
In The Background of the New Testament and Its Eschatology.
Edited by W. D. Davies and David Daube. Cambridge: University
Press, 1956. Pp. 96-114.

Houlden, J. L. Ethics and the New Testament. Harmondsworth, Eng.:
Penguin Books, 1973.

Kraemer, Hendrik. The Bible and Social Ethics. Facet Books, Social
Ethics Series, No. 5. Philadelphia: Fortress Press, 1965.

Kümmel, Werner Georg. "Der Begriff des Eigentums im Neuen Testament."
In Heilsgeschehen und Geschichte. Marburger theologische
Studien, no. 3. Marburg: N. G. Elwart Verlag, 1965. Pp. 271-77.

Lillie, William. Studies in New Testament Ethics. Edinburgh: Oliver
& Boyd, 1961.

Marshall, L. H. The Challenge of New Testament Ethics. New York:
Macmillan Co., 1947.

Sanders, Jack T. Ethics in the New Testament: Change and Development.
Philadelphia: Fortress Press, 1975.

Schnackenburg, Rudolf. The Moral Teaching of the New Testament.
Translated by J. Holland-Smith and W. J. O'Hara. New York:
Herder & Herder, 1965.

Sharp, Douglas S. Epictetus and the New Testament. London: Charles
H. Kelly, 1914.

Smith, Charles Ryder. The Bible Doctrine of Wealth and Work in Its
Historical Evolution. London: Epworth Press, 1924.

Theissen, Gerd. "Wanderradikalismus: Literatursoziologische Aspekte
der Überlieferung von Worten Jesu im Urchristentum." Zeitschrift für Theologie und Kirche 70 (1973):245-71.

_____. Sociology of Early Palestinian Christianity. Translated
by John Bowden. Philadelphia: Fortress Press, 1978.

Theological Dictionary of the New Testament. S.v. "πένης, πενιχρός,"
by Friedrich Hauck, and "πτωχός, πτωχεία, πτωχεύω," by Friedrich
Hauck and Ernst Bammel.

Wilder, Amos Niven. Eschatology and Ethics in the Teaching of Jesus.
New York: Harper & Bros., 1939.

B. Gospels and Acts

Bartsch, Hans-Werner. Wachet aber zu jeder Zeit! Entwurf einer
    Auslegung des Lukasevangeliums. Hamburg: Herbert Reich, 1963.

Batey, Richard. Jesus and the Poor. New York: Harper & Row, 1972.

Brown, Schuyler. Apostasy and Perseverance in the Theology of Luke.
    Analecta Biblica, no. 36. Rome: Pontifical Institute, 1969.

Buchanan, George Wesley. "Jesus and the Upper Class." Novum Testa-
    mentum 7 (1964-65):195-209.

Bultmann, Rudolf. The History of the Synoptic Tradition. Translated
    by John Marsh. Rev. ed. New York: Harper & Row, paperback
    edition, 1976.

Cadbury, Henry J. The Making of Luke-Acts. London: S. P. C. K., 1961.

_____. The Style and Literary Method of Luke. Harvard
    Theological Studies, vol. 6 Cambridge: Harvard University Press,
    1920; reprint ed., New York: Kraus Reprint Co., 1969.

Davies, William D. The Setting of the Sermon on the Mount. Cam-
    bridge: University Press, 1966.

Degenhardt, Hans-Joachim. Lukas, Evangelist der Armen: Besitz und
    Besitzverzicht in den lukanischen Schriften: Eine traditions-
    und redaktionsgeschichtliche Untersuchung. Stuttgart: Verlag
    kath. Bibelwerk, 1965.

Derrett, J. Duncan M. "Ananias, Sapphira, and the Right of Property."
    Downside Review 89 (1971):225-32.

Dibelius, Martin. Studies in the Acts of the Apostles. Edited by
    Heinrich Greeven. Translated by Mary Ling. London: SCM Press,
    1956.

Dupont, Jacques. Les Béatitudes: Le problème littéraire-Les deux
    versions du Sermon sur la montagne et des Béatitudes. 2d ed.
    Bruges: Abbaye de Saint-Andrè, 1958.

Grant, F. C. The Economic Background of the Gospels. London: Oxford
    University Press, H. Milford, 1926.

Haenchen, Ernst. The Acts of the Apostles: A Commentary. Translated
    by Bernard Noble and Gerald Shinn. Philadelphia: Westminster
    Press, 1971.

Heuver, Gerald D. The Teachings of Jesus Concerning Wealth. Introduction by Herrick Johnson. Chicago: Fleming H. Revell Co., 1903.

Holtzmann, H. "Die Gütergemeinschaft der Apostelgeschichte." In Strassburger Abhandlungen zur Philosophie. Freiburg in Breisgau: J. C. B. Mohr (Paul Siebeck), 1884. Pp. 25-60.

Jeremias, Joachim. The Parables of Jesus. 2d rev. ed. New York: Charles Scribner's Sons, 1972.

Johnson, Luke T. The Literary Function of Possessions in Luke-Acts. Society of Biblical Literature Dissertation Series, no. 39. Missoula, Montana: Scholars Press, 1977.

Kent, Charles Foster. The Social Teachings of the Prophets and Jesus. New York: Charles Scribner's Sons, 1917.

Légasse, S. L'appel du riche (Marc 10, 17-31 et parallèles): Contribution à l'étude des fondements scripturaires de l'état religieux. Paris: Beauchesne, 1966.

McCown, Chester Charlton. The Genesis of the Social Gospel: The Meaning of the Ideals of Jesus in the Light of Their Antecedents. New York: Alfred A. Knopf, 1929.

Mathews, Shailer. The Social Teaching of Jesus: An Essay in Christian Sociology. New York: Macmillan Co., 1897.

_____. Jesus on Social Institutions. New York: Macmillan Co., 1928.

Mealand, David L. "Community of Goods and Utopian Allusions in Acts II-IV." Journal of Theological Studies, New Series, 28 (1977): 96-99.

Minear, Paul Sevier. Commands of Christ. Nashville: Abingdon Press, 1972.

Peabody, Francis Greenwood. Jesus Christ and the Social Question: An Examination of the Teaching of Jesus in its Relation to Some of the Problems of Modern Social Life. New York: Grosset & Dunlap, 1900.

Percy, Ernst. Die Botschaft Jesu: Eine traditionskritische und exegetische Untersuchung. Lunds Universitets Årsskrift, N. F. Avd. 1, Band 49, Nʳ 5. Lund: C. W. K. Gleerup, 1953.

Perrin, Norman. Rediscovering the Teachings of Jesus. New York: Harper & Row, paperback edition, 1976.

Rauschenbusch, Walter. The Social Principles of Jesus. New York:
    Association Press, 1925.

Taylor, Vincent. The Gospel According to St. Mark. London: Mac-
    millan & Co., 1959.

Thurman, Howard. Jesus and the Disinherited. New York: Abingdon-
    Cokesbury, 1949.

Turner, Nigel. "The Relation of Luke 1 & 2 to the Hebraic Sources and
    to the Rest of Luke-Acts." New Testament Studies 2 (1955-56):
    100-109.

Williams, Francis E. "Is Almsgiving the Point of 'The Unjust
    Steward?'" Journal of Biblical Literature 83 (1964):293-97.

Winter, Paul. "Some Observations on the Language of the Birth and
    Infancy Stories of the Third Gospel." New Testament Studies 1
    (1954-55):111-21.

C. Pauline Epistles, Including the Pastorals

Barrett, C. K. A Commentary on the First Epistle to the Corinthians.
    New York: Harper & Row, 1968.

Chadwick, William Edward. The Social Teaching of St. Paul. Cam-
    bridge: University Press, 1906.

Conzelmann, Hans. First Corinthians. Translated by James W. Leitch.
    Bibliography and references by James W. Dunkly. Edited by George
    W. MacRae. Philadelphia: Fortress Press, 1975.

Davies, William D. Paul and Rabbinic Judaism: Some Rabbinic Elements
    in Pauline Theology. New York: Harper & Row, Torchbooks, 1967.

Dibelius, Martin, and Conzelmann, Hans. The Pastoral Epistles. Trans-
    lated by Philip Buttolph and Adela Yarbro. Edited by Helmut
    Koester. Philadelphia: Fortress Press, 1972.

Enslin, Morton Scott. The Ethics of Paul. New York: Abingdon Press,
    paperback edition, 1957.

Georgi, Dieter. Die Geschichte der Kollekte des Paulus für Jerusalem.
    Theologische Forschung, no. 38. Hamburg: Herbert Reich—
    Evangelischer Verlag, 1965.

Heinrici, G. "Zur Geschichte der Anfänge paulinischer Gemeinden."
    Zeitschrift für wissenschaftliche Theologie 20 (1877):89-130.

Judge, E. A.   "Paul's Boasting in Relation to Contemporary Professional Practice."   Australian Biblical Review 16 (1968):37-50.

_____.   "St. Paul and Classical Society."   Jahrbuch für Antike und
Christentum 15 (1972):19-36.

Kelly, J. N. D.   A Commentary on the Pastoral Epistles: I Timothy, II
Timothy, Titus.   New York: Harper & Row, 1963.

Nickle, Keith Fullerton.   The Collection: A Study in Paul's Strategy.
Studies in Biblical Theology, no. 48.   Naperville, Ill.: Alec
R. Allenson, 1966.

Rolston, Holmes.   The Social Message of the Apostle Paul.   Richmond,
Va.: John Knox Press, 1942.

Sampley, J. Paul.   "Societas Christi: Roman Law and Paul's Conception
of the Christian Community."   In God's Christ and His People:
Studies in Honor of Nils Alstrup Dahl.   Edited by Jacob Jervell
and Wayne A. Meeks.   Oslo: Universitetsforlaget, 1977.   Pp. 158-
74.

Sanday, William, and Headlam, Arthur C.   A Critical and Exegetical
Commentary on the Epistle to the Romans.   International Critical
Commentary.   5th ed.   Edinburgh: T. & T. Clark, 1902.

Schrage, Wolfgang.   "Die Stellung zur Welt bei Paulus, Epiktet und in
der Apokalyptik.   Ein Beitrag zu 1 Kor 7,29-31."   Zeitschrift
für Theologie und Kirche 61 (1964):125-54.

Sevenster, Jan Nicolaas.   Paul and Seneca.   Novum Testamentum, Suppl.
4.   Leiden: E. J. Brill, 1961.

Theissen, Gerd.   "Soziale Schichtung in der korinthischen Gemeinde:
Ein Beitrag zur Soziologie des hellenistischen Urchristentums."
Zeitschrift für die neutestamentliche Wissenschaft 65 (1974):
232-72.

_____.   "Die Starken und Schwachen in Korinth: Soziologische
Analyse eines theologisches Streites."   Evangelische Theologie
35 (1975):155-72.

D.   Other

Buchanan, George Wesley.   To the Hebrews: Translation, Comment, and
Conclusions.   Anchor Bible, vol. 36.   Garden City, N.Y.: Doubleday & Co., 1972.

Dibelius, Martin.   James.   Revised by Heinrich Greeven.   Translated

by Michael A. Williams. Edited by Helmut Koester. Philadelphia:
   Fortress Press, 1976.

Malherbe, Abraham. "The Inhospitality of Diotrephes." In God's Christ
   and His People: Studies in Honor of Nils Alstrup Dahl. Edited by
   Jacob Jervell and Wayne A. Meeks. Oslo: Universitetsforlaget,
   1977. Pp. 222-32.

Reicke, Bo. The Epistles of James, Peter, and Jude. Anchor Bible,
   vol. 37. Garden City, N.Y.: Doubleday & Co., 1964.

V. Works on Later Christian Authors

A. Clement of Alexandria

Bardy, Gustave. Clément d'Alexandrie. Paris: J. Gabalda, 1926.

Capitaine, Wilhelm. Die Moral des Clemens von Alexandrien. Jahrbuch
   für Philosophie und spekulative Theologie, Erganzungsheft 7.
   Paderborn, 1902.

Clark, Elizabeth A. Clement's Use of Aristotle: The Aristotelian Con-
   tribution to Clement of Alexandria's Refutation of Gnosticism.
   Texts and Studies in Religion, no. 1. New York: Edwin Mellen
   Press, 1977.

Hagen, Odulphus Josephus van der. De Clementis Alexandrini sententiis
   oeconomicis, socialibus, politicis. Utrecht: Dekker & V. D.
   Vegt, 1920.

Lilla, Salvatore R. C. Clement of Alexandria: A Study in Christian
   Platonism and Gnosticism. London: Oxford University Press,
   1971.

Markgraf, _____. "Klemens von Alexandrien als asketischer
   Schriftsteller in seiner Stellung zu den natürlichen Lebensgütern." Zeitschrift für Kirchengeschichte 22 (1901):487-515.

Marrou, Henri Irenée. "Morale et spiritualité chrétiennes dans le
   Pédagogue de Clément d'Alexandrie." Studia Patristica, 2, pt.
   2, 538-46. Texte und Untersuchungen 64.

Mehat, A. "Pénitence seconde et péché volontaire chez Clément
   d'Alexandrie." Vigiliae Christianae 8 (1954):225-33.

Patrick, John. Clement of Alexandria. Edinburgh: William Blackwood
   & Sons, 1914.

Paul, Ludwig. "Welche Reiche wird selig Werden?" Zeitschrift für
    wissenschaftliche Theologie 44 (1901):504-44.

Prunet, Olivier. La morale de Clément d'Alexandrie et le Nouveau
    Testament. Paris: Presses Universitaires de France, 1966.

Tollinton, Richard Bartram. Clement of Alexandria, A Study in Chris-
    tian Liberalism. 2 vols. London: Williams & Norgate, 1914.

Völker, Walther. Der wahre Gnostiker nach Clemens Alexandrinus.
    Texte und Untersuchungen 57.

Wagner, Wilhelm. Der Christ und die Welt nach Clemens von Alexandrien:
    Ein noch unveraltetes Problem in altchristlicher Beleuchtung.
    Göttingen: Vandenhoeck & Ruprecht, 1903.

B. Cyprian

d'Alès, Adhémar. La théologie de Saint Cyprien. Paris: Gabriel
    Beauchesne, 1922.

Alföldy, Géza. "Der heilige Cyprian und die Krise des römischen
    Reiches." Historia 22 (1973):479-501.

Benson, Edward White. Cyprian: His Life. His Times. His Work. New
    York: D. Appleton & Co., 1897.

Boutet, Joseph. Saint Cyprien, Évêque de Carthage et martyr (210-258).
    Avignon: Aubanel Frères, 1923.

Fichter, Joseph H. Saint Cecil Cyprian, Early Defender of the Faith.
    St. Louis: Herder Book Co., 1942.

Hinchliff, Peter. Cyprian of Carthage and the Unity of the Christian
    Church. London: Goeffrey Chapman, 1974.

Koch, Hugo. Cyprianische Untersuchungen. Arbeiten zur Kirchenge-
    schichte, no. 4. Bonn: A. Marcus & E. Weber, 1926.

Ludwig, Joseph. Der heilige Märtyrerbischof Cyprian von Karthago: Ein
    kulturgeschichtliches und theologisches Zeitbild aus der
    afrikanischen Kirche des 3. Jahrhunderts. Munich: Karl Zink
    Verlag, 1951.

Monceaux, Paul. Histoire littéraire de l'Afrique chrétienne depuis
    les origines jusqu'à l'invasion arabe. Vol. 2: Saint Cyprien
    et son temps. Paris: E. Leroux, 1902.

_____. Saint Cyprien, évêque de Carthage (210-258). 2d ed. Paris:

J. Gabalda, 1914.

Sage, Michael M. Cyprian. Patristic Monograph Series, no. 1. Cam-
    bridge, Mass.: Philadelphia Patristic Foundation, 1975.

Sullivan, Daniel David. The Life of the North Africans as Revealed
    in the Works of St. Cyprian. Catholic University of America
    Patristic Studies, vol. 37. Washington: Catholic University of
    America, 1933.

Turner, Cuthbert Hamilton. Studies in Early Church History. Oxford:
    Clarendon Press, 1912.

Watson, E. W. "The De Opere et Eleemosynis of St. Cyprian." Journal
    of Theological Studies 2 (1901):433-38.

C. Others

Barnes, Timothy David. Tertullian: A Historical and Literary Study.
    Oxford: Clarendon Press, 1971.

Brown, Peter. Augustine of Hippo: A Biography. Berkeley: University
    of California Press, paperback edition, 1969.

Burnaby, John. Amor Dei, A Study of the Religion of St. Augustine.
    London: Hodder & Stoughton, 1938.

Chadwick, Henry. "Justification by Faith and Hospitality." Studia
    Patristica, 4, pt. 2, 281-85. Texte und Untersuchungen 79.

Dibelius, Martin. Der Hirt des Hermas. Die apostolischen Väter, vol.
    4. Tübingen: J. C. B. Mohr (Paul Siebeck), 1923.

Donfried, Karl Paul. The Setting of Second Clement in Early Chris-
    tianity. Novum Testamentum, Suppl. 38. Leiden: E. J. Brill,
    1974.

Giet, Stanislas. "La doctrine de l'appropriation des biens chez
    quelques-uns des Pères." Recherches de science religieuse 35
    (1948):55-91.

Grant, Robert M., ed. The Apostolic Fathers: A New Translation and
    Commentary. New York: Thomas Nelson & Sons, 1965-68. Vol. 2:
    First and Second Clement, by R. M. Grant and Holt H. Graham.
    Vol. 3: Barnabas and the Didache, by Robert A. Kraft. Vol. 6:
    Hermas, by Graydon F. Snyder.

Lightfoot, Joseph Barber, ed. The Apostolic Fathers. 5 vols. London:
    Macmillan & Co., 1885-90; reprint ed., Hildesheim: Georg Olms
    Verlag, 1973.

Nöldechen, E. "Tertullians Verhältnis zu Klemens von Alexandrien."
Jahrbücher für protestantische Theologie 12 (1886):278-301.

Richardson, Cyril C., ed. Early Christian Fathers. New York: Macmillan Publishing Co., paperback ed., 1970.

Wrede, William. Untersuchungen zum Ersten Klemensbriefe. Göttingen:
Vanderhoeck & Ruprecht, 1891.